AUTUMNS
IN THE
GARDEN

Autumns
in the Garden

THE COACH
OF CAMELOT
& OTHER KNICKS STORIES

IRA BERKOW

TRIUMPH
BOOKS

Library of Congress Cataloging-in-Publication Data

Berkow, Ira.
    Autumns in the garden : the coach of Camelot and other Knicks stories / Ira Berkow.
        pages cm.
    ISBN 978-1-60078-866-6
    1. New York Knickerbockers (Basketball team)—History. 2. Basketball players—United States—Biography. I. Title.
    GV885.52.N4B43 2013
    796.323'64097471—dc23
                              2013008098

This book is available in quantity at special discounts for your group or organization. For further information, contact:

    Triumph Books LLC
    814 North Franklin Street
    Chicago, Illinois 60610
    (312) 337-0747
    www.triumphbooks.com

Printed in U.S.A.
ISBN: 978-1-60078-866-6
Design by Prologue Publishing Services, LLC
Page production by Patricia Frey

For Dolly

CONTENTS

INTRODUCTION

AUTUMN IN NEW YORK, late September 1967, a sweet time of year, the green leaves already beginning to change gloriously into coats of crimson and gold and purple in deeply wooded Central Park, the brassy Manhattan symphony of cars and trucks and yellow taxis honking and police cars and the occasional ambulance wailing, glittering and blinking neon signs vying for attention, the subways and elevated trains rumbling, and the masses of people, bundled and brief-cased, hurrying, elbowing, waving, or giving fellow citizens and tourists the bird, as the case may be. With a nip in the air—sometimes having to pull up the collar of my jacket to buttress the wind—I arrived in New York City from the Midwest, marveling at the vibrancy of this miraculous metropolis.

I had been hired to write sports for Newspaper Enterprise Association, a national feature syndicate with 750 newspaper outlets nationally and internationally. I was on the cusp of a new phase in my journalistic career—I had worked for the previous two years as a sportswriter for the *Minneapolis Tribune*—but little did I know—little did New Yorkers know, I have no doubt—that coincidentally the New York Knicks were on the cusp of wonderful things, including their only two National Basketball Association championships, ending in the 1969–1970 and 1972–73 seasons, and losing to the Lakers in the 1972 Finals after their star center, Willis Reed, was unable to play due to a knee injury.

As of this writing, the Knicks have never won another championship. They've tried, to be sure, gotten close, but circumstances and rivals, including such adversaries as the aerodynamic Michael Jordan, the balletic Hakeem Olajuwon, and the ever-lurking Reggie Miller, have succeeded in frustrating their dreams and goals.

Barely two months after I had dropped my luggage down in my new apartment in Greenwich Village, the Knicks, on December 27, 1967—in the midst of holiday cheer—and wallowing in the NBA standings, fired their head coach, Dick McGuire—a man so low-key in conversation that he was nicknamed "Mumbles." They elevated William "Red" Holzman, who was the team's head scout.

With some trades—particularly the obtaining of Dave DeBusschere, the rugged forward—and inserting the third-string guard, Walt "Clyde" Frazier, as the starting point guard, and taking advantage of the considerable assets of Willis Reed, Bill Bradley, Dick Barnett, and Phil Jackson, among others—and with an unequivocal emphasis on defense, the Knicks began to excel.

It was a spectacular time for people, like me, who relished good basketball. It was a wonderful team, with appealing and generous teamwork, with sometimes three and four passes to set up a shot, something one didn't often see in the pros. The Knicks' home games were played in the old Garden, a musty, smoky arena, soon to be torn down. A new, gleaming Garden, atop Penn Station, would be erected. The first Knick game there would be played in February 1971.

The standing-room-only crowds at the Garden began to draw celebrities, who didn't stand, naturally. Dustin Hoffman, who had recently starred in *Midnight Cowboy*, sat behind the Knicks' bench, and the players called him "Ratso," for the character, Ratso Rizzo, that he played in the film. There was Woody Allen, a knowledgeable and fervent fan. One afternoon in the '70s, I accompanied Walt Frazier to P.J. Clarke's, a popular bar and restaurant in Manhattan, where Clyde was having his pregame meal.

At a nearby table a man sat reading a newspaper, which he held in front of his face. Periodically, I'd look over and the paper would be lowered and I saw the man was staring in awe at Frazier. When I looked at him, he brought the paper back to cover his face, obviously a little embarrassed to be gawking. This newspaper thing went on until Frazier and I left the restaurant. I recognized the man at that other table. It was Woody Allen.

The great screenwriter William Goldman was a knowing and loving fan who had season courtside seats and rarely missed a game. "When you get excited about sports as I do, you develop expectations and images in your mind of how well a game can be played," he told me, "and you root for it to be played that way. When it's not, it's disappointing. When it is, it's thrilling. Like life."

From NEA, where I had become the sports editor and sports columnist, I went to *The New York Times*, in March 1981, where I wrote feature stories and the "Sports of the Times" column, along with, at various times, that stellar array of co-columnists, Red Smith, Dave Anderson, Robert Lipsyte, George Vecsey, Harvey Araton, Bill Rhoden, and Selena Roberts. And, besides keeping an eye on the world of sports in general, I continued often writing about and covering the rises and falls of the Knicks, the comings and goings of a wide assortment of players and coaches. Until my retirement from the paper in February 2007, a full 26 years after I began at *The Times*, and nearly 40 years after I made New York City my home.

This book is not, nor is it meant to be, a history of the New York Knicks. It is no more and no less than the issues and personalities that interested me, amused me, intrigued me, sometimes vexed me—a columnist ought always to be on the lookout to be vexed. It was also a great learning experience—witnessing first-hand how pressure was dealt with, how strategies evolved, how people in the glare of the spotlight handle success and failure, hope and disappointment.

I was gone from the scene by February 2012 when one of the most remarkable moments in all my days of covering and following sports occurred. It was when Jeremy Lin emerged into stardom, and "Linsanity" swiftly possessed the sometimes cynical city. This bespectacled former economics major from Harvard, one of the few Asian Americans to ever make an NBA roster, who had been cut from two other NBA teams, was fresh from the D-League and finally got his chance to play only when the Knick guards ahead of him succumbed to injury, suddenly emerged as the most unlikely of stars, passing beautifully, defending, driving through crowded lanes for lay-ups, hitting game-winning shots, scoring 38 points against Kobe Bryant and the Lakers, and propelling the slumping Knicks into a terrific winning streak.

Because of a dispute between the MSG Network and Time-Warner, the games were not seen on most television sets in New York. I found an Irish bar on Third Avenue near my apartment and it had a feed for the Knicks game. Because of Lin, and the great uproar his games caused from

Chinatown to uptown to points around the globe, the network and Time-Warner resolved their issues.

Near season's end, Lin suffered a knee injury and missed the playoffs—the Knicks lost in five games to the Miami Heat—but for reasons beyond the ken of many Knick fans, the owner of the team, James Dolan, in his inscrutable fashion, refused to match the offer that the Houston Rockets had made for Lin, then a free agent. And Lin was gone, vanished from the Manhattan scene. An added sour note to Lin's leave-taking was that, before Dolan's decision, his teammates Carmelo Anthony and J.R. Smith were critical and derisive of Houston's proposed three-year, $25 million contract for Lin. Anthony said it was "ridiculous" and Smith said that "some guys [would] take it personal, because they've been doing it longer and haven't received any reward for it yet." It was really none of their business what contract negotiations a teammate—he was a teammate at that time—was involved in. Both Anthony and Smith are paid handsomely by the Knicks, and both came off as mean-spirited and envious of Lin's popularity and good fortune.

Notwithstanding, the Knicks, behind Anthony, Smith, Raymond Felton, Tyson Chandler, and coach Mike Woodson, had now become NBA contenders. And fans and celebrities like Woody Allen, Spike Lee, and Bill Goldman continued to find joy and excitement in the now-refurbished Garden.

And among the Garden rafters, the ghosts of the old Knick title teams are recalled. Replicas of the uniforms of Frazier, number 10; Barnett, number 12; Earl Monroe, number 15; Reed, number 19; DeBusschere, number 22; and Bradley, number 24, hang there and flutter along with Red Holzman's number, 613, in homage to the regular-season victories he amassed as the Knicks coach. (The only other retired numbers are those of Dick McGuire—who was, like Monroe, 15—and Patrick Ewing's number 33. However, McGuire played before the championship era, and Ewing after it.)

While Holzman was invariably unobtrusive in his public persona, he ran a tight ship with the Knicks. I remember one time that I was in his office before a game. It was in October 1972. His office was situated next to the team's locker room, with a door that led into it. Frankie Blauschild, the Knicks traveling secretary, walked from the locker room through the door into Holzman's office.

"Frankie, what's that commotion I hear in the locker room?" Holzman asked.

"Oh, Red, that's Sargent Shriver," said Blauschild. "You know, he's running for vice president."

"What's he doing in the locker room?"

"He just wants to say hello to the players."

"You know we have a policy: no one in the locker room before a game except team members."

"I know," explained Blauschild, "but it's Sargent Shriver."

"I don't give a damn if it's General Shriver," said Holzman. "Get him out of there."

And he did.

I.

KING RED AND SOME OF HIS KNIGHTS

THE COACH OF CAMELOT

May 10, 1986

SOMETIMES IT SEEMS LIKE Camelot, as if it might have happened only in our imagination: the Knicks of the very late 1960s and the first part of the 1970s. The champion Knicks of 1970 and 1973. King Red and the Knights of the Round Ball.

But surely it all occurred. The history books tell us that, and, as if for added confirmation, last Tuesday William "Red" Holzman was inducted into the Basketball Hall of Fame in Springfield, Massachusetts.

Every game night at Madison Square Garden, in that time almost before memory, was bursting with a sellout crowd of 19,500. People of recent times who were lost and wandered in off the street and found themselves witnessing a basketball game of the depleted Knicks in an often-hollow Garden must have wondered what it was like in those storybook days.

"You make a few steals or work for a few good plays," Walt Frazier once said, "and you have the feeling that it's going to be one of those nights. The whole team gets into it, and then the crowd picks it up, and you come to the sidelines for a timeout and listen to that standing ovation, and it just makes you jingle inside."

And at the sideline was Holzman, the coach, an average-sized man in an oversized world, a man with a receding hairline and conservative dark suit and tie, a man who originally didn't want to be coach of the Knicks, who had turned down the job a few times, and was finally convinced in December 1967 that he had to take it. He was then a scout for the team, and had been for 10 years. He had seen six Knick coaches dismissed in that

3

period, and understood how uneasy lies the head that wears the coach's crown. He was dismissed once as a coach himself—he had been shown the door as coach of the St. Louis Hawks in 1957.

But Holzman took the Knicks, then in last place, and began to build a winner, constructing the parts of Frazier and Bill Bradley and Willis Reed and Dick Barnett and Dave DeBusschere, and reviving, it was said, the concept of team play. To basketball lovers, the Knicks were not only a treat, they were a clinic.

Holzman was a man of little outward ego, trying often not to call attention to himself, other than for aphorisms he coined, such as: never take a haircut from a bald barber; never make a point with your finger raised when the waiter is bringing the check; and the best feeling in the world is to wake up early in the morning when you don't have to go anywhere.

Shortly after Holzman had begun to win with the Knicks, this interviewer had what he hoped would be a discussion with him on how he worked his coaching magic.

"What have you done to help your team's success?" he was asked.

"Some stuff I've done has evidently appealed to them." "What do you mean 'stuff'?" "Offensive and defensive stuff," he explained.

The conversation continued in this fashion, and as it did, Holzman began to slowly disappear in a cloud of his own modesty. As if, now, he were not King of the Court, but Merlin.

The "stuff" Holzman employed, in fact, was a large dependence on defense, a mastery of matchups, diligent repetitions (during one 25-day stretch in the earliest days, the Knicks played eight games and had 21 two-hour practices), and he had the ability with that team to communicate and motivate.

"The real genius of Holzman lies in his handling of players," Bill Bradley once wrote. "Most men would have failed as coach of the New York Knickerbockers. Great college coaches often cannot make the adjustment from coaching boys to controlling men. Holzman does not beg players to do good deeds, nor does he set up elaborate codes of conduct. He expects everyone to act as a responsible adult, and he treats players accordingly."

They were terrific players in those days, and some of them became coaches and general managers and memory experts and one would become a star of tax reforms. "But as smart as they were," said Danny Whelan, who was the Knicks trainer, "I remember Red sometimes over his Scotch wondering if he'd ever be able to teach 'em what he was always hollering, 'See the ball,' 'Hit the open man.'"

Eventually, that team did. But times and players changed, and a group began arriving with whom Holzman couldn't make his notions stick. With this group came the long, long nights at the Garden, when Micheal Ray Richardson and Ray Williams were a backcourt of coachly impenetrability, when Bob McAdoo was firing away as if in a gym alone, and when Spencer Haywood made plays such as the following: he picked up a loose ball near half-court with a defender on him. Frazier, then at the end of his Knick days, was under the basket by himself, arms outstretched. But Haywood decided that he was going to score himself instead of passing the ball. He took about five giant steps, and dunked. But the basket didn't count. He was whistled for traveling, and Frazier's shoulders slumped, and his eyes twirled in his head.

Holzman was dismissed in 1978, Reed became the coach for a year and a few games, and then Holzman was urgently called back, and dismissed again. His last year was 1982, and when he finished, he had more victories, 696, than any coach in National Basketball Association history other than Red Auerbach, who had 938.

After 41 years in professional basketball, as a player (he was a guard with the Rochester Royals on two championship teams), scout, coach, and general manager, Holzman is currently a quiet consultant for the Knicks, doing little in the Hubie Brown regime. And, at 65, he seems to be taking his semiretirement contentedly.

Holzman recently spoke about a recurring dream he once had.

"I dreamed I was playing in a league and not doing well," he said. "My passes were bad, my shooting was off, and the man I was guarding was scoring. But teams I had played for, Rochester and Milwaukee, still wanted me. And I thought, well, I guess it's not so bad, how many people at 57 years old are still playing in the league?"

Holzman smiled. "When I turned 60, the dream mysteriously ended. In my dreams I finally retired."

RED HOLZMAN'S SECRET

August 8, 1981

"DID YOU SEE THE Knicks signed Red Holzman to a new two-year contract?" a fan asked the other day. "I don't know why. The parade has passed and he's still waving at it."

That's one view held by a number of people on Holzman as a basketball coach. There's another. "Red's amazing to have stayed this long and still be a great coach," said Al Cervi, a teammate of Holzman's with the old Rochester Royals and a former National Basketball Association coach. "The players today are so individually inclined, I get tired watching them. I don't know how Red does it. If it was me, dear God, I'd be put in jail." On Monday, Holzman celebrates his 61st birthday. He is the oldest coach in the league, the oldest in point of service—17 seasons on the bench, plus 18 as a player (one of the league's pioneers), scout, consultant, and general manager—second only to Red Auerbach in coaching victories (Holzman has won 663 games to Auerbach's 938 in 20 seasons) and the only coach active who has won more than one NBA championship.

The Knicks under Holzman won titles in 1970 and again in 1973. But in the following few years they deteriorated. The championship players retired or slipped, the new players couldn't match their team skills. No one doubted that. But then fingers began to point at Holzman: he's tired, he can't handle the new breed of player, he's a fossil. He was fired as coach.

Once considered a certified genius for the delicious team concept the Knicks had used with such success, Holzman was now forced to hand in his certified genius card. And before the 1977–78 season, Willis Reed became the new coach. Reed was big and strong and young and black— the majority of Knicks were black and it was believed he would relate well.

As a rookie coach, Reed had reasonable success. But Knick management felt he should have done better. Reed was dropped. Many coaches were considered. Then, to the surprise of most, Red Holzman, who had been relegated to a small, distant "consultant's" office in Madison Square Garden where he remained without complaint—the ultimate company man—was brought back as coach of the Knicks.

Last season, the Knicks won 50 games and made the playoffs, though they were soundly beaten by Chicago in the opening round. "We'll do better this season," said Holzman, sitting down to dinner at Pippo's, a favorite restaurant near his home in Cedarhurst, Long Island. He was with Selma, his wife of 39 years.

"I know people miss those championships, so do I," he said, "but people forget that we won with a veteran team, and those guys had been together for some time. This team is young, and most of the guys are now just getting to know how to play together. And physically, they're more talented than the guys used to be. They're capable of so much."

The waiter appeared with drinks, compliments of an acquaintance of Holzman's at a nearby table. Holzman waved thank you. He now talked about the current players. "I enjoy coaching them because most of them like to play, and want to learn," he said. He said it's frustrating for them and for him when, after working hard in practice, one of them will make a costly mental error to lose a game. "You want them to squeeze the ball, and they lose it," he said. "You've got to be patient. That's what they've taught me—patience. I've just got to keep talking to them."

Nevertheless, he still longs for a game he once knew. "I envied the Celtics last season," he said. "You love to see a team that can pass and think. Bill Fitch did a great job. I don't think he's been given proper credit for it. And Larry Bird. He's one of the best players I've ever seen. He's not fast, he's not a great jumper, but he's a winner."

The mention of Bird recalled Bill Bradley. "Another great team player," he said. "And people didn't realize how good Bill was, or how tough. I remember one night in San Diego he had a terrible virus but insisted on playing, and he played well. Most guys would have stayed home. He came to the bench about four times and threw up."

On occasion, Holzman will shoot with a player after practice. At 5'10", he is still trim. One day Marvin Webster, the Knick center, and Holzman put $10 apiece on the floor for a shootout from the top of the free throw circle. "Marvin went first and made nine out of 10," said Holzman. "He went to pick up the money. I said, 'Just a minute.' Then I shot. I still shoot the old two-hand set. I made nine out of l0. He couldn't believe it. I don't know if Marvin had ever seen a two-hander before."

"I remember you telling me about that," said Selma. Did he think he could get the two-hander off in a game today? "I bet Walt Frazier I could. We played one-on-one. He blocked every shot. I faked every way I could, but I never got a single shot off."

"Red," said Selma, "you never told me that!" Holzman shrugged. She laughed. "People talk about the game changing," he continued. "It doesn't change as much as it might seem. The basics are still there. You've got to play good defense. You've got to hit the open man. You've got to pass and think. And the players still take pride in winning, no matter how much money they make. You try to tap that pride. Coaching today is as simple as that."

Holzman tries to keep things as uncomplicated in his private life. "People say, 'Red, how come you only have one suit?'" he said. "Well, I've got a bunch of suits. They just all look the same. Why change?"

When Selma wanted to buy a color television set, he resisted. "You'll get used to it," she promised. He has. Holzman relies on several life axioms, in and out of basketball. "If you come late, you play late," he says. He is a stickler for promptness. He also says, "Never talk money with your wife at night." That last one is crucial, he says. "Otherwise you'll get no sleep."

The meal finished, he lit up a long greenish cigar and suddenly remembered something. He hailed the waiter. Holzman told him he wanted to buy the people at the next table a drink. They had bought earlier.

"Hey, Red," called his friend at the table. "Just when we're leaving, you buy us a drink?" He looked embarrassed only for a moment. "I'm not so dumb," he replied genially. And that, basketball followers, is how he does it.

RECALLING RED'S
WIT AND MODESTY

November 27, 1998

IN AN EARLY SCRIMMAGE in the Knicks training camp in the mid-1960s, the chief scout, Red Holzman, watched one of the rookies he had scouted—the team had followed his enthusiastic advice to draft the player high—and now anticipated that he would be a productive member of the team. On the sideline, Scout Holzman noticed a flaw in the player that he hadn't noticed before. He had trouble getting through screens on his left. During a break in the action, Holzman went onto the court to demonstrate to the player how it's done.

"You have to look out of the corner of your eye and then fight through the screen," Holzman told the player.

"I can't look out of the corner of my eye," the player said.

"You can't?" Red said, skeptically. "What's so hard?"

"I'm blind in the left eye," the player said.

Holzman looked around to see if anyone was in earshot. No one was.

"C'mere," he said, and led the player to a corner of the gym. Holzman whispered, "Don't ever tell anyone you can't see, okay?"

"Okay," the player said.

This story is revealed for the first time, since Holzman, even some 30 years after the incident, and after enough successful draft suggestions—from Willis Reed to Walt Frazier—and enough successes as the coach of the Knicks to win two National Basketball Association championships and earn him a place in the Basketball Hall of Fame, even after all that, was still a little embarrassed about the player, who never played in the league. But in a relaxed moment at dinner one night he told the story, with the self-effacement and humor that had become as much a part of him as was Selma, his wife of over 55 years.

This week, the MSG Network has been broadcasting a half-hour retrospective on Holzman who, as every basketball—and perhaps sports—fan knows, died on November 13, at age 78, losing a battle to leukemia. His death came just four months after Selma died.

To say that he missed Selma would be a gross understatement. Just a week before he died, he attended the wedding of George Kalinsky, the longtime official photographer at Madison Square Garden. Holzman had not been feeling well, and Kalinsky called to inquire after him. "I'm okay," Holzman said. "But I was thinking about the gift I gave you and June. I don't know if it was appropriate. Selma would have done better."

What made Holzman a successful coach? The reason as I see it, and I covered the team in its glory years and grew in friendship with Red after he left coaching in 1982, was that he gave people a boost, was sensitive and thoughtful of their feelings, left them with their dignity and even when being critical did so with an underpinning of humor.

But he could be tough. And many years after he had coached Phil Jackson, the former Bulls coach called Holzman with condolences after the death of Selma. Holzman recalled Jackson saying, surely recalling his days as a player for Holzman, "Red, if you need someone to scream and holler at, call me any time."

If a friend hadn't called him in a while, he'd phone the friend. "Where've you been?" he asked. He wouldn't put the guy on the defensive by saying, "How come you haven't called?" It was more like, You must have been lost in the wilds of Borneo and couldn't get to a phone.

At dinner one night in a restaurant in Madison Square Garden, the waiter and Holzman greeted each other. "Is your soup hot tonight?" Holzman asked. The waiter said, "Of course, Mr. Holzman, absolutely." I wondered about that question, never having heard it before. Then I realized what the coach had done. The soup wasn't hot the last time he was there, he didn't want to embarrass the waiter, but wanted to make sure the soup was hot this time. When the soup arrived, it was piping hot.

Sometimes, though, his humor could be wry. Even on his deathbed. His daughter, Gail Holzman Papelian, recalled that when her father was admitted to the hospital for the last time two weeks ago, he was put into a bed in a room with another man. The other man kept talking and talking. Red turned to Gail, with an irritated nod toward the man. "Doesn't miss a detail," Holzman said quietly.

I once invited Holzman to lunch with Jackie Mason. Holzman was a great fan of Mason's. Mason, however, has no interest in any sport other than boxing. When I introduced the comedian to Holzman, I said, "Jackie, this is Red Holzman. He was the brilliant coach of the Knicks."

Mason looked at Holzman. "Doesn't look so smart to me," he said.

Red loved it.

CLYDE'S ULTIMATE COOL

February 6, 1987

THE MEMORIES OF WALT "Clyde" Frazier playing his quietly exciting basketball for the Knicks come back in a flood for any fan, especially now, the day after he had been elected to the Basketball Hall of Fame.

There was the time he hit this clutch shot with one second left to win the game, the time he threw that pass or got that rebound or made that steal to turn the game around.

And of course, there was the seventh game of the National Basketball Association championship series in 1970, when, with Willis Reed ailing, Frazier scored 36 points, grabbed seven rebounds, and added a sensational 19 assists as the Knicks won their first title.

He ran the offense. "It's Clyde's ball," Reed once said. "He lets the rest of us play with it sometimes."

Frazier did it in his seemingly cool fashion. But for all that, the game that sticks out in this reporter's memory is one in which he played against the Knicks.

After 10 years with two championship teams in New York, he was sent to the Cleveland Cavaliers as compensation for a free agent, Jim Cleamons, on October 3, 1977.

Frazier, at 32, was past his salad days, the team chemistry had changed, and he was distraught—he had built his life here, and now learned of the deal second-hand—and was incommunicado for several days before reporting to the Cavaliers, the lowly Cavs. Shortly after, he returned to Madison Square Garden, this time in a strange uniform. When he was announced before the game, the cheers nearly brought the roof down.

Clyde, cool Clyde, showed, customarily, little emotion. But he was pumped. He scored 28 points, made five steals, as the Cavaliers won in overtime 117–112. As the buzzer sounded ending the game, Clyde, cool, cool Clyde, thrust a fist in the air and leaped and yelped and raced off the court, with the crowd again cheering madly for this special opponent.

But he wouldn't have many more great basketball days, and he never quite seemed to heal from a stress fracture to a foot, or from his sudden departure from New York, and although he hung on for a few more seasons, he would never be the Frazier we knew.

His easy style made it seem to some that he wasn't always trying as hard as he could. Some said that he could make so many steals because he gambled and, if he missed, well, there was Willis Reed to back him up.

But Frazier was clever as a defensive player. He would, for example, lull a player into a sense of security. He would capture the rhythm of an opponent's dribble. And although he could make the steal now, he might decide to wait, to use the steal off the dribble for a crucial moment later in the game. Thus those clutch, late-game snatchings. One player he had trouble with, however, was Lenny Wilkens, who, ironically, was one of those who was nominated for the Hall, but didn't get the required number of votes.

Once, before heading off to do a piece on Wilkens—then the coach of Seattle—I asked Frazier if he had a question for him.

"You know, Wilkens was a lefty and he always went left," said Frazier. "But I could never stop him. Ask him why."

I did. "He always knew I was going left," said Wilkens, "but he never knew when." Frazier delighted in the response. Frazier was able to laugh at himself, and in that way, although he greatly enjoyed the world of the star in Manhattan, could retain some perspective.

Despite his pink Eldorado ("the Clydemobile") and his black mink coat and his wide wardrobe of lids and kicks and suits (including the black cowskin suit with poncho and silver studs), there were moments when Frazier could still be seen as the kid who grew up in Atlanta, the oldest of nine children—he and his brother, Keith, the youngest, were the only boys in the family.

Walt helped his mother diaper and cook for the babies, and then went into the schoolyard where he learned to dribble an erratic basketball that kept bouncing off the stones.

And he was the guy who didn't sulk and quit when he didn't make grades and lost eligibility for a time at Southern Illinois. Instead, he played with the varsity only on defense, and labored so hard at it that he would become a superb defensive player. And when he came to the Knicks, after having led Southern Illinois to the National Invitation Tournament championship in 1967, he seemed lost in the big city, and on a team in disarray. He was often afraid to shoot. But with the help of a new coach, Red Holzman, Frazier regained confidence, a career opened up, and he would be rated among the best guards ever, with Oscar Robertson, Jerry West, and Bob Cousy.

Frazier once recalled a time when he picked up two kids hitchhiking in the Catskills, where he had a basketball camp. The kids—they were about 12 or 13 years old—sank into the white leather seats of his Cadillac. They were coming from playing basketball and were very quiet.

"I got a feeling they knew who I was," recalled Frazier, "but they didn't say anything. Cool cats. I didn't say anything, either. I stopped to let them out, and they thanked me for the ride. As I drove away, I saw them in the rearview mirror. They were jumping up and down and slapping palms. Cool cats to the end."

With his election to the Hall of Fame, Clyde Frazier, the ultimate Cool Cat, can now forgivably slap palms, too.

THE FRAZIER ROLE MODEL

October 5, 1976

WHENEVER SOMEONE WISHES TO make a statement about an exploitive black sports star, Walt Frazier's name is trundled out. In a recent article, for example, on *The New York Times* op-ed page, William Serrin wrote:

"But the problem is one of private people, too. The [young blacks of Detroit] did not learn what they know by themselves. Magazines said that wearing wide-brim hats and carrying canes was black cool. The basketball player, Walt Frazier, who did not sweat, was cool...Black people like Fred Williamson and Jim Brown found they could make a bundle making violent, sex-filled movies. And the young blacks started acting in the fashion of the Hollywood actors, and it was no longer acting. It was violence and death on Detroit's East Side."

Lumping Frazier with those alleged catalysts of mayhem is muddleheaded. The marauding black youths of Detroit, to say the least, impose themselves on others. No one says to Walt Frazier, "Get away from me," except, perhaps, a man he is guarding on the basketball court. Frazier's cool is marked by restraint.

Frazier has never been called for a technical foul, for example, in his entire nine-year career in the National Basketball Association. He almost never even grimaces at a call by a referee, let alone complains about it. He has never gotten into a scuffle on the court; his reserve was dramatically demonstrated to a nationwide television audience when, a few seasons back, an opponent on the Baltimore Bullets slugged Frazier in frustration.

Frazier simply continued on in the game.

A few years ago I was at a game the Knicks played in Atlanta, Frazier's hometown. I noticed that Frazier left the pregame warm-up drills to talk with a member of the band that played at courtside. The band was made up of inmates of a nearby Georgia prison.

After the game I asked Frazer who it was he spoke with. He said it was a guy he had played with on his high school basketball team.

I asked Frazier what the difference was between himself and guys like that fellow. Frazier said that he determined long ago not to grow up standing on the corner, nodding and talking jive. He wanted to make something of himself and he knew it would take work. He came to the belief that "cool" was the answer. That is, a positive "cool."

"Cool is my style," he has said. "I almost never show any emotion on the court. A guy might harass me and it might be working, but if you look at my face, I always look cool. So they never know what I'm thinking.

"Some cool is natural, but a lot is learned.

"Cool is a quality admired in the black neighborhoods. Cool is a matter of self-preservation, of survival. It must go back to the slave days, when often times all a black man had to defend himself with was his poise. If you'd show fear or anger, you'd suffer the consequences. Today, the guy respected in the ghetto is the guy who resists the urge to go off—who can handle himself in a crisis, who can talk his way out of a fight."

One also wonders about Serrin's point about clothes. Is he saying that wearing wide-brim hats stirs up hostile blood in young blacks?

It is a truism in ghetto life as elsewhere, that the wearing of prized clothing is a step toward pacifism. Few dudes are inclined to tear up snazzy duds in a scuffle.

Frazier says he was always conscious of being neat as far back as grade school. He remembers when the blue-suede shoe fad came out, he bought himself a pair of those sharp brogans. "I was proud of them and brushed them all the time," he said. "My mother said I'd better be careful because I was brushing all the suede off."

Like many of us, the better Frazier dresses, he says, the better he feels. Even on the court. The neater he feels in his uniform, he says, the better he usually plays.

It is a matter of pride and self-respect. Psychologists tell us that we must respect ourselves before we can or will respect others. And who should judge how wide another's hat brim ought to be?

As for being an example to youth, Frazier says, "The only thing about me that I'd want kids to identify with is that I'm my own man. I don't use people and I don't let people use me.

"I believe what Bill Russell says: black kids can look up to a black athlete as an athlete, as someone who has worked hard and developed his talents, a man who has accomplished something he wanted. But a father should set an example for a kid, or an uncle or a religious or neighborhood leader.

"My example is that I'm Walt Frazier. I do my job well."

THE HALL DESERVES THE PEARL

November 5, 1989

EARL MONROE WAS THE only basketball shooter I ever saw whose ball seemed to deflate when it hit the rim. Then it just flopped through the net, like a dead fish.

That wasn't the only thing unusual about his game. Another was the way he moved. Like a Tinker Toy. All askew elbows and knobby knees and various parts traveling at their own odd pace and rhythm. And yet the whole coming together in a most graceful and startling fashion.

He came upcourt bouncing the ball in his high, unconventional way, then spun here, twisted there, went between three or four or five bodies, and, like Houdini from a trunk, impossibly emerged and tossed off a deft pass or flipped up one of his mackerel-flop shots.

I liked what Woody Allen once wrote about him. Monroe, he said, "resembles an animated cartoon character whose feet never touch the ground." And yet, he added, Monroe demonstrates "the indescribable heat of genius that burns deep inside him. Some kind of diabolical intensity comes across his face when he has the ball."

"He was a nightmare to guard," said Walt Frazier recently. "Earl didn't know what he was going to do next, so how could I?"

I once asked Monroe, after a routinely spectacular shooting night, if he just knew that anything he shot would go in.

"A few times tonight I was fooled," he said.

"That the ball didn't go in, or did go in?" "Both," he said. Earl Monroe—known widely and fittingly as Earl the Pearl—is recalled now because on Wednesday the nominees for the Basketball Hall of Fame were announced, and Monroe was among the 15 people named. The article in

The New York Times about it noted that Bob Lanier, Elvin Hayes, Nate Archibald, Calvin Murphy, and Al McGuire were all listed for the first time, and some like Ann Meyers and Dave Bing and Walt Bellamy were nominees last year. The story went on: "Monroe, a Knick backcourt star for almost nine seasons and rookie of the year as a Baltimore Bullet, has failed in his election bid the last three years."

"I made it in my third try," said Frazier, "and I thought Earl would, too. He certainly deserves it."

There is a linking between Frazier and Monroe that began as opponents, and continued as teammates. Both came into the National Basketball Association in 1967, and retired the same year, 1980. Frazier, during his 13 seasons, averaged 18.9 points per game and accounted for 5,040 assists. Monroe averaged 18.8 points per game and had 2,416 assists.

But cold, impersonal numbers do not convey the feeling of excitement and pleasure that Monroe—and Frazier—provided. And the overall excellence they manifested.

And when the Knicks obtained Monroe in a trade with the Bullets in 1971, skeptics warned that the Knicks would need two basketballs for their two backcourt stars.

"It didn't happen because we had too much mutual respect for each other," recalled Frazier. "We didn't let our egos get in the way of trying to win. When he was hot, I got him the ball, and vice versa."

Monroe's coach with the Knicks, Red Holzman, said that because of Monroe's "flamboyant style, people tended to miss how good he was on defense."

But it was indeed his style that stood out. It was showy without being irritating, confident without being cocky. It was all, one understood, part and parcel of the inner man.

The first time I ever saw Monroe play was when he was still in college, at Winston-Salem in 1966, and he was trying out in Minneapolis for the United States team in the Pan-Am Games. I remember being amazed that he would turn his back to the basket while dribbling in the backcourt—it was a cardinal sin in the game's canon—but he never had the ball stolen, and seemed to know exactly where the hoop was at all times. He was a true and unfettered original.

He and Elvin Hayes were the best players in the tryouts, and neither made the team. I thought a Congressional investigation should have been made into it, though Congress, apparently, had other things on its mind at the time. What, I can't imagine.

Monroe, in his first year with Baltimore, had difficulty assimilating his unusual and eye-catching talents into a veteran team, and had problems with the NBA in general. As a star rookie, opponents roughed him up. Meanwhile, some teammates thought he controlled the ball too much. And Monroe hated the travel, especially the beds. Sleeping on some mattresses, he said, was like falling into a hole. Others were like riding the humps of a camel. "I'm thinking of quitting after this season," he told me.

But he stayed, of course, and went on to have a spectacular career. One that ought to end with his being remembered on a wall in the Basketball Hall of Fame.

·   ·   ·

Monroe was slected to the Basketball Hall of Fame in the balloting that year.

BILL BRADLEY USES OLD LESSONS IN A NEW ARENA

May 1, 1983

WASHINGTON, D.C.—IN SENATOR BILL Bradley's large new white office with high ceilings and high windows, there is an echo. "Listen," he says. And the sound of the word is faintly reheard. The Democratic United States Senator from New Jersey is standing near the center of the room, a yellow pencil behind his ear, a blue lightweight suit casually worn, his vaulted left eyebrow raised, and he laughs in his throaty manner at the sound. That, too, reverberates lightly. There are other echoes in the room, these silent. They depict what the senator, with characteristic irony, refers to as his "past life."

A desk plaque, a kind of inside joke, reads "Senator Bill Bradley," then right below it "Former New York Knick." And on the floor against the wall—he has been in this office in the Hart Building for only a month, so papers and photographs are piled around the room awaiting shelves and carpenters—can be seen, amid pictures of sober civilian scenes, two enlarged black-and-white photos of him in a Knicks jersey and shorts. One picture shows him racing across the basketball court, arms pumping in triumph, just after the Knicks had beaten Los Angeles to win the 1970 National Basketball Association championship.

In the other photo he has leaped into the broad arms of Willis Reed, the former Knick center. Bradley, his legs wrapped around Reed's waist, is facing the camera and his mouth is open with a yelp of glee. The Knicks had just won the 1973 NBA title.

Senator Bradley walks behind his desk and eases his 6'5" body into a plain, hardback chair. "A back injury from my playing days—I couldn't take sitting in a big leather chair for long," he explains. He smiles. "That's the way it is with us old jocks."

Senator Bradley was named recently to the Naismith Memorial Basketball Hall of Fame. The senator, along with Dave DeBusschere, the other starting forward on the Knicks' two championship teams, his former roommate and still a close friend, will be among six men inducted tomorrow into the hall at Springfield, Massachusetts.

"I think I'm a senator today as much because I had the experience of playing professional basketball for 10 years on the road in America as for any other college experience or for anything I studied," he said.

Senator Bradley, by his own estimation, had grown up relatively sheltered in Crystal City, Missouri, a suburb of St. Louis. The only child of Warren Bradley, a well-to-do banker, and Susan Crowe Bradley, a former junior high school teacher, Bill Bradley enrolled at Princeton, became an All-America basketball player, was a starter on the United States Olympic championship team in 1964, then a Rhodes Scholar at Oxford in England, played for the Knicks from 1967 to 1977, and, at age 35, won election to the Senate in 1978. Now 39—he will be 40 on July 28—he is one of the youngest senators and, by most accounts, one of the most capable on Capitol Hill.

"I played with a team—the Knicks—at a time when the people on it were not only great basketball players, but good people," he said, "so the experience for me was remarkable, living and traveling with them 100 days of the year and getting to know them." Blacks and whites, men from all over the country, from a variety of backgrounds. DeBusschere from a working-class family in Detroit; Reed a black from the rural South; Walt Frazier a black from Atlanta. Earl Monroe was a black from Philadelphia, and Phil Jackson a white man from Montana.

"I remember one night when I had been in the Senate for only about four or five months," said Senator Bradley. "It was about 11:00 PM and the Senate was still in session. I was sitting around the Democratic cloak room, which is just off the Senate floor, and a lot of senators were there.

"I looked around and saw one guy joking, another guy was quiet, another one was talking. And it occurred to me that this wasn't a lot different from the Knicks' locker room, in that it really was a matter of people getting along together in a small space, each of whom has his own individual agendas but who must subsume that individual agenda in a broader, more general context—if they're actually going to get anything accomplished.

"That process still fascinates me—how to get people with different backgrounds, different experiences, different personal agendas to agree on a shared goal and work toward it."

As a professional, he had a career average of 12.4 points per game and made one midseason All-Star team, but he was the ultimate role player. Never the most gifted athlete—most of the NBA players could run faster and jump higher—he understood that he needed constant motion to frustrate his defender, he developed an uncanny ability to get open for a shot off a screen, and he was deadly with a jump shot. If need be, he might hold another player's jersey or step on his toe, when the referee's vision was blocked.

It was suggested that he was the least talented, grabbiest, and smartest player in the NBA, and each of those explained the other. "None of that's true," Senator Bradley said with a laugh. "A reporter called me after I had been named for the Hall of Fame and asked me what I thought had been my contributions to the game," he said. "I had never prior to that question ever thought that I had made a contribution to the game, not like somebody who breaks the DNA code or makes a contribution to medicine.

"I think my whole orientation was to view myself only as a part of a larger whole, which was the team. And while you always looked at individual stats, you didn't really pay that much attention to them.

"But of course I was flattered and pleased that an honor like this would happen to me. And I'm especially glad to go in with DeBusschere. I figured that for six years I walked behind him and carried his bag, I might as well walk behind him and carry his bag into the Hall of Fame."

But playing well wasn't the only thing. Winning was essential. "Certainly winning is important," the senator said. "If you didn't win, you wouldn't have proved anything by the way you played. It was winning by playing the way you did that was the key. In amateur sports you could take a lot of satisfaction from your efforts. You could tell a grade school or high school student—as I tell my daughter, Theresa Anne, who's six—'Go out and play and do something just as well as you possibly can, as well as your ability will allow, and then be satisfied with your performance, regardless of whether you won or lost.'

"But not in professional sports, because the nature of it, the reason you're playing is to win. Now, there were other levels of the game for me, obviously, in addition to winning—such as playing in a certain manner." He meant the humanness of the experience; not only knowing where your teammate was going to go to be open for a pass, but being congenial to even discussing personal problems with him off the court.

"But winning justifies your success," he said. "Some people justify their success if they don't win by their individual achievements. I didn't."

But is there not an overemphasis on winning in America that has influenced it greatly? "Some of that has been exaggerated," he said. "There is a flip side to winning, of course, and that's losing. And part of personal growth is being able to deal with that. Losing has a flavor, a taste all its own. And in some sense it is as much responsible for the personal growth component in sport as is winning. And simply because you emphasize winning doesn't mean that you don't have a healthy respect for the personal growth potential in losing, and coping with that."

Bradley, too, "lost." With Princeton in 1965, he went to the semifinals of the National Collegiate Athletic Association and lost to Michigan. He struggled in his rookie year with the Knicks—the highest-paid player in the game at the time—and made bad plays at the end of several games that contributed to Knick losses. And he was disappointed in not winning four straight championships with the Knicks. He thought they might have.

"I still think that sports are overwhelmingly positive," he said. "I think that elements such as commercialism and overemphasis in certain segments has become like many of the areas of our life. And the problems associated with those areas are part of sports as well. But I think that still the dominant motive for playing and the dominant experience of the game is positive.

"And the motive is to excel, and the experience provides the range from discipline to dedication to community to what else that it always had when you are with the right group of people at the right time.

"And I always said that I think sports as a model for other things—as a metaphor—is limited. That's why I have to be pushed by a writer to even draw a parallel to my own experiences. But the parallel I've chosen to draw is a very personal one. Not what sports means for America, but what sports meant for me, and how that related to what I do now.

"The practice really did establish habits for me that carry over into what I do now. I work very hard now." He often puts in 16 to 18 hours of work. "And I work because I want to be the best senator I can be. In a way it's like when I starting practicing basketball four or five hours a day when I was 13. I wanted to be the very best basketball player I could be."

The senator no longer plays basketball. "I just don't have the time," he said. He also has said that much of the fun would be gone for him when he would want to make a move he once made, and now could not. "I haven't really shot since 1977, when I walked off the court in Detroit in Cobo Arena. An odd thing is, the last shot I took was a jump shot which I hit from the left baseline. It was a kind of symmetry because that was the first jump shot against the same team, the first shot I took as a pro in 1967. So, 10 years later, the same team, the same shot.

"The only time I touch a ball now is when I'm visiting a high school and someone throws me a ball and says, 'Shoot.' Sometimes I'll be campaigning for a Democratic candidate and we'll have a meeting in the high school. We may be discussing the military budget or the health of the economy and it never makes the local news. But if a free throw shooting contest is arranged, that's always covered. So the candidates want me to do that, and so I do. That's the extent to which I do any playing at all."

Bradley has recently lost about 30 pounds. He now weighs 212, about three pounds fewer than when he played with the Knicks. "Basically, I lost the weight by not eating," he said. He was once an aficionado of junk foods. "I try to jog a few times a week for about 30 minutes a time. Or I'll ride an exercise bicycle. My athletic experience now is no different from about 80 million other Americans who are in sports to try to flatten their stomachs and widen their arteries."

His interest in pro basketball remains, but on a sedentary level. "I watch the playoffs when they get down to the end," he said. "It's then that you really see the psychology of the game. You see what the team that has gotten to know each other will do in a period of stress. And more times than not that team will win over the team that has really not been through the pressure cooker."

It was mentioned that Larry Bird of the Celtics plays in a manner reminiscent of Bradley.

"The most distinguishing characteristics of Bird," he said, "is that he always moves and the ball doesn't stay in his hands very long. And obviously those are the two things I can identify with as a player."

For the most part, Bradley has downplayed his participation in sports, though he says he remains very proud of it. "But I wanted to prove myself in a different field—in the Senate—and I had to prove myself by the standards of the institution." So he refused to rely on his celebrity status from basketball as a crutch.

"But I am still often referred to in newspaper stories, as 'Senator Bill Bradley, the former New York Knick.' I laugh about that, but I have the feeling it will be with me the rest of my life."

Senator Bradley, like some intensely hard-working people, uses humor as a release—at times, a zany sense of humor. Once, when he was with the Knicks, he went to a party dressed in a priest's frock, and supposedly heard confessions. He was also known for his unconcerned sartorial style of dress. Walt Frazier remembers Bradley's raincoat, for example. When it wasn't raining, he would roll it into a ball and carry it under his arm.

He was also known as "Dollar Bill," because of his frugality. Rumor had it that he had kept the first dollar he ever made. He seemed to enjoy the ribbing and attention of the other players in regard to his unusual habits. It made the boy from the suburbs feel a part of the team.

It was mentioned to him that when he played on the All-Star team, he had said to Pistol Pete Maravich "to do something crazy when you get in the game."

"Did I say 'crazy'?" asked Bradley. "Maybe I did. Or maybe I said, 'Do something different.' You can't take yourself too seriously. And that episode illustrates that not only did I feel that as a player, I feel that in this job. You have to have a sense of humor about who you are and what you do. You maintain a personal stability that way. It relieves tension, to recognize that you can't always do everything, and that you do the best you can for as long as you can. And recognizing that you alone are not responsible for things happening on the court, or in the Senate. Ultimately, it's the recognition that the institution goes on. When you see yourself that way, it's hard to take yourself too seriously—though you can take what you're doing seriously."

Looking at the photo of him jumping into Reed's arms, he was asked if he has had such a moment of elation since. "That's a feeling that's never been duplicated," he said. "It's a clear-cut victory, something that rarely happens in life. We had established ourselves as the best in the world. But it's like anything. It lasts about 24 hours. But the moment is intense."

What's the closest he has come to it since? "Haven't." He thought for a moment. "Afterward you experience a whole range of satisfactions and achievements and series of accomplishments," he said. "The point is, the moment depicted in that photo was a peak in that narrow category of experience—basketball. Then life goes on."

A SNORKELER'S TALE

November 10, 1984

WHEN THE LANDSLIDE RE-ELECTION victory for Bill Bradley as United States Senator from New Jersey was apparent last Tuesday evening, one of the television commentators discussed the senator's style.

He spoke of the great respect that the tall, dark-haired man with the oddly upturned left eyebrow had earned from both sides of the aisle in the Senate, of how hard he had worked to gain a firm grasp of issues, and of the tremendous popularity he had attained in his state. The commentator also mentioned that Bill Bradley's speaking voice was rather flat, though he had been endeavoring to improve it, and that his sense of humor could be wooden.

Dave DeBusschere and his wife, Gerri, smiled when that last point was made. That's not quite the Bill Bradley they know.

"He's not a joke teller; some people just aren't," said Gerri DeBusschere. "But Dave and I enjoyed his kind of wacko sense of humor, especially when he was with the Knicks."

Dave DeBusschere, now the Knicks executive vice president and director of basketball operations, was Bill Bradley's roommate on the road when they played together, from 1968 through 1974.

"I remember when a man began writing and calling Bill at hotels," said Gerri, "and Bill would whisper to the guy on the phone, and they'd have meetings in coffee shops. Dave finally asked Bill who the guy was. Bill said, 'He thinks I'm not Bill Bradley. He thinks I'm really an Albanian spy.' And Bill encouraged him."

On the road in basketball, Bradley, the Princeton graduate and Rhodes Scholar, also involved himself in such issues as prison reform, the economy, and foreign affairs. Unlike most of the other players, who were dapper, he seemed to have little time for sartorial concerns. He would sometimes forget to bring extra socks and would borrow DeBusschere's, and when a button broke on his shirt he'd replace it with a paper clip. His raincoat was generally wrapped up in a ball and carried under his arm. On seeing it, Dick Barnett would make a sound like a foghorn, an esthetic appraisal of sorts.

After the 1974 playoffs, the DeBusscheres, Bradley and his wife, Ernestine, and another couple, the Nick Kladdises of Chicago, went to Greece on vacation. Gerri DeBusschere recalls that everyone except Bradley took at least one suitcase—the DeBusscheres had one suitcase just for their scuba-diving equipment. "Bill came with a little gym bag," she said. "He didn't even have a bathing suit. He swam in his Knick practice shorts."

The three couples rented a cabin cruiser and embarked from the port of Piraeus for a two-week trip around the Greek islands. They lay on the deck and watched the islands go by, and Dave and Bill, particularly, would don snorkeling masks and flippers, drop down, and explore the Aegean. From the boat one afternoon, they saw a church on a hill of a tiny, isolated island. They decided to get a closer look.

The island was so small that there was no place to dock the boat, so it remained about a quarter of a mile out to sea. Bradley and DeBusschere swam to shore. DeBusschere came up first, and saw a man sitting on a beach chair, reading a book.

DeBusschere took off his mask, and the man jumped up, his book dropping out of his hands. The man's mouth was agape, and he pointed frantically at DeBusschere.

DeBusschere thought that there might be something wrong with him, or that he was frightened that someone who was 6'6" was suddenly rising from the sea.

"Then," DeBusschere recalled, "the man stuttered, 'You're, you're, you're Dave...Dave...Dave DeBusschere!'"

DeBusschere was surprised that anyone on this little island could speak English, let alone recognize him.

"Then Bill came out of the water right behind me," DeBusschere recalls. "The guy says, 'Oh, my God! Bill Bradley too! I can't believe this!'"

The man sputtered that he had season tickets under the basket, and that he had been postponing his vacation until after the playoffs, and that he was on this island because he had been so overworked that his wife had said he needed to go to a secluded place for a rest.

"And to see you guys here is—"

"Sure," Bradley said with understanding, "and Willis Reed will be here in a minute."

"The whole team is coming up," said DeBusschere.

The man said, "Wait, wait right here. I've got to get my wife. She'll never believe this. Oh, my God!"

The man flew off down the beach, screaming his wife's name.

Bradley turned to DeBusschere and said with a grin, "Let's leave."

DeBusschere nodded. The pair clamped on their masks and disappeared back into the water.

Gerri DeBusschere happened to be watching this from the deck of the boat. She sees the man now racing back along the beach, dragging his wife by the hand.

He returns to the spot where his chair is, and where his book is lying in the sand. Otherwise, the beach is deserted.

He goes to the water's edge, looking around and pointing. Meanwhile, Bradley and DeBusschere have returned to the boat and are hiding in a cabin below deck. Nick Kladdis revs up the motor, and the boat heads farther out to sea.

On the beach, the man is waving wildly, while his wife is looking at him and then looking at the receding boat.

Bradley and DeBusschere never saw him again. The next season, they looked for him under the baskets at Madison Square Garden, but he wasn't there.

"The guy's wife probably thought he had flipped," said Gerri DeBusschere, "and he never came up to Bill or Dave and said, 'I saw you in Greece.' He was probably too embarrassed. He probably thought he hadn't really seen them, and that he was just suffering from being overworked."

THE BIG PLAYER WHO DID
ALL THE LITTLE THINGS

May 15, 2003

WHAT ONE REMEMBERS ABOUT Dave DeBusschere, the basketball player, the one player who was perhaps most responsible for the emergence of the champion Knicks in the early 1970s—the Camelot years of the Knicks—is that he could be a Hummer or a BMW, depending on the situation in a particular night.

Burly, rock-jawed, his thighs so muscular they seemed cast in marble, he could be a force in what the players called "the butcher shop," the rebounding area under the basket where welts sprouted and blood spilled and, as Kipling might have said, you had to be a man, my son.

Or he sank shots from so far out the basketballs seemed to be launched from Section 310 in Madison Square Garden. And if a defender dared try nuzzling up to him, DeBusschere drove around him with grace and power and surprising alacrity, given that he was 6'6" and 235 pounds.

On defense, he had the amazing ability to make his man disappear. As Donnie May, a teammate, said in the 1970 book on the Knicks, *Miracle on 33rd Street*, by Phil Berger, "Guys like DeBusschere, for six, seven, eight minutes of a game, you don't even see the man he's guarding. He cuts him off from the ball, takes him right out of the game."

DeBusschere off the court possessed a sense of humor, a sense of balance, a solid sense of himself. I remember a night in the locker room before a game when he was talking with several teammates, discussing "homer" referees who called, he said, "these terrible charging fouls." DeBusschere, wearing only a jock strap, impersonated a referee calling a charging foul—slapping his right hand behind his neck and pointing with his left hand and skipping across the floor. Everyone was laughing.

"In college once a guy called that on me," he said. "'Get your hand up. Get your hand up.' I said, 'I didn't foul him. I'm not getting my hand up.'" More laughter.

After a game, he'd be open for an even-handed discussion with reporters—win or lose—but first he had to have his cold bottle of brew. (His father owned a bar in Detroit, and DeBusschere, all his life, was comfortable with a beer in his hands.) Yesterday afternoon, a phone call came with the shocking news: Dave DeBusschere, age 62, had died of a heart attack.

It was a difficult notion to grasp. Dave DeBusschere. A monument of strength and vitality and, in the mind's eye, everlasting youth. And genuineness. He might have been criticized for his stewardship as general manager of the Knicks in the 1980s. He might even have been criticized as a basketball coach; he was given the reins of the Pistons at the improbable age of 24, while still a player, in only his third season in the NBA, and couldn't influence a team of egotists to simply play like a team. But I've never heard anyone knock Dave DeBusschere the man. Teammates like Willis Reed, Walt Frazier, Phil Jackson, Earl Monroe, and Bill Bradley have expressed admiration for him. Bradley, his roommate on the road, has said that DeBusschere was "like a brother to me."

Red Holzman was the coach of the Knicks when, on December 19, 1968, he and general manager Eddie Donovan engineered a deal with the Pistons for DeBusschere. In return, the Knicks sent center Walt Bellamy and guard Howard Komives to Detroit.

"We were a good team, and Dave made us a terrific team," Danny Whelan, the trainer for the Knicks in that era, said yesterday.

Frazier said, "He was the final piece of the puzzle."

The Knicks won the NBA championship in 1970 and again in 1973, the only titles in the history of the franchise. Holzman once told me something in confidence that, under the circumstances, I don't think he would mind my revealing.

"When we made the trade, sending Bellamy to Detroit for Dave," Holzman said, "I was so happy I got drunk for three days." That was only a figure of speech to express his pleasure, for although Red enjoyed his Scotch, he also liked to keep his wits about him. The fact is he had a game to coach the next day.

Holzman, in his 1987 autobiography, *Red on Red*, said about DeBusschere: "He was very intelligent, wasn't hungry about his points, and helped younger players.

"When we traded for him, we believed DeBusschere was a great player. Dave turned out to be even better than we thought. All too often a player comes to a team in a deal and you find there are problems; he's got bad hands, poor training habits, stuff you never notice before coaching or playing against him. Dave had no problems. All the players respected him for his ability and leadership qualities. For all-around play, I rank him as one of the best all-time forwards."

After the trade, Holzman said, the roles of the Knick players became more defined. Reed moved from forward to center, and Frazier, who had been the third guard, stepped in as a starter.

Once DeBusschere joined the team, the Knicks won 10 straight games, then a club record. "He was so astute in basketball," Whelan said, "that on the first night he joined us, he almost knew the plays."

In his life after basketball, DeBusschere and his wife, Geri, saw their three children grow up. He became a real estate executive, his hair turned gray, but when he was seen periodically at courtside at Knicks games, he still looked sturdy enough to take perhaps a dozen rebounds a game. The fans greeted him with cheers. He was named to the Basketball Hall of Fame and was chosen one of the 50 best players in NBA history. Now he is gone.

"I'm heartbroken at the news," Whelan said. "Just heartbroken."

He is not alone.

THE CAPTAIN RESURFACES

March 3, 1988

WILLIS REED MADE A joke, one of several Tuesday night.

He could afford it; he was rolling. He had been named the head coach of the Nets the day before, and in his first game on the bench his team was beating the Los Angeles Clippers by some 30 points with two minutes left.

Buck Williams, the star forward he inherited, had just been called for his fifth foul.

Reed took him out of the game. "Take a rest," Reed told Williams, "so you'll be ready to play McHale and Bird tomorrow."

In the past, of course, regardless of how well rested any of the Nets were—and this could go for virtually every team in the National Basketball Association—no one was rested quite enough to successfully engage the Celtics in that old barn in Boston with that old laundry hanging from the rafters.

And the Nets? Dear Lord, one of the game's most deplorable outfits.

And yet, well, why sustain the suspense. Yesterday they went to Boston and knocked off the Celtics 117–107. Did it in rather cavalier fashion. Did it without Buck Williams, even, who had pulled a hamstring in a collision with Larry Bird with about seven minutes left in the first period, and was lost for the rest of the game.

Did it with, or for, the new coach, Reed.

What next? After Tuesday's triumph, Reed wasn't letting a 29-point victory inflate his head.

"Look what happened in Washington when Wes Unseld took over a few weeks ago," he said. "They won for him right away, then they settled back and have had trouble winning."

Regardless, euphoria is where you can find it. And right now, it's great to be a Net. Who would have imagined it?

Meanwhile, on the night of his coaching debut in New Jersey, Reed talked about nervousness and was asked about the night in which he is perhaps most famous for—until, of course, last night in Boston. It was May 8, 1970. "I was very, very nervous," he said. "I walked out there without being able to walk too well and there I was, having to face probably the greatest all-around center in the history of the game. I would've had problems if I'd had two good legs.

"But everyone thought, 'Well, the Captain's here. Everything is going to be all right.' It was some predicament."

He remembers coming through the tunnel and onto the court and receiving that huge roar from a full house of nearly 20,000 fans, cheering for the man known widely as the Captain.

That was Madison Square Garden, when, suffering with a recently injured hip, he hobbled onto the court. The fate of a team, the Knicks, was waiting that night.

It was the seventh and deciding game of the NBA championship series. On the other side of the court was the purple-clad foe, the Lakers, and their sizable Dipper, Wilt Chamberlain.

Reed sank two quick jump shots—his only field goals of the game—and, pumped by Captain Courageous, the Knicks beat the Lakers for the title.

On Tuesday night at Byrne Meadowlands Arena, it was a little more of the same. Very little. Nervous, Willis? "Well, competition always makes you nervous."

But he appeared relatively loose now, reminding a visitor that, after all, this wasn't for the championship.

It was the reverse. The loser would be the undisputed worst team in the NBA. These Angelenos were in last place in their division, with 12 victories (and 40 losses) for the season. The Nets were last in their division, also with 12 victories (and 42 losses). These were the two foulest records in the NBA.

So, once again, the Captain was being called to save the situation.

Before the formal introduction, Reed came onto the arena floor. Encompassing him were some 20,000 seats, as in Madison Square Garden, but here about 18,000 of them were vacant.

A round of applause and cheers, generous but dispersed, greeted the Captain, that very nice large man, now wearing glasses, and garmented not in intimate basketball apparel, but in a brown herringbone sport coat and mustard-colored slacks.

Familiarly, there was still that slight limp, the limp that had torn at the hearts of Knick fans on that night many Mays ago.

"Go, Willis, do it Captain!" someone now yelled, someone, perhaps, like some old Japanese soldiers from World War II, still scattered in basketball caves and barely aware of the passage of time.

Reed was back as a head coach in the NBA after nearly 10 years away, after having spent a year as head man with the Knicks, and then was fired. He's been a college coach and a pro assistant since then.

Before he knew it, the Nets were off to a terrific start, with a 14–0 lead. Would he debut with a shutout? "What bad shooting!" groaned Gene Shue, the Clipper coach. "My God, what bad shooting!"

It didn't get much better for the rest of the night for the Clippers. The Net defense, as Reed later pointed out, looked "great," but he admitted it was a little hard to tell how great because of the level of the adversary.

Meanwhile, Reed had good words for several Nets, including the euphonious Dudley Bradley, who sparked the team defensively. There was also the expected generous assortment of bumbled plays on both sides.

He knew that the next night, in Boston, he'd be facing a healthy sampling of reality, as he once faced Chamberlain.

"One night you think, 'What a team, this is great,'" he said, smiling after the victory Tuesday. "And the next night, 'Is this basketball?'"

"Those are the frustrations of being a coach. I've learned at least that."

After two games, what frustrations can the Captain possibly be thinking of?

WING-O!

January 13, 1990

AS HE LAY IN a ward in Harlem Hospital, with five other patients and no telephone, he said he remembered how the crowd at Madison Square Garden would chant his name: "Wing-O! Wing-O!" It usually came late in the game. He had sat at the end of the Knicks bench, his bony knees nearly hiding his eyes, as he heard the appeal for him to play. "Ah man," he said now, "that felt good, but it made me a little embarrassed." And he smiled, a familiar, gentle smile.

Harthorne Nathaniel Wingo Jr., a name that has the lilt of poetry, pulled his bedcover higher on his blue pajamas. Beside him on a nightstand lay his cane.

"Those were great days," he said. "Great days. But I don't see many of the guys anymore." Wingo—Wingy to friends and teammates—was one of New York's most endearing athletes, from 1972, when he joined the Knicks, to 1976, when he was released. He is 41 years old, and all of that seems long ago.

Why had this rather routine player been so popular? Well, there was his name, which gave flight to imagination. And his attitude: he was a hard-working, high-jumping, sweet-tempered man. He was 6'8", thin as a pipestem, and uncomplaining as a substitute player. Indeed, he touched us because he was Cinderella, and still happy on occasion to haul coals in the castle.

He had been discovered only a few blocks from the Garden, wheeling clothes racks in the garment center. He had journeyed from his home in Tryon, North Carolina, where he grew up playing on dirt courts, and hoped to find a way to play professional basketball. It was his dream.

When he began making a name for himself in the Rucker Tournament in Harlem, two scouts from the Knicks appeared. It was arranged for him to play for Allentown of the Eastern League, while still living here. "Then one day," Wingo said, "my agent called me and said, 'Why don't you come downtown to my office so you can sign a contract with the Knicks.' I screamed so loud everyone in the Bronx must have heard me, and Manhattan, too."

"He was one of my favorites," said Red Holzman, the former Knicks coach. "He always gave everything he had, in practice or in a game. And wherever he went, people loved him. I remember seeing him in a summer league in Los Angeles, and even there people were hollering, 'Wingo! Wingo!'"

Harthorne Nathaniel Wingo Jr. had some good games for the Knicks, rebounding and playing aggressive defense, though he was never a star shooter. "And the guys were wonderful, like Bill Bradley," Wingo said. "Bill was head of the players' union, and our lockers were next to each other. He'd ask, 'Everything okay, Wingy, need anything?' Imagine, him a Rhodes Scholar and being that way to me, who dropped out of junior college."

Wingo's "biggest thrill" came, he said, "when we won the championship in Los Angeles in 1973."

"In the last game," he recalled, "Dave DeBusschere sprained his ankle and Henry Bibby and I carried him to the locker room. That was the only time I got on the court that night. That was my highlight." He laughed. "But I got the ring. That's what I wanted."

He no longer has the ring, however. His former wife does. She also has his trophies. And he hasn't seen her in several years. His salary with the Knicks ranged from $25,000 a year to $45,000, and that went, he says, "when I bought over-my-head jewelry and cars and stuff to try to impress her."

In fact, in the last several years, not much has gone very well for Wingo. After the NBA, he played four years in Italy and then he came back, failed in another tryout with the Knicks, and went from job to job. His money is gone. About a year ago he worked as a "temp," as he said, arriving at an office in the morning, receiving an assignment for menial labor somewhere, and then returning in the evening to pick up his $25.

"And I got tired of that," he said. "Then I guess I kinda gave up. I stayed in a lot. I didn't like going out at night because that's when you get in trouble. I'd seen some terrible things on the streets, shootings, beatings, drugs. But I stayed clean. And I'd be in bed and at all times of night I'd hear gunshots. I just turned over and tried to sleep."

Last December 12 Wingo woke up and found he couldn't move his right leg. It had stiffened up. He was also suffering from pneumonia, and was taken to the hospital. Now, Wingo has no job, no home of his own—he sleeps in the living room of a cousin's apartment in Harlem—and has an arthritic hip that will probably need surgery.

He hopes to leave the hospital soon, and expects $16,000 from the NBA for a licensing program. This is back money due him because the NBA Players Association had been unable to locate him. "I'd like to work with kids," Wingo said. "Nothin' extravagant. It's so easy to mess up— too easy. And maybe I could do a little somethin' for 'em, somethin' good."

DAY OF A PRO BASKETBALL
PLAYER—YAWWWN

February 2, 1972

DANNY WHELAN, GRAY-HAIRED TEAM trainer and handyman, is alone in the New York Knicks locker room in Madison Square Garden. It is 10:30 AM. The room, with greenish carpet and light wood lockers built into the wall, is clean and tidy. Stools have been turned upside down and placed on the low shelf of each locker. Practice begins in half an hour. At 1:00 PM, the team will board a bus to the airport for an away game tomorrow.

Whelan is packing the blue traveling uniforms. Jerry Lucas is the first player in. He wears a tawny suede jacket, brown corduroy bell-bottoms, work shoes.

"Stayed up late to see you on the Johnny Carson Show last night," said Whelan. "Disgusting."

"Yeah," said Lucas. He had come on at the end of the show. "I got two minutes of air time. In between 32 commercials. They had promised me 14 minutes. I couldn't do my stuff in two minutes. And I didn't want to talk."

Lucas has some tricks. One is taking names from a telephone book and changing them into words and sentences.

"I would never go on that show," said Whelan. "The nerve. You should've gone around the corner to the Cavett Show. I woulda."

The talk is low. Dave DeBusschere comes in.

"I fell asleep, Luke, how'd ya do last night?"

"I did the Casper the Ghost act."

"Benched?" asked DeBusschere.

"Almost. Got two minutes." Lucas shakes his head. DeBusschere shakes his head.

"I saw films of that Ohio State–Minnesota fight," said DeBusschere, as rookie Dean Meminger and Eddie Miles stroll in.

"They were sure dukin' it, weren't they?" says Meminger, who sports a sparse goatee.

"See that one guy knee the other?" asks DeBusschere.

"These college kids are all hepped up for the game," says Meminger. "They only play one or two a week. The coach says, 'Don't you guys take nothin' from the other guys.'"

"They'd go out there like bulls and see red," says Miles.

Phil Jackson walks in. "The announcer said that one guy spit on the guy on the floor. I didn't see that."

"You can't see everything on television," says Miles.

Jackson sits down. Looks over *The New York Times*, then throws the paper across the room at the wastebasket. The paper flutters all over the floor. A couple of guys laugh.

"A lotta times it's the referees' fault," says DeBusschere. "Especially homers on the road. They call these terrible charging fouls." In jock strap, he impersonates a referee calling a charging foul—slapping his right hand behind his neck, pointing with left hand, and skipping across the floor.

"They're ruining the game with that stuff," said Meminger.

"How come, Luke, they didn't give you no time last night?" asks Jackson.

"Arrgh," says Lucas, diligently taping his ankles. "After the show I did my tricks for 'em. Great, they said, great. The greatest stuff we've ever seen. Come back next week. I told 'em to forget it."

"Right," said Whelan. "The Cavett Show's the answer."

"Bradley not here yet?" says coach Red Holzman, momentarily extracting the butt of a thin cigar from his mouth as he walks in.

By 11:00, all the Knicks are on the court. The Garden is eerily empty, save for a few maintenance people. Kenny Mayfield, a small guard who plays in the Eastern League and who has hopes of making the Knicks next season, is a regular 12th man who plays mostly defense in drills. The players wear reversible red-and-blue sleeveless sweatshirts.

The practice is swift, no nonsense. They run through plays. Then have a quick scrimmage.

"Get in front of your offensive man, Earl," shouts Holzman to Monroe, as they practice the press.

Clyde Frazier, later, shouts "Get it up, Get it up," in anticipation of a nonexistent 24-second clock.

Mayfield blocks a DeBusschere shot. "Way to do it, Kenny," calls Meminger from the sideline. "Who is that chump, anyway." DeBusschere grimaces.

"I know you're a great outside shot, Luther," Holzman says to Rackley, later, "but you could've had a step-in."

Practice ends at 12:30. The team hurriedly showers and dresses. DeBusschere employs a hand hair-dryer. Bradley drinks a beer. The team leaves for the waiting bus.

Another exciting day in the life of a pro basketball team.

II.

A QUARTET OF THE 2013 KNICKS

THE FUTURE OF YOUNG MELO

April 1, 2002

CARMELO ANTHONY WATCHED WITH interest the film clips on television last year of the Raptors star Vince Carter taking the morning and afternoon off before an important playoff game that evening and flying by private plane to Chapel Hill. Carter made the arrangements to receive his diploma from the University of North Carolina and fly back to Philadelphia for the game.

Carter felt it was important for him, and as a symbol to others, to attend the graduation ceremony. Some criticized him for not giving full focus to the playoff game. Others believed Carter's gesture indeed sent an important message.

At the time, Anthony was a high school basketball star in his junior year at Towson Catholic in Baltimore, his grades falling below C, myriad distractions keeping him from diligence with his schoolbooks.

"What Vince Carter did influenced me a lot," Anthony said yesterday, shortly before working out with the McDonald's All-American team at Basketball City in preparation for an All-Star game at Madison Square Garden on Thursday. "He showed that you could do both, play basketball and graduate from college." Carter had left North Carolina after his junior year to turn pro.

Anthony, 17, is a lithe, 6'7" small forward with carefully braided hair and a winning aplomb. He is, according to authorities like Tom Konchalski, who puts out the highly regarded H.S.B.I. Report, "one of the two or three best high school basketball players in the country."

Anthony transferred before this school year from Towson Catholic to Oak Hill Academy in a remote area of southwest Virginia. He brought his grades up drastically, to mostly As and Bs, and played with such skill, such displays of leadership, on one of the top-rated teams in the country, that he has been discussed as an NBA lottery pick, or at least a first-round draft choice.

"I'm 90 percent sure that I'm going to college," he said. "I want to be the first person in my family to go to college. After a year or two, we'll see if I'll stay or not. But I will definitely graduate. Carter did it, Shaq did it, Isiah Thomas did it. Others did it. My mother wants to me do it, and I want it for myself."

He has chosen Syracuse, he says, for reasons both hoops-wise and academics-related. He liked Jim Boeheim as a coach and a person, and was impressed with a particular department at Syracuse.

"I know people like Bob Costas and Marv Albert went to the Newhouse School of Communications there," Anthony said. "It's supposed to be one of the best. I want to go into communications, too, but behind the camera, not in front of it. I like video stuff. Maybe one day I can make movies."

Like a good business major, however, he also knows exactly what top NBA draft picks make. "Four point six million a year for three years guaranteed," he said. Kwame Brown, the first pick last season for the Washington Wizards, Anthony said, "got $11.9 million."

"That's a lot of money," Anthony said, "but my family has survived until now, and another year or two won't make that much difference."

He grew up in a tough Baltimore neighborhood, where, he said, drugs and shootings were commonplace. "Some guys with as much or more talent than me went the other way," Anthony said. "But I had a strong mom, and good coaches and friends to help keep me straight."

It sounds like a cliché if the facts of the circumstances weren't so real, and perilous.

Anthony's mother, Mary, is a housekeeper at the University of Maryland. He is the youngest in his family and his three siblings—two brothers and a sister—are all employed.

"My father died when I was three," Anthony said, "and I never thought we were rich. But I never thought we were poor, either."

When people see Anthony play, they invariably draw comparisons to Tracy McGrady, who went straight from high school to the pros. A few months ago, Anthony had the opportunity to talk with McGrady.

"His advice to me was, 'Do what's in your heart, but college won't hurt,'" Anthony said. "He told me he struggled at first because his coach with Toronto, Butch Carter, didn't believe in high school kids jumping to the pros.

"But when making my decision, I look at the Kobe Bryants and Kevin Garnetts, who do get a lot of playing time right away, and people like Jermaine O'Neal, who spent three years on the bench."

Anthony's eyes also widened when he watched the Final Four games Saturday night. "I want to be there next year; it would be a great thing to play in," he said.

He took special interest in two Maryland players. "I loved Juan Dixon's game; he's from Baltimore, too," Anthony said. "I loved his leadership, his poise—so cool. His face never changes expression. And Chris Wilcox, he plays hard every minute."

So he is leaning toward college, for the time being, and not the "league," the inside name for the NBA.

"College will help me mature, it'll broaden my interests and help me as a basketball player," Anthony said. "Like, I feel I can do everything Tracy does. Except right now he does it all better. I have a lot of work ahead of me."

SHEED UNSUBDUED

January 14, 2001

RASHEED WALLACE, THE PERPETUALLY nonplused Portland Trail Blazer, said something at the beginning of the fourth period last night against the Knicks in Madison Square Garden that would not be approved of in mixed company—which means when referees are around. He was whistled for a technical foul, his 21ˢᵗ of the season, more than double anyone else in the National Basketball Association. He is on his way to topping his over-the-top total of 38 technicals last season—again, more than double the total of anyone else.

"What's wrong with the guy?" one fan said, turning to a companion. "Court rage," came the reply.

Yes. Perhaps it will one day soon enter the psychological lexicon as, say, *ragus courtus*, a wild-eyed companion to other maladies brought on in stressful situations in the modern era, from road rage to air rage to shopping rage, the last when bargain hunters go bonkers. Wallace's agitation is generally brought on because of too many people being on the basketball court—mainly, three. By coincidence, they all wear referees' shirts.

Wallace has emerged as one of the best players in the NBA, and as combustible as Vesuvius on a bad day.

"Rasheed is one of the main reasons we are where we are," Trail Blazers coach Mike Dunleavy said. Where they are is possessing the best record in the tough Western Conference, 27–11, and the second-best record in the NBA, behind only the 76ers, whom they beat by 18 points on Wednesday in Philadelphia.

The Trail Blazers were on a 10-game winning streak when they met up with the odd Knicks. On Thursday, the Knicks found the Houston

Rockets restful, and went to sleep, losing a close game. To the Blazers' surprise, and perhaps even embarrassment, they awakened the Knicks, and took a whupping 91–78.

Wallace, who had been averaging a team-best 20 points per game, along with nearly nine rebounds, wound up with just 13 points, but 13 rebounds. Shortly after his technical foul, and with the Blazers down by 21 points and some nine minutes left in the game, Dunleavy sent Wallace to the bench.

"Rasheed had played big minutes in the last several games on this road trip," Dunleavy said, "and I thought the game was out of hand at this point and wanted to give him a rest. We have a game tomorrow in Detroit. I wanted to conserve some energy for him. But if we had got back in the game, I'd have sent him back in."

Dunleavy has acknowledged that the technicals are a problem. It was illuminated in the playoffs last season in the first game of the Western Conference Finals against the Los Angeles Lakers—the series that surely decided the NBA champion. Wallace got his second technical midway (two techs and you're out of the game) through the third period, and the Lakers went on to win.

Dunleavy said that there were two games this season in which Wallace had suffered two technicals.

"I don't know what it is, competitiveness or a sense of unfairness in bad calls, or what," Dunleavy said, "but I've told Rasheed that no matter what happens on the court that he doesn't like, from either referees missing a call in his opinion or an opponent pulling something that irritates him, he has to keep his head. If he doesn't, the other guys win. I don't mean they necessarily win the game, but they win if the idea is to get him either in trouble in the game, or ejected."

The referees are thin-skinned when it comes to Wallace. He was famously ejected in Game 1 of the Laker series because he stared at a referee who had warned him not to and earned his second technical. It was the kind of look you might see by someone you had just poked with an umbrella when crowding onto a subway.

"I don't know if he's a hothead or if he's just very intense," said Chris Childs, the Knicks guard who himself has had technical-foul contretemps in the past. "I'll tell you this, though, he has all the tools, all the skills. I don't think the foul calls have been affecting his play too much, by the record. He matches up great against the best power forwards in the league, like Garnett and Duncan and Malone. He gives them all problems because he's so long."

Wallace, in his sixth year in the league, is 6'11", strong at 225 pounds, and quick. Quick tempered, as well.

Some around the team say that the temper can be viewed as passion. And the Blazers are reluctant to put too tight a rein on him, not wishing to risk turning their lion into a lamb.

This, however, doesn't seem likely to happen in the near future.

Before the game, Wallace was approached in the locker room by a reporter. "Do you have a moment, Rasheed?"

"Don't talk before the game," he said.

After the game, several reporters waited around Wallace's area in the locker room until he had come out of the shower and dressed.

He put on his coat and scooped up some personal items and began to walk out.

"Do you have a moment, Rasheed?" a reporter asked.

"Nope," he said.

Maybe it's passion. Maybe it's also a case of locker-room rage.

JASON KIDD, PASSING DREAMS

December 26, 2001

MOST YOUNG BOYS, WHEN they dreamed heroic daydreams, imagined themselves as the Red Baron gunning down flying foes, or Sherlock Holmes cracking a case, or, at this time of year, perhaps Santa all a-bundle spreading cheer and largess as he wriggles down chimneys. Or, if basketball was the springboard to wonderland, then it was scoring the winning basket in a big game. Not so, though, for Jason Kidd.

For Kidd, it wasn't scoring the winning hoop, it was whipping the pass that produced the score. It was, in a fashion, dreaming of being the co-pilot, or Dr. Watson, or Rudolph the Red-Nosed Reindeer. It was the unselfish guy, or quadruped, who gloried in making the other guys look good. Someone once said that to be successful, you must keep true to the dreams of your youth. Kidd, the new, spectacular passing wizard of the surging Nets, has.

That's why his coach, Byron Scott, recently said, "Christmas came real early for us; this was in July, when we got Jason. Like I told my wife when I buy her a new car, 'This is your Christmas present, birthday present, Thanksgiving present.' That's what Jason was, basically."

The trade that brought Kidd to the Nets and sent Stephon Marbury to the Phoenix Suns has been a gift not only to Scott, but also to Kidd's Nets teammates and to their fans, those few, that is, who brave the wilds of North Jersey to show up at games at Continental Arena. The Nets are at the bottom of the NBA in home attendance, while the team has become one of the most entertaining in the league.

The man is at the center of this 16–9 team. "In almost every game—in almost every practice, for that matter—Jason will do something that none of us has ever seen before," Scott said.

Like perhaps a pass in a preseason game against Washington in which Kidd, at full speed on the fast break, threw a bounce pass between the legs of the man defending him and into the hands of a streaking Kerry Kittles, who scored on a slam dunk.

Or the rocket pass to the hefty center Todd MacCulloch, whose strong hands handled the pass for another basket. MacCulloch has especially good hands, so Kidd knows he can handle the "fast ball," as Kidd call it. Kidd will, however, throw a softer pass to another player. You have to know your customer—want to know your customer—and act in a split second.

And there are the underhand passes from near half-court that result in spine-tingling alley-oop dunks by the emotive, though sometimes overly fervent second-year ace, Kenyon Martin. The half-filled arena echoes with exultation.

Kidd's passes, even the flamboyant behind-the-back and through-the-legs tosses, are not only for show; they are invariably for a purpose, and can come off the dribble or not, right-handed or left-handed.

Scott, who played on the Lakers with Magic Johnson, one of the great point guards in NBA history, said Kidd and Johnson were much alike as floor leaders and passers. "The only thing Magic had over him, I think, is that he was about five inches taller," Scott said.

Kidd, built like a running back at 6'4", 212 pounds, is in his eighth season in the NBA, and, at age 28, in his prime.

"Jason always gives you the ball in your rhythm, in your stride," Keith Van Horn, the Nets' leading scorer, said. "His timing and court vision are unparalleled in this league. It makes you more alert, and naturally that improves the play of everyone."

Van Horn was asked if he always gets the ball when he is open. "Only," he said, "if I'm more open than anybody else."

Kidd described his job this way: "To get the ball to the guy who's got the hot hand, whether he's open or not." Even if the player thinks he's not open, Kidd will somehow get him the ball in good shooting position.

It is not uncommon even for a rival player to have witnessed a sensational Kidd pass thread through the opposition, then mutter to him, "How did you get it through there?"

You would not need Freud to figure out, however, why Kidd is the way he is. As a boy of seven or eight, trying to break into games with older boys at the Grass Valley School on Golf Links Road in Oakland, California, Kidd learned that if he threw passes to the guys who could shoot, he would be beloved.

"As time went on," he recalled, "I went from being one of the last picked to up near the first."

As a boy, Kidd would practice passing against a wall beside his house. "I'd aim at a spot and try to hit it," he said. "Sometimes I'd see a fly on the wall. I squashed a lot of flies. Of course, I missed a lot of them, too. But it's all trial and error."

The difference between Kidd and Marbury, the Nets' point guard for the previous two and a half seasons, is striking. Marbury looked to shoot first, and passed when he was done with the ball. Kidd thinks shot second.

"Passing, and the desire to pass, can be catching, like a cold," Kidd said. All of his teammates get into the act. Often, a shot is taken only after all five players have touched the ball.

"I've told all of our guys that when one of you is hot, you'll get the ball," Kidd said. "The others have to be patient. They'll get their turn."

Even Kidd gets his turn. As in the final minute of a game against Minnesota last week, when he stripped Kevin Garnett of the ball and dribbled at the speed of light downcourt to score on a jaw-dropping drive. The Nets won the game in overtime.

"Well, at that point, there was no one else to pass to," Kidd said.

CAMBY SHOWS HOW
TO PUT FAMILY FIRST

May 1, 2001

FOR SEVERAL YEARS NOW, Marcus Camby, the New York Knicks center who springs as quickly as a Champagne cork pops, has been an avid viewer of Court TV, following the cases closely, parsing the arguments, weighing the evidence.

Most recently, he was discussing with a reporter the case involving Mark Chmura, the former Green Bay Packer who was on trial, charged with sexually assaulting a teenage girl in Wisconsin.

"The laws are really strict on this in Wisconsin," the reporter said. "I think he might get time."

Camby shook his head. "I think he'll get off," he said. "Spree tells me the laws are tough in Wisconsin, but I don't think the evidence is there." His teammate and friend Latrell Sprewell is from Milwaukee. Camby turned out to be astute in his observations, because Chmura was found not guilty.

Little did Camby know that within weeks he, too, would be involved in a terrifying criminal situation. It happened just hours after Camby, who sprang up for 18 rebounds, helped lead the Knicks to victory over Toronto in the first game of their first-round playoff series in Madison Square Garden.

In the dark of early morning on Monday, April 23, Camby was awakened at 3:30 at home in Westchester County to learn that his mother and two sisters were being held hostage by a man wielding a kitchen knife in the two-story brick house Camby had bought for his mother in South

54

Windsor, Connecticut, a Hartford suburb. Police officers arriving on the scene said they heard "screams and noise" inside.

Camby dressed swiftly and then sped north in his black Mercedes to his family's home. After an eight-hour ordeal, with Camby on the scene, the police negotiated with and then arrested Troy D. Crooms, a onetime boy-friend of Monica Camby, Marcus' 21-year-old sister. Crooms is charged with first-degree sexual assault, kidnapping, burglary, and possession of a weapon.

One week later, the searing trauma for the Camby family has subsided somewhat, though it has hardly been erased. Camby played in unchar-acteristically lackluster fashion Thursday in the Garden in Game 2 and didn't travel to Toronto for Game 3 on Sunday. Instead, he watched on television as the Knicks won, preferring to stay behind to clear his head and comfort his family.

Yesterday, however, he practiced with the team for the first time in four days.

He said he is prepared to play Game 4 of the series tomorrow in Toronto. "It's been depressing, but I hope to get back to a normal life," he said after practice, standing against a wall in the gym at SUNY-Purchase, sweat stains on his blue workout jersey. In Game 2, he said, "mentally I wasn't there."

Yesterday, however, he said his family was encouraging him to play, and he said he had "tried to smile and laugh with the guys."

"I'm more upbeat," he said, "and I'm ready to go."

Coach Jeff Van Gundy spoke to Camby after the incident and said with compassion, "If you are in a frame of mind to play, we welcome you. But if you aren't, you must be honest, for your good and the good of the team."

After the second game, in which Camby scored just two points and had just two rebounds, he decided, as Van Gundy expressed it, "to step back, which was fine, to get him and his family healthy again."

"I told him not to come back until he feels he can play effectively," Van Gundy said. "And if something changes in him between now and game time, to let me know. It's important that he doesn't go out there and put us in a position to fail."

Sprewell thought Camby demonstrated in practice yesterday the kind of focus and energy the team is accustomed to seeing in him. "I paged him sometime after the incident," Sprewell recalled, "and we talked a little, but I wasn't sure what to say. I thought I'd just let him handle things at his own pace."

So, wisely, has Van Gundy. In fact, beyond the Camby situation, Van Gundy seems to be doing a lot of very bright things, overcoming, for example, such obstacles as injuries and the stifling of Vaulting Vince Carter, and a weaving of substitutions in combat that would have made Chief Sitting Bull sit up.

Some frenzied fans wondered why Camby, making $7 million per year, couldn't summon the spirit and energy to play despite the family problems.

Such fans were also contemptuous of center fielder Bernie Williams spending time away from the Yankees to be bedside with his seriously ailing father in Puerto Rico.

"If some people are so unknowledgeable about human events," Van Gundy said, "if they feel a player has more responsibility to his team than to his family, well, I don't know what to respond to that."

That response is full and sufficient.

III

A MEDLEY
OF MARQUEE
KNICKS

THE INCANDESCENT KING

February 2, 1984

BERNARD KING ON THE basketball court combines the late with the latest.

His face is a study of concentration—eyes narrowed, goateed jaw set firm, like the portrait mask of a somber Pharaoh.

When he walks, it is all hips and shoulders, the way a break-dancer on a street corner struts.

King would be strictly comical if he weren't so sensational.

Last night, King scored 50 points in the Knicks' 105–98 victory over the Mavericks. It was his second straight 50-point game in consecutive nights.

Tuesday night in San Antonio he scored 50 points, as he led the Knicks to a 117–113 victory over the Spurs. His point total was the most by any Knick in 16 years, or since Willis Reed scored 53 in 1967.

It is significant that King achieved that sum in a close game. "Bernard," said Dave DeBusschere, director of Knick basketball operations, "is a big-shot person."

King's two 50-point nights followed his performance Sunday in the National Basketball Association All-Star Game when he scored 18 points in 22 minutes and was instrumental in the East beating the West in overtime.

And that followed the first half of his seventh NBA season, a period in which he has unquestionably established himself as one of the best players in professional basketball.

The Knicks are on a hot streak, as reports describe it, winning four straight games and five of their last six, and they are eight games over .500 at 26–18. King might seem to be on a hot streak but he has been incandescent all season—remarkably enough, he has been even more glowing this week.

For the record, King, at age 27, is averaging more than 24 points, up from his career average of 21.9. He is near the top of the league in scoring.

He plays what is known as small forward—he stands 6'7" and weighs 205 pounds—and thus is not required to be a primary rebounder. That role falls to the muscleman on the opposite side of the court, Truck Robinson. Still, King has been pulling down 5.6 rebounds per game.

On defense, on occasion, he will get faked out, he might find himself out of position, and he might lose his man in a series of screens, but watching him fervently scramble to find his way would make even the hard-hearted begin to squeeze for him.

On offense is where he is brightest.

King is fast and strong and determined. He seeks a favorite spot on the baseline, urgently calls for the ball, and with his back to the basket, with two guys on him, two guys taller, he can still wheel and fake and, with a quick release on the way up, flip in a jump shot, or a jump hook, or whatever that odd shot is.

Like bed sheets tied together for an escape out a window, the shot seems hastily constructed due to necessity, and eminently effective.

"I played center in high school, and usually against bigger guys," said King recently. "I had to find a way to get the shot off. And I'm still doing it."

On the open court, there are few as spectacular as King.

"When I get an outlet pass at half-court and I see daylight, it gets me excited," said King. When he ends his dribble and springs, he seems able to go around his man in midair.

"I really don't understand how he gets some of those shots off," said DeBusschere.

King has a theory, at least in regard to the drives. "I've got high hips and a sway back," he said, "and I wonder if that doesn't make me more flexible."

As with any exceptional athlete with longevity, however, there comes a certain degree of introspection. And King has understood what it takes for him to excel.

One thing is concentration. "It seems that his mind never wanders, unlike most players," said Albert King, his brother who plays for the Nets.

Bernard King rarely smiles on the court and rarely banters.

"I know I've got this evil look," said King. "But in college it was worse."

At the University of Tennessee, where he made All-American, he said he "went out to try to demolish the other team. I saw them as my enemies. Now, I just want to go out and play as well as I can and help the team play as well as it can."

Cedric Maxwell, the Celtic forward, and King were NBA rookies in 1977. They'd line up before a game, and King would be wearing his normal glare, which Maxwell had never seen before.

Before one game, Maxwell stared at him and said, "Are you crazy?"

King said nothing.

The two are friends now, and Maxwell appreciates King, who is well spoken and genial off the court. On the court, Maxwell will impersonate King's menacing look, but it still gets no rise out of him.

In practice, King is regularly matched up against Louis Orr, a Knick forward on the second unit. "He never takes a breather," said Orr.

Last year, King injured his ankle and was out for 14 games. The Knicks went on to win nine of those games. Until then they had played mediocre ball, with King designated to take the majority of shots.

When he returned to the lineup the Knicks had established a balance in scoring and King did not disrupt the rhythm. He looked to pass, shot when he was open. King, said Hubie Brown, the Knick coach, "is the consummate professional."

King is remarkable on another level: he was able to arrest a problem with alcohol.

After the 1980–81 season with Golden State, he won the NBA's Comeback Player of the Year Award, and he was only 24 years old.

The season before that, in 1979–80, King, then with the Utah Jazz, played only 19 of the 82 regular season games, and averaged just 9.3 points per game. But in the 1980–81 season, he overcame his personal problems, problems he no longer wishes to discuss—some who know him well say he was courageous—and he played the full year, scoring 21.9 points per game.

He's been right ever since.

"I'm not as good as I'd like to be," said King, "and I feel that I have to prove something to myself every night."

THE KNICKS, THE ROCKETS, A MILLENIUM

June 7, 1994

IN THE MADNESS OF the moment that engulfed the Knick players and fans in Madison Square Garden Sunday, the unfettered John Starks, still aglow in sweat from the comeback victory in Game 7, told an interviewer at courtside, "After these tough playoff series we've had, Houston will be a breeze."

"He said that?" asked Charles Smith. "Good old John. That adds a little fuel to the fire." It was now Monday afternoon. Smith had driven to SUNY-Purchase where he and the rest of the Knicks were meeting the team bus for the trip to Houston for the National Basketball Association Finals starting Wednesday.

"This is not going to be a breeze by far," said Smith, hoping to toss a little water on the fire. "Houston is very explosive."

Other players drove up. Greg Anthony, attired in a green-and-black pinstriped outfit, put a different spin on Starks' statement. "We don't feel as much pressure being in the championship as we did having to get there," said Anthony. "And especially after the frustrations of losing out in each of the last three years. But this is the moment we've all dreamed of, ever since we were kids."

Pat Riley, the coach, arrived, natty as always in raked hair, and said his job now was to "calm them down from last night and the high of getting here."

He was reminded that they were only four victories away from the championship.

"Four wins is a millennium," he said. "This is the toughest team we've faced."

Charles Oakley showed up in a canary-yellow shirt and canary-yellow pants and wearing dark glasses, surely to deflect the glare of his wardrobe. And limping slightly, the result of a furious season spent partly crashing into the stands and partly into other players.

Then came Patrick Ewing. He wore that broad Caribbean smile and, while the news media flocked to him, he said, "Excuse me." He wasn't talking. He didn't have to. For the game he played Sunday night was the finest he has played in the nine years and 750-some games he has been a New York Knick, and it echoed from the rooftops of all the boroughs.

While Ewing has been an All-Star, it was believed here that he was never quite as good as he might be. Sunday he was all he could be, and that was simply magnificent. While he had scored all those points over the years and got all those rebounds, he never quite combined the great ballplayer's savvy with his great physical skills.

"When I heard Patrick come past our bench, and yell to Riley, 'Call 'em for me!' when we were down in the last quarter," said Smith, "then I knew how much he wanted to win."

So frustrated, so angry over the years in never being able to get to a championship final, Ewing seemed to have added ball bearings to his legs Sunday as he grabbed 11 offensive rebounds—11 more than he had taken in the previous two games—and whipped the ball around when double-teamed; timed blocks perfectly; wasn't suckered into chump fakes, and made passes, including a full-court baseball pass to a streaking Derek Harper, that were reminiscent of Larry Bird, or Magic Johnson, or Nolan Ryan.

He played with a winner's crafty focus, particularly when he had five fouls. In the playgrounds, the phrase is, "He played right."

And the next time he turns around, he will be staring into the hungry eyes of Hakeem Olajuwon.

A memory returns of Ewing in the locker room after a game against Olajuwon a few years ago. He was asked, "Had you ever been out-rebounded by that many before in your career?"

"How many was it?" he asked in reply.

"Twenty-five to three," he was told.

Ewing's eyebrows rose. "He did that?" Ewing paused. "Well," he said, "he's a big guy."

In most of their encounters, Olajuwon has outplayed Ewing, outscored him, outrebounded him, outmaneuvered him.

And while it takes more than one against one to win a championship, this one-on-one, between two of the best centers in basketball, will be intriguing. If Ewing plays as he did Sunday, he might not think the superb Olajuwon is quite as big as he once did.

The last time Knick fans, meanwhile, were treated to such a clash of centers in a final—treated to a final of any sort—was in 1973, when the locals beat the Lakers. And Willis Reed and Wilt Chamberlain roamed the arena. Reed, now the general manager of the Nets, said, "It's going to be a great chess match, but I'm rooting for the Knicks. I mean, it's the only team I ever played for, and I gave up my good knees for that team."

It was no breeze then. It will be no breeze now.

.   .   .

Houston beat the Knicks in seven games, with Olajuwon outscoring Ewing in each game, and topping him overall in assists, though Ewing had more rebounds and more blocked shots in those games. Olajuwon was the unanimous MVP selection of the Finals.

EWING'S LAST GAME AT THE GARDEN

April 10, 2002

HE HAD COME BACK to Madison Square Garden in a basketball uniform for possibly the last time. He had 15 seasons here as a Knick, 15 seasons filled with great expectations, 15 seasons that, invariably, ended in a certain sense of unfulfillment. Fifteen seasons in which there was always the opportunity for this star player to embrace the fans, and the fans to embrace him, but it was 15 years, in many ways, of lost opportunities.

And last night, Patrick Ewing returned to New York and the basketball arena in which he spent a great part of his professional career, and returned in the blue-and-white uniform of the Orlando Magic. He had been here earlier this season with the Magic, and last season he showed up as a Seattle SuperSonic, but in each instance, there was the distinct possibility that he would appear here again, and he did.

Now, however, there were signs and suggestions, veiled and otherwise, that this would be the final time around for Ewing. At age 39, and after 17 seasons, with sore knees and diminished skills, he has played fewer and fewer minutes.

Once affectionately called the Beast of the East by his Knick teammates, he has become less than fearsome. Recently he spent one full game on the bench, never getting a call from the coach, Doc Rivers. On Monday night, he played five minutes, scored two points and had two rebounds in Orlando's victory over Houston.

When he returned for the first time to the Garden, he got a two-minute standing ovation, and the cheers were repeated last night. It was, to some looking on, a triumph of sentimentality over their reality.

Ewing was truly one of the most ambiguous stars in Gotham annals.

He regularly guaranteed a championship at the beginning of the season, or the playoffs. But he was unable to follow through on those promises. Joe Namath guaranteed a championship, and achieved it. Mark Messier guaranteed a victory in Game 6 of the 1994 Eastern Conference Finals against the Devils, and later drank from the Cup. Fans simply wished Ewing would just shut up about it. It was false, and annoying, bravado.

Then he was nowhere to be found when Charles Smith went up four times against Michael Jordan and Scottie Pippen for that rebound and tip in the 1993 playoffs, and he missed that finger roll against Indiana in 1995. And he couldn't pull it off against Hakeem Olajuwon in the 1994 Finals.

But that was only winning and losing at basketball. A fan can, at bottom, understand that. But it's harder for the knowledgeable fan to swallow the fact that Ewing could have been one of the best defensive centers, as he was in college, but preferred being the shooter. So he went for the fakes and didn't master the pass out of the double-team.

Fans dream of the accessible superstar. If you're aloof but come through in the clutch and help provide championships, you're forgiven. Like Joe DiMaggio. If you have a drinking surliness at times but win championships, you win the heart of the public. Read Mickey Mantle.

And if you can lead the team to a title and do it with dignity and grace, like Willis Reed, you are adored. And if you have a New York flair, like Clyde Frazier, you're given the high sign on the subway (or as you tool down Fifth Avenue in your burgundy-and-antelope Rolls).

But Ewing never seemed to make an effort to connect to the city. And if you're a superstar, you either win championships, or you give the impression that you have a spiritual bond with the locals. Unlike Ewing. Lodged in memory was the time just a few years ago when he was host to a charity lunch for disadvantaged youth at the Garden and refused to sign autographs for the kids. He said he never signed autographs before a game. The Knicks indeed had a game. Ewing, however, was on the injured list.

Yet no one sweated more in a game than Patrick Ewing. And sometimes, to his dismay and befuddlement, there were boos. The feeling was, he was very good, but he could have been better and helped make his teammates better.

But not last night. Rivers, in a surprise, started Ewing, believing this might indeed be his farewell appearance. The relatively sparse crowd gave

Ewing a warm, generous ovation. He waved back. Rivers kept him in the game more than usual, 19 minutes. At times the fans chanted his name enthusiastically. Ewing, perspiring as of old, scored but six points and pulled down five rebounds as Orlando won 108–97.

Ewing was gracious after the game. "I appreciated the start," he said, "and the opportunity for the fans to show their appreciation for what I'd done here."

Much, but not all, had been forgiven, if not forgotten. Probably on both sides.

ALLAN HOUSTON'S PASSION

April 10, 2002

ALLAN HOUSTON APPEARS TO be one of nature's noblemen. He is the kind of guy who would never think of reaching across someone's plate and snaring a chicken leg on the dinner table.

His gentle, even demeanor strikes you as someone you could tell your troubles to, like a shrink, or a barber. He is not about to interrupt you to make his point. Allan Houston raising his voice seems as implausible as hockey fans at Carnegie Hall.

And his eyes—his wide, brown, doe-like eyes—are filled with compassion, understanding, serenity. So on those occasions when he mutates into a monster, it is bewildering, and, if you are a Knicks fan, wondrous.

"At halftime," Chris Childs said—referring to Friday night's game when the Knicks trailed the Heat in Game 6 at Madison Square Garden, and had been booed with a profound and insightful passion by their adoring fans—"Allan came into the locker room all emotional. He was just saying things. He was upset. And you could tell it in his eyes. His eyes were speaking loudly."

"At halftime," Houston said after the game, in which the Knicks mounted an astonishing comeback to win by 72–70, and send the series to Game 7 this afternoon in Miami, "I felt that we had to stay together as a team. Just keep doing all the good, fundamental things we knew we could do. And I had to attack the basket more."

Attack he did. Not wild, like a wildebeest. More like Hannibal, coolly charting out the best positions for his elephants, and decisively heading tusks-first into the breach.

It was truly a team effort, as they posit in the textbooks, but in this case, and in more and more cases over the past few years, Houston has assumed a leadership role, both on the court and in the locker room. In typical understated fashion, he seems to have emerged, like the top patriarch in the Eastern Orthodox Church, first among equals.

And when Houston at times on the court becomes as passive as a rag doll, or, in another instance, hostage to a gooey defender like Dan Majerle, the team must hurdle that barrier, of a lost or nugatory leader. Not good.

Such was the case in Game 5, when he attempted but two shots in the second half, as the team lost in the closing minute. Houston is the team's high scorer, at about 20 per game. He scored 12 in that game. In the first half of the game Friday, which the Knicks had to win to dodge elimination, he shot 3-for-9—hitting one three-point shot—and had taken no free throws. Not good.

"I had heard all that stuff about how good Majerle was guarding me," Houston said, "and I heard guys telling me, 'Majerle can't guard you.' I heard lots of things. But I knew I just couldn't keep settling for jump shots. I'm always better when I become more aggressive."

With just 46 seconds gone in the third quarter, Houston sank a three-point shot. But he was looking to drive. Shortly after that three-pointer, he swept to the hoop and hit a twisting layup through and over a host of arms. Within a half-minute, he drove again, but found Charlie Ward under the hoop with a dish that Emeril Lagasse would have loved. There was another assist by Houston.

And after a timeout, it was Houston who went to each of the other players on the court and whispered a reminder of a play to come. The Knicks, with others like Latrell Sprewell, Larry Johnson, Patrick Ewing, and Ward picking up the pace with shots, steals, and rebounds, chopped the deficit, amazingly, to four, back up to seven on an Anthony Carter three-pointer, but Houston had the last word in the period, hitting a spinning, fadeaway jump shot seconds before quarter's end.

Knicks fans were on their feet. Their screams could be heard in Bergen County. Suddenly, no greater love had they.

And, as history now records, the Knicks came back in the fourth quarter to tie the game at 70–70, and, with 17.6 seconds left, Houston, taking it upon himself to do something special, drove to the hoop again, was fouled, and, with that delicious combination of frost and fire—ice cream and hot fudge—Houston sank the two final points of the game, for a team-leading 21 points—5-for-6 from the field, including a pair of threes and three free throws.

Now the Knicks go back to Miami, a team that they view (and are viewed in return) with the ardor reserved for a neighbor who keeps running over your lawn with his truck. And has a dog that barks all night, to boot. But it was in the deciding game of last year's playoffs, which also went the full length, when Houston again emerged the hero with a last-second shot that bounced up and then in, a moment in Knick lore that ranks with Willis Reed's limp.

Houston, in fact, twisted his ankle on a drive in the last half Friday. But you would not have known it by watching him.

"It's still sore," he said after the game, "but it'll be ready in Miami. And the team that can execute under pressure, that can make the big plays, the plays you dream about and pray about, that team will win." He said Friday night's game demonstrated how the Knicks stick together, do not get rattled, make the big plays under pressure.

There is a saying in sports that you must let the game come to you. But not if you are the star. Not if you are the leader. You must take the game by the lapels, and demand satisfaction.

Houston, who was a virtual bystander in Game 5, did what a star has to do in Game 6. He did what a leader has to do. That is, he did it.

Game 7 awaits.

•　　•　　•

The Knicks beat the Heat in that series but then lost to Indiana in the Eastern Conference Finals.

FOR MARK JACKSON, DÉJÀ VU OF SORTS

February 24, 2001

WHEN MARK JACKSON RETURNED to the Knicks lineup early in the second period last night, after a hiatus of 677 regular season games since he was traded away in 1992, the sellout crowd of nearly 20,000 in Madison Square Garden stood and applauded.

"I felt very grateful," Jackson said. "Basically, I felt like clapping for them. They were missed."

The fans' hope that Jackson would make the Knicks monsters didn't materialize, and he had little effect in his 13 minutes, scoring no points in the 88–84 overtime loss to Phoenix.

Charlie Ward, whom Jackson will replace as the starting point guard, probably beginning tomorrow against Sacramento, didn't do appreciably more in 34 minutes.

It is an odd situation, but one that Jackson has been in before with the Knicks. That is, a new guy, a veteran point guard, shows up in a trade and replaces the guy who has been the starting point guard for the last few years. The difference this time: Jackson is the veteran who has just been traded to the Knicks—from Toronto for Chris Childs—and will assume the first-string operations, relegating Charlie Ward to secondary status.

Eleven years ago, on February 21, 1990, the Knicks traded for Maurice Cheeks. And soon, Jackson, the Rookie of the Year in his first season and an All-Star in his second, found himself suddenly the No. 2 point guard in his third year.

When Cheeks, then 33 and a four-time All-Star, arrived, Jackson, then 24 and with a generous opinion of himself, was less than delighted in his new role. The fact, however, was that the Brooklyn-born Jackson had not quite honed his New York moxie, while Cheeks' considerable Chicago-bred basketball intellect, which had helped the 76ers win the title in 1983, was still in fine feather.

Jackson had been seen as a showboat, from wayward flashy passes to going into a goofy, arms-spread, kamikaze-like dive. Fans hooted. There was none of either of that last night, however.

When Cheeks arrived, Jackson was asked, "What can you learn from Cheeks?"

"I can learn from him, and he can learn from me," Jackson responded. However Jackson meant it, it came out sounding haughty.

Charlie Ward is 30, a seven-year veteran who exhibits a maturity that is not frequently fashionable in sports. He has been a very good but not a great player.

"Hopefully, the trade will turn out good for us," he said. "But right now, everything is just speculation."

Jeff Van Gundy, the Knick coach, called Ward after the trade and told him Jackson would be the starter. How did he feel?

"He's starting and rightly so," Ward said. "He's an outstanding player. He beat us in a lot of ways when he was with Indiana."

But every player has his pride. Doesn't it hurt to lose the starting job?

"I've thrown out my ego," Ward said. "Ego equals pride and pride can get in the way of achievement because it leads to selfishness. I find no problem with sacrifice. Sacrifice means something to me, and I relish it."

Ward is a deeply religious man who studies the Bible, and he has apparently read, "Pride goeth before destruction."

Jackson 35, in his 14th season, has been with four teams in nine-plus years after having been traded from New York. He is a respected, heady elder statesman in the league, and he is fourth in career assists.

He finally got to the finals for the first time last season with Indiana. He remains a limited player, particularly on defense.

"Oh, man," said Latrell Sprewell, reacting to the Jackson trade. "Finally, someone who knows how to find guys in the open court and can really fill the lane."

Van Gundy was less effusive. "Charlie has done a great job for us as a starter," he said. "But it's well documented that Mark makes the other players better with his passing."

But how much of a liability can Jackson's defense be? "We have a few guys who are laterally challenged," he said. "And Mark is one of them. We just have to cover for them."

Jackson, who didn't start last night because Childs passed his physical late, said he was excited about his return home.

If he saw a game film of himself when he last wore a Knick jersey, and one today, what would he see? "I'm bigger," he said with a smile, "my shorts are longer. But I'd look deep, and see a guy who knew some things then, as opposed to a guy today who has lived some things, and gone through the wars."

Last night was merely another battle.

LATRELL SPREWELL STARTS FRESH

May 7, 2001

PHILADELPHIA—RESURRECTION IS PROBABLY TOO strong a word, even among the pious Knicks, but if there is a sports equivalent, it must be one Latrell Fontaine Sprewell, braids and all. Just two and a half years ago he was widely reviled as the symbol of virtually every evil commonly associated with modern athletes, as well as Generations X, Y, and Z—unfettered emotionally, disrespectful of authority and simply spoiled rotten.

Yet not only has the intense, 6'5", swift-as-a-slingshot Sprewell gained the respect of the people who employ him and the people who seek to undo him, but he has also inspired an army of impostors. You see it every day on the streets of New York, the town thick with people of all ages and sexes wearing Knicks jerseys with Sprewell's name and No. 8 on their backs.

On Saturday, Jeff Van Gundy, the Knicks coach, put what was probably the finishing touches on Sprewell's remarkable image reclamation project. "I think the biggest person of influence in this organization is Latrell," he said.

Brian James, an assistant coach with Toronto, which knocked the Knicks out of the first round of the National Basketball Association playoffs on Friday, said, "He sacrificed his offense for most of the series to guard Vince." He referred, of course, to Vince Carter. "And then when they needed offense, he decided it was up to him."

Charles Oakley, the voluble Raptors forward, said, "Sprewell's got attitude. And that's what you need in this league."

Indeed, with the Knicks down 70–59 heading into the fourth quarter of the last game, Sprewell scored 12 points, with resounding dunks and clutch jump shots, and finished with a game-high 29 points, in a losing effort, 93–89.

His passion, his propulsion, his entire performance, was riveting. It was the entirety of his considerable energies and talents merging in a most positive way. It was the reverse of those energies and talents that went into that fateful afternoon of December 1, 1997, when—he says he was provoked, the victim contends otherwise—he attacked and choked P.J. Carlesimo, then his coach with the Golden State Warriors.

Sprewell was fined and suspended from the NBA for a year (it was later reduced) and only reluctantly apologized for his shocking action. "I think it's fair to say I had a bad day," Sprewell said. Fair to say. He also said, "I'm looked on as a negative person. That's not me."

Then he came to New York under this somber cloud, the reception mixed at best. He went about proving that not only was he still one of the best players in the league, but he was also one of the most candid, and with impressive leadership qualities.

When, early on, Van Gundy wasn't starting him, Sprewell complained, and legitimately. When Van Gundy finally saw the light, Sprewell went about proving himself astute in analyzing talent.

When he was asked last season about the Knicks' record being better in the playoffs without Patrick Ewing, Sprewell said, "Numbers don't lie."

Sprewell, at age 30, doesn't back down, which is admirable when funneled properly. When he came to New York, he wore his hair in cornrows and braids. Allen Iverson, who wears his hair in a similar style, had said that people think it's "supposed to be some thug image."

Sprewell doesn't care. "I just like to be different," he said. "I know some people might be threatened by the hairstyle, but I like not being like everybody else."

At this, a reporter jokingly ran a hand through his own rather unruly mop and asked, "Well, what do you think of my 'do?" Sprewell smiled his disarming smile. "If it works for you," he said, discreetly.

He has understood what he had to do on the court—play hard, play team ball—and off the court—be reasonably accessible to the news media, be courteous to fans. He has done all of that, and done it without seeming either obsequious or reticent. He has, in brief, maintained his dignity and independence. So independent, in fact, that he rarely answers his telephone at home. When Van Gundy wanted to tell him he had been named to this year's Eastern Conference All-Star team, he had to drive to Sprewell's house.

"I made a mistake," Sprewell had said about his throttling of Carlesimo. "We all make mistakes in life. I've paid the price."

It hasn't always been smooth sailing since then. In March 1998, while sitting out his suspension, he lost control of his car and was charged with reckless driving. In 1999 he was a week late to training camp and never called the team as to his whereabouts.

Before joining the Knicks after his suspension, Sprewell met with commissioner David Stern. He expressed contrition and reassured Stern that he would be a positive influence.

He has been true to his word, and more. When, for example, Sprewell made pointed criticisms Saturday of the Knicks team as presently constituted, saying "something has to be done" to get the team "some size and some kind of toughness," Van Gundy was all ears. "He's earned every right to express his opinion," Van Gundy said, "because he's all about winning."

The guy who said there are no second acts in American life just didn't live long enough to appreciate the revival of Sprewell.

OAKLEY THE ENFORCER

February 17, 1999

USED TO BE THAT after having played against the Knicks, opponents needed respirators and paramedics in order to leave the arena. And the major cause of such mayhem was Charles Oakley, all 6'9" and 245 foreboding pounds of him.

"Every time I went to the basket, I knew I was going to be hit by Charles Oakley," recalled Grant Hill, who said this yesterday with a kind of respect, and maybe some admiration, too. "So I always made sure I knew where he was on the court, to be prepared."

Every player in the league knew that he was going to be hit by Charles Oakley—still does. But it is Charles Oakley in a different uniform, the shocking purple of the Toronto Raptors, and not the orange, white, and blue of the Knicks. And last night, Oakley returned to Madison Square Garden, the scene of so many of his greatest collisions, clobbers, and clouts, for the first time since having been traded for Marcus Camby over the summer.

Oakley had expressed unhappiness about being traded from the team he had been a part of for 10 years—or at least the seemingly abrupt manner in which he was traded—but then Oakley wears unhappiness as a kind of badge.

Grumpiness is one of the elements that made Oakley so endearing to Knick fans. One always got the impression that Charles' shoes, or shorts, fit too tight. Whatever the reason, his fervent style featured his invariably diving headfirst into the stands for balls, crashing into and flummoxing fans. It was never a good idea to sit with a drink or a box of popcorn in your hands in the first five rows of a Knicks game with Oakley on the court.

One fan, who has sat courtside for 25 years, wrote of him, in the *New York Observer*, last year: "Oakley has been a consistently tremendous ballplayer for New York who has contributed mightily night after night. Of course, I'd hate to wake up in the middle of the night and find him hovering over my bed with that look on his face, but on the court he's worth every cent they pay him."

That was Woody Allen's assessment, and most Knick fans would surely agree with it. But times change, and the Knicks sought a younger, springier player—Oakley is 35, Camby 24.

Patrick Ewing, the Knicks center, said that he missed Oakley, though Oakley wondered. "He never told me that," Oakley said.

In last night's game, which the Knicks won 95–85, Oakley scored 11 points, had seven rebounds, and did not dive into the stands until a full four minutes had passed in the first quarter. Same old Oak.

After the game, Ewing was asked if the two former teammates had spoken.

"We chit-chatted for a minute," he said, smiling, "and then he tried to take my head off." Same old Oak.

There was significant interest in Oakley's return to the Garden, and he received a standing ovation when introduced before the game. At halftime, the Knicks put on a highlight film tribute of Oakley's career, which had to include some of his most arresting fouls.

Oakley, who was never a great shooter (though a competent one when standing in one spot), who often fell down when he tried to dribble, who was a decent passer when he wasn't trying to be fancy and flinging the ball behind his back and over the scorer's table, was a good defender, a ferocious rebounder, and a general terror.

He holds the National Basketball Association career record of 30 flagrant fouls—that is, contact deemed excessive, or unnecessary, or both—since that infraction was instituted nine seasons ago, followed by those Righteous Brothers, Charles Barkley, with 26, and Dennis Rodman, 21. Oakley has been suspended twice because of the thumping number of flagrants in a given season, also a record.

"I know some people been building this up like a Tyson–Evander Holyfield rematch," he said before the game, "but it's not. I don't carry a grudge and I'm not gonna bite anyone's ear off." And true to his word, he didn't.

Oakley held back from saying it was exciting returning to the Garden, but at one timeout, he headed for the Knicks bench by habit. He made five turnovers that he felt hurt his team.

"I'm trying to fit in any kind of way," he said. "It's a young team and it's something new. It's not easy."

Before the game, he said, "I'm not gonna get caught up in trying to score 20 points. I'm just gonna try to help my team win."

Which is what Charles Oakley has always done. Often to the benefit of the team he was playing for, as well as to the good fortune of those in the neighborhood selling medical supplies.

A FAMILY IS DEVASTATED ONE MORE TIME

December 11, 2005

COUNTRY CLUB HILLS, IL — ON a clear and frigid morning in this snow-covered suburb south of Chicago, the first of the Knick players to come down the aisle at the packed Leak & Sons Funeral Home chapel on Saturday was the 6'6" forward Quentin Richardson.

In a dark suit, he appeared at the entrance and walked in with his arm around his sister Rochelle. They stopped for a moment as Rochelle, seeing the open casket of their brother Lee Richardson Jr. at the front of the chandeliered chapel, began to sob.

She covered her face with a black-gloved hand, and Quentin pulled her closer, his head bowed.

It was the 34-year-old Rochelle who, shortly after Lee, 31, was shot and killed in an apparent robbery attempt last Monday, told the *Chicago Sun-Times*, "I don't believe I'm doing this again." Her and Quentin's brother Bernard, then 23, was shot and killed in a robbery attempt on a Chicago street 13 years earlier. Quentin, the youngest of five children, was 12 at the time.

That same year, the Richardson children lost their mother, Emma, to breast cancer and their grandmother Ada to natural causes.

Lee Richardson Sr., a 62-year-old retired city transit worker, was with Lee Jr. in front of the family's house as one of the assailants shot his son four times. Lee Sr. was not injured.

Quentin, who joined the Knicks in a trade with the Phoenix Suns before this season, learned of the shooting while the team was preparing to play in Seattle.

He quickly made arrangements to return to the Sheldon Heights neighborhood on Chicago's South Side, where he was reared and attended the Whitney M. Young Magnet High School. He won a state championship there and went on to star at DePaul.

At five minutes to 11:00 on Saturday morning, five minutes before the services were to begin, Larry Brown, the Knicks coach, and Isiah Thomas, the team president, who grew up on the West Side of Chicago and saw his share of violence on the streets, appeared in the doorway of the funeral home.

Following them was a parade of mostly tall men, their heads nearly touching the ceiling. It was the entire Knicks team, including Eddy Curry and Channing Frye, both 6'11", as well as guards Stephon Marbury and Nate Robinson.

Players paid their respects to the family members in the front rows, then took seats among the congregation, which filled a hallway and two rooms, including one where there was a closed-circuit television.

One of the funeral directors estimated the crowd size at a few thousand, as people came to remember Lee Jr., or Lil Lee, as the family called him, even though he stood 6'4" and weighed 280 pounds.

Brown observed the proceedings from a doorway between the two rooms.

"I couldn't sit," he said later. "Something like this makes games insignificant."

The Knicks, who are having their problems winning games, lost at Phoenix on Friday night. But they were intent on showing their concern for their teammate, so they caught a bus at 5:30 AM in Phoenix, then flew three hours to Chicago, arriving just in time for the funeral.

Everyone there surely knew the details of the killing and something of the life of Lil Lee, who had only recently returned from New York. It was there, as an aspiring music producer, that he had hoped to make some deals; he was promoting a singing group, The Catalysts.

Lee Jr., who never married and who was not a gifted athlete like Quentin, had joined the Navy, serving honorably before returning to pursue business interests.

He was described by an aunt, a woman who identified herself as Angie, as "jolly, kind, loving, and protective; he wasn't afraid of anything."

On the afternoon of December 5, Lee Jr. and his father drove into the garage in an Infiniti. As they walked to the house, according to the police, they were accosted by men with guns who told them to lie on the ground. Then Lee Jr. was told to roll over, virtually on top of his much smaller father. At that point, Lee Jr. grabbed for one of the robbers' guns, and he was riddled with bullets.

Three men, all from Chicago, were arrested after a car chase, according to the Chicago police. The three have been charged with murder and attempted robbery.

On Saturday, The Catalysts were called on to sing gospel songs and hymns in tribute to Lee Jr. Several pastors spoke, and there was a call and response. Then Rochelle, representing the immediate family, rose to speak. The crowd was hushed.

"People who did this to my brother, who perpetrated this hideous, hideous, horrendous crime, did not know my brother," she said. "To know him was to love him. He cared about family, about people."

Then she addressed the broader issue: "We have to stop this insanity, this violence in our neighborhoods. We have to stop it now. Please. And we can stop it. It doesn't have to be this way. We can't just turn our heads when we see our young people acting delinquent. We have to plant a seed. It's up to us to stop this cycle of tragedy and death. I don't want my brother to be just another statistic."

A short while later, the Knicks contingent filed out of the chapel, on to another game, but, undoubtedly, not the same as it had been early Saturday or the day before.

Outside in the cold, in a suit without an overcoat, Thomas said that Quentin's sister Rochelle had said it best.

"We've got to find a way to stop these senseless murders," he said. "It's happened too many times, in too many places, to too many families."

IV.

THE ODDEST COUPLE: STARKS AND REGGIE

MILLER AND MOUTH VS. STARKS

May 24, 1994

SWEET, CUDDLY REGGIE MILLER, the man who John Starks punched in the mouth with his head last year, is coming to town again. Lovable Reggie Miller, who whispers such sweet nothings into the other players' ears that he makes their thumbs quiver for his throat, has got his wish.

"I want the Knicks," he said last week, as he waited for the outcome of the Knicks-Bulls series. And so Miller, who is also the ace of the Pacers, leads his team to the Garden for Game 1 of the Eastern Conference Finals.

Miller was last seen by these eyes recently after a shower following a workout in Market Square Arena in Indianapolis. Dripping wet, he looks like anything but the big, bad actor that he is often made out to be. He is skinny to a fault, possessing a build that appears constructed from ice-cream sticks. A media guide proclaims that he is 6'7", 185 pounds, but it might exaggerate his weight by about 100 pounds.

Never mind. He is one terrific shooter, clutch player, tough dude, and one Very Big Mouth.

"I used to watch Westerns with my dad and we always talked about the guy wearing the black hat," Miller said. "My father used to say, 'See that gun? It might be a seven-shooter.' I'd say, 'But Dad, it only holds six bullets.' 'Yeah, but you don't know that. And he might have a little Derringer there in the back.'"

So Miller said he came to respect and admire the man in the black hat, and, metaphorically at least, has donned one of his own.

"I like being the bad guy," he said. "Nothing wrong with that. We have too many guys making commercials, being the good guy." He laughed the hollow laugh of a horse thief. "Everyone can't be the good guy. Someone has to be the bad guy."

And so Miller nominated himself. "I love being booed," he said. And so he will surely fall head over heels with the Garden throng, who remember him well from the head-butting incident with Starks in a Game 3 of last year's playoffs, which resulted in Starks being banished from the premises.

Such considerations of rabbit ears for this year are important then, because when Starks left that game, early in the third quarter, the Knicks were ahead 59–57, after a Starks jump shot. They ended up losing 116–93. Starks, who has been known to lose his head—and not just into someone else's teeth—is aware that Miller remains a Pacer.

Does this make him jumpy?

Naw, he said, after practice at SUNY-Purchase yesterday. "I'm past all that," said Starks, in a mood so serene that one would hardly have known it was the same person who had to be held back by teammates on the bench in a game in Chicago just four days ago lest he chase a referee around the court. "Over the years you learn, you grow, you mature. You know how to defuse things."

Sure, he knows that Reggie will "talk noise and try to throw me off my game," but it will go in one ear, he promises, and out the other.

What gets Starks mad, he said, is not the talking, but "the cheap shots: the elbows, and stuff like that."

He does have respect for his rival as a competitor, though. "He's fierce and aggressive," Starks said. "We're similar players. We play with a lot of heart and play very hard."

While cheap shots and taunting, meanwhile, are officially banned by the league, they are still a part of the game. So taunting must be subtle. Unlike what Scottie Pippen, for example, did with Patrick Ewing, after his dunk that knocked Ewing to the floor. He then stood over his face and shouted something scatological that, in a family newspaper, must read, How's this! Technical on Pippen!

If, for example, Charles Oakley will again call Reggie Miller "Cheryl," referring to Reggie's older sister, herself an Olympic basketball player, then he must do it very quietly, or in sign language. But if the Knicks want to bandy insults with Miller, then they might suffer. For, as Pat Riley, the Knicks' wizened sage, says, "You can't do anything to faze him. You just have to let him flap his lips."

The more Miller is loathed, meanwhile, the jollier he gets. "If I could," he said, "I'd play all 82 games on the road."

Ignored, he might go into a funk. Besides, the Knicks need all the players they can keep in the arena, and wouldn't find it advantageous for a Ewing or Starks or Oakley or Harper to be thrown out of a game—as each has been during the playoffs this year or last.

As for Starks as Trash Talker, well, last year against the Nets he accused Drazen Petrovic, a Croatian, of complicity in the World Trade Center bombings. Petrovic had no idea what he was talking about. And then hit a jump shot.

JOHN STARKS HAS FOUND AN ANSWER

December 29, 1994

IN THESE DIRE TIMES, with the Mighty Oak felled, the Knicks need leadership to steady their season. So John Starks took it upon himself to provide such guidance. Against the Nets Tuesday night at the Meadowlands, while Charles Oakley and his toe were nestled in a Manhattan hospital after surgery, Starks immediately took charge, or what he considered to be charge.

With little more than a minute gone in the game, and the score 0–0, Starks was fouled from behind by Kenny Anderson at half-court to prevent a fast break. Starks then took dead aim and heaved the ball against the 24-second clock above the basket. Why the 24-second clock should receive such treatment only Starks knew. But he later explained.

"I was just letting my teammates know that we have to play hard," Starks said. "I was trying to show that even without Oak we have to be aggressive as a team."

What he did do, however, was control his actions from that point forward and help the Knicks break a five-game losing streak, as he shot well from outside, drove hard to the hoop, and scored 22 points.

Starks, at age 29, marches to the beat of his own flutist. One that Pat Riley, among others, doesn't march to. "We've been through three years of John Starks, and trying to get him to act consistently mature on the court," Riley said. "He's got to act like a professional. We can talk to him until we're blue in the face, but he's got to take more responsibility for himself. Enough is enough."

Starks, as Riley has also said, can and has provided leadership by inspired play. From my seat, it appeared to inspire no one when Starks flung the ball off the clock—except perhaps the Nets, when Armon Gilliam sank a pair of free throws for the first points of the game.

And who did he inspire or lead, for example, when he threw the ball at Pete Myers in Chicago on Christmas Day and was properly ejected from the game? Who did he inspire or lead when he chased a referee in the passageway after a recent game against the Nets? Or leg-whipped B.J. Armstrong in the playoffs last season?

While Starks may sometimes be wrongheaded one must also appreciate him, and give him the benefit of the doubt. And Knick fans, for the most part, do. Which is why he has been so little booed in his widely publicized shooting struggles. He has taken such off-the-mark shots—like the infamous airball in Philadelphia that might have won the game—that they look like he's shooting at another basket.

But many of us feel the way Wayne Embry, the general manager of the Cavaliers, feels about him. "I really admire him because he pulled himself up from nothing," Embry said recently. "He's a tough player. He plays hard. He's just going through some mental blocks, like most players at one time or another. He'll come out of it."

The story of Starks' attending four different colleges in Oklahoma, not being drafted by a National Basketball Association franchise, bagging groceries, bouncing around the Continental Basketball Association and the World Basketball League, being cut by the Warriors, and eventually becoming an All-Star with the Knicks underscores Embry's assessment.

He has suffered bad times, and weathered them. "When it rains, it pours," Starks said a few games ago. "And right now it's pouring."

Starks was talking reflectively about the game that night, but when a reporter asked what he had thought about on taking a last shot that clanged off the rim, Starks turned suddenly. "You're trying to get into my head!" Starks said. "What if I said I was thinking I wanted to kill you? I wouldn't have to tell you about it!" While that response might have been a little excessive, it does reveal how quickly Starks can spin off, on or off the court.

But it is his high-pitched emotional approach, he believes, that has spurred his success. For much of this season, however, he had been at wit's end to escape his shooting slump.

So after his solid game Tuesday, he said, "I'll give the credit to God. I tried it my way and it didn't work. I'm just trying to do the things I'm capable of doing and let things flow. I'm just putting it in His hands and you can see, He's doing a good job."

But surely, Starks will be in for more good nights and more bad nights. And Starks must understand that He has provided a balance to nature.

HE'S BAD, HE'S BIZARRE...
HE'S REGGIE MILLER

May 8, 1995

YES, SOME PEOPLE REVEL in being loathed. Maybe it's simply that they crave attention—any attention. If they saw their photograph in a post office, they might complain that it wasn't taken from their good side. When hissed, they beam. If they are told to leave a birthday party, they sit on the cake. Reggie Miller, the Inimitable, the Implausible, the Impossible, is surely one such entity.

"I love being booed," Reggie Miller said. "Maybe it goes back to my childhood." He said he used to watch movies and "root for the bad guy."

If there is a greater villain today in all of Gotham than Reggie Miller, his name does not come quickly to mind. And it thrills him the way night-fall made Dracula tingle.

We all know the story now, of how the Knicks yesterday afternoon were ahead by six points with 18.7 seconds to go in Game 1 of their playoff series against the Indiana Pacers, and couldn't win.

We all know the story now, of how the Knicks, one of the most imma-ture teams to ever contend for championships, were raising their arms in triumph, as the Madison Square Garden crowd of 19,763 cheered. After all, the game was over, wasn't it? With a six-point lead with 18.7 seconds left?

But they neglected that Miller is one of the best long-range shooters in the game, one of the best clutch shooters in the game, and the game still had some game left. And Miller, who comes from Los Angeles by way of Transylvania, could still smell blood.

"Things weren't looking so good," Miller admitted. "But in the game of basketball, it's never over until the horn goes off."

The Pacers called a timeout, and coach Larry Brown spoke with his huddled masses about trying to get a basket, then quickly fouling and hoping to get the ball back, and, well, he revealed this after the game: "Realistically, I thought we had no chance. I couldn't imagine us coming back at this point. But a coach has to keep coaching."

Indeed, and Reggie—cocky, cool, as skinny as a noodle—kept playing. He took a pass from Mark Jackson and sank a three-point shot: 105–102 Knicks. Anthony Mason took the ball out of bounds under the basket. "I saw him falling in bounds and he was having trouble finding someone to throw it to," Miller said. "I know he was going to throw it somewhere, I didn't expect him to throw it to me."

Ah, but Mason did throw it to him. Miller had a short shot, but this wasn't to his taste. He turned and dribbled out to three-point range and let loose a shot that flew right through the hoop. "I wanted to drive a stake through their heart," said the cuddly Reggie.

Both shots took a total of 3.1 seconds on the game clock. In the stands, Grant Hill, the standout Detroit Pistons rookie, said he looked down to sign an autograph with the Knicks ahead by six, and when he looked up the game was tied.

"Reggie loves the pressure," said Hill. "A lot of guys in the league don't want that last shot. They're running the other way from the ball. Reggie wants the ball in his hands with the game on the line."

Reggie wasn't finished. After John Starks missed two free throws, Mason fouled Miller with 7.5 seconds left.

Now the home crowd was screaming at Miller as he stepped to the line, and what they were screaming was not "New York Loves Reggie!"

He made the first free throw. He made the second free throw. The crowd was silenced and stunned. And within seconds, it was over.

Well, not quite. Miller couldn't resist gilding the 107–105 losers. As he ran into the locker room, he shouted, "Choke artists! Choke artists!"

In the past, Miller has taunted opponents, particularly the Knicks. There was the legendary needling of Starks two years ago, which resulted in that volatile Knick punching Miller in the mouth with his head. For the butt, Starks was ejected. Another time, Miller grasped his hand to his throat in mute declaration that the Knicks had choked. But how he could produce. He scored 25 of his 39 points in the fourth quarter last year at the Garden—including five three-pointers—in the Pacers' come-from-behind Game 5 victory over the Knicks that will remain forever a sports classic.

"Funny," said Hill, "but Reggie was quiet until the last 18 seconds of the game." In fact, Miller had made only one basket in seven tries in the first half, and had nine points. Juiced in the second half from fans' howls of execration, he finished 7-for-18, with 14-of-15 from the free throw line, for 31 points.

"It was wild," said Brown. "I don't think I ever saw a game like this."

"It was bizarre," said Knick coach Pat Riley, who looked as if he had just seen, well, someone who resembled a dude with a black cape. "It was a bizarre ending."

Miller, who had outscored the Knicks by 8–0 in the closing seconds, was asked if he still enjoyed being the bad guy?

"Yes, indeedy," he said, with a very toothy grin.

A Garden Finale
Starts with a Boo

April 6, 2005

SKINNY AS A STRAND of linguine, as welcome as a termite, as fearless as Fosdick, Reggie Miller returned to Madison Square Garden last night for what was expected to be the last time as a player, having announced he would retire at season's end.

And if it was the swan song for Miller, the Indiana Pacers shooting guard, then it meant that it was the last time that Miller, 39, would have an opportunity to make the Knicks and their fans miserable.

"And starting at guard, in his last ever game"—the boos began as the public address announcer began his introduction—"in Madison Square Garden"—more boos—"No. 31, Reggie Miller!"

As he ran out to the free throw line, the boos turned to cheers and a standing ovation, in grudging homage, perhaps, in respect for sure. Even Spike Lee, the filmmaker and Miller's courtside foil, cheered from his seat.

Miller loved to torment the Knicks. And, to be fair, he tormented other opponents, but he seemed to save his best moments for the Garden.

Even though he wound up with only 13 points and shot just 3-for-15, he wasn't needed to pull the game out. The Pacers (39–34) led throughout by comfortable margins and beat the Knicks 97–79. And now Miller will no longer taunt the Knicks world with those dagger-in-the-heart game-winning shots, or his contemptuous gestures.

"Sentimental?" Miller said, responding to a question about his final appearance at the Garden. "Well, it does take on a little more meaning because of my history here, because I had some of my best moments in games in this city, and because it's the most famous stadium in the world."

It may be too painful to recall for New Yorkers, but there was the playoff game on June 1, 1994, when Miller bombed in 25 points in the fourth quarter to steal a victory from the Knicks, and then, to add insult to injury, gave the choke sign to Lee.

On May 7, 1995, he infamously poured in eight points in 8.9 seconds, erasing a six-point Knicks lead and giving the Pacers a 107–105 victory in the first game of their playoff series.

On June 2, 2000, he scored 34 points in a Game 6 victory over the Knicks and sent the Pacers into the NBA Finals.

And the boos flooded the gym.

His greatest thrill in the Garden? He mentioned none of his individual achievements, but talked about the great rivalry between the Pacers and the fine Knick teams. "But it was a big thrill to win our first conference playoff series against them, in, I think it was '95 or '96," he said. "We'd lost a couple before that, and weren't sure we'd ever do it."

John Starks, who had his considerable battles and frustrations with Miller, said, "He believes he can do anything at any time on the basketball court. Some guys don't want to take that last shot."

Rick Carlisle, the Pacers coach, explained his theory on why Miller has played so well in the Garden. "Great venues bring out the greatness in great players," he said. "There's been a lot of magical moments in Madison Square Garden, from boxers to singers to everything else."

This is Miller's 18th season in the NBA, and even at the end of an All-Star career, he is among the best.

In recent games, with a shot still as quick as a twitch, he scored 31 against the Miami Heat and 39 against the Lakers. He has topped 30 points in a game five times this season. Only three other NBA players have scored more than 30 points at age 39, and none of them were shooting guards. Kareem Abdul-Jabbar was a center, Karl Malone was a power forward, and Michael Jordan was playing small forward.

"We're seeing something now that I believe we will never see again in this league," Carlisle said. "He's playing this well at this age at the No. 2 position. It's more demanding than forward or center. There's much more running involved. And this takes nothing away from a player, say, like Michael Jordan."

Carlisle has been deeply impressed by Miller's work ethic. "He has regular routines and works as hard as anyone I've ever seen at keeping his body in the best shape possible," he added. At game's end last night, the crowd began chanting "Reggie! Reggie!" Did he ever expect that? "The fans showed their appreciation, and I appreciated that," he said. But, he added, "there were a few" rather crude aspersions. Just for balance, surely.

And so, for the Knicks and their followers, it was a fond farewell to Reggie Miller. Well, farewell, anyway.

V.

MJ:
A FLYING
NEMESIS

M. JORDAN: FIRST IN FLIGHT

May 15, 1989

MICHAEL JORDAN, TO THE surprise of most, used wheels yesterday morning when he arrived at Chicago Stadium, and not wings. He motored into the parking lot before Game 4 of the playoffs in his red Ferrari, but the license plate was suggestive of the most notable propensity of the occupant:

"M-Air-J," and below it the state name, "North Carolina," and above it the state motto, "First in Flight."

When Wilbur and Orville Wright departed their bike shop in Dayton, Ohio, in 1903 to go fly the first airplane, they chose Kitty Hawk, North Carolina, as the historic site. No way it was just coincidence. The Wright Brothers must surely have figured that one day years and years later Jordan the Flying Machine would grow up and make his home in North Carolina and have license plates that read, "First in Flight." Historians should look into the matter.

All that, however, is merely prologue. For yesterday, there was concern among the faithful of the Chicago Bovines that Jordan might in fact be grounded.

It was reported that he had injured a groin muscle in his left thigh in the second quarter of the game on Saturday afternoon, even though he went on to score a total of 40 points in the game. One of his baskets included a typical "M-Air-J" shot in which he flew along the baseline as if he were a kite being blown by a strong wind.

The 6'6" Jordan moved so gingerly on the court near game's end—this before the injury had been revealed—that one observer wondered if he had a pebble in his size 13 shoe.

Rick Pitino, for one, harbored doubts that anything was seriously wrong with Jordan. The Knick coach knows a psychological ploy when he hears it—and sees it with his own eyes. A guy scores 40 points and he's injured. Impossible. But then, yes, Michael Jordan is impossible.

Now, at about 10:30 AM, "M-Air-J," in white sweater, black slacks, black loafers, and sockless, stepped out of the car and was met by a handful of reporters.

"How's it feel, Michael?" he was asked.

"Feels a lot better," he replied. "Had treatment for about four or five hours last night on a machine." "What kind?" "I'm not a doctor and I don't know the technical term, but I call it 'electrostem'—that and I iced it." "Will you play?" "I'll play sore," he said, "but I'll play."

In the Bulls locker room, he went immediately into the trainer's room to continue treatment. The trainer, Mark Pfeil, had explained that the treatment was known as "micro-current electro nerve stimulant," which, in a word, is supposed to be very good stuff.

When Jordan, now in shorts, slid onto the table, he made a little "ooh" sound of pain.

The trainer's room is a fairly small facility off of a small locker room. Jordan and the trainer, Pfeil, were joined there by the Bulls coach, Doug Collins, who looked worried. Then Jerry Krause, the general manager, went in. He was followed a few minutes later by Jerry Reinsdorf, the team owner, and, shortly, Keith Brown, director of ticket sales. It was getting as crowded in there as that ship cabin in *A Night at the Opera*. It seemed that the only way to get out was to step over a Marx Brother.

Pfeil persevered, nonetheless. He kneaded Jordan's legs.

"His legs are so strong and so well defined," Pfeil said later, "that you can easily isolate his muscles. It's like working on an anatomy chart."

The problem now, said Pfeil, was that when Jordan stretched his leg, it pulled on his muscle and gave him pain. "You tired?" someone asked him. "Never feel tired when you're about to win a series," he said. And he smiled.

When he came onto the court to warm up before the game, he still seemed to move a bit carefully. But in the game, it appeared that he was not hurting, not at all. Some pro scouts in the stands thought he might not be reaching quite the altitudes he normally did, but that was niggling. In fact, it might even be better for him. For one thing, he doesn't have as far to fall when he descends to earth. The other is, the closer one flies to the sun the more hazardous it is to your health.

In the first period, he scored eight points and had three rebounds as his team took the lead 27–22.

"I didn't know what to expect," he said later, about his groin muscle injury, "and so I favored it at the beginning.

"As I continued, I got more confidence. Once I did, it was full speed ahead."

Full speed ahead meant that head-spinning assortment of drive shots and jump shots, of clothesline passes on the fast break for baskets, of steals and rebounds, of him breaking the Knicks' full-court press by dribbling left and right and in and out of holes, reminiscent of the broken-field work of that other Chicago dignitary, Gale Sayers.

And, of course, he spent great bunches of time in the air. Sometimes people say he gets away with taking steps. This is true. However, some of those steps are taken in the air. Rulesmakers have not yet addressed this part of his game. So for now it's legal.

And every time the Knicks drew close to the Bulls, Jordan did something that, like star-crossed lovers, brought them farther apart.

In the fourth quarter, with the Knicks only four points down, Jordan scored 18 of his team's last 25 points.

In the end, he pumped in 47 points—the high scorer by double of anyone else in the game—pulled down 11 rebounds, had six assists, as the Bulls beat the Knicks 106–93, for a 3–1 lead in their four-of-seven-game series.

"It's the playoffs," Jordan said after the game, "it's not time to be injured, it's not time to think about it."

And so "M-Air-J, First in Flight," soared again. Gerald Wilkins, Trent Tucker, Patrick Ewing, and the other Knicks couldn't bring him down. Only the Red Baron might have had a chance.

JORDAN TUNES IN ON KNICKS

May 18, 1993

"I JUST MET MAYBE the only person in America who doesn't know who Michael Jordan is," said the visitor as his host opened the door of a hotel suite here Sunday afternoon.

"You did?" said the genuinely curious host, a basketball player for the Chicago Bulls named Michael Jordan. "Who's that?"

"Ran into a couple in the lobby," said the visitor. "It was Abba Eban and his wife. He was in town to make a speech. I told him I was here to see Michael Jordan. I asked if he'd heard of you, and he said he has. But his wife said, 'Who's Michael Jordan?'"

Jordan smiled. "That's good," he said. "They won't be after me for anything. By the way, who's Abba Eban?"

Aha! In life, one learns that one way or another, things always even out.

Jordan, who would later be interested in hearing about the star Israeli diplomat, had other concerns at that moment. He was watching the telecast of the Knicks-Hornets playoff game.

And his rooting interest showed a certain ambivalence. While he openly seemed to want Charlotte to win this game and tie the series at 2–2—the better, surely, to help wear both teams down—he wasn't that crazy about the Hornets winning the series. After all, with the Bulls up three games to none against the Cavaliers, it was a good bet that Chicago would advance, as it did last night, and play one of those two teams.

"If we play Charlotte," he said, "I'm in hot water with tickets."

Jordan was raised in North Carolina, and went to the University of North Carolina. Would the Knicks be a bigger challenge? "My challenge," he said, "is only to win a third straight championship."

As the Knicks began to squander a 15-point lead, spectator Jordan, in sweatshirt, jogging pants, and red-and-white sneakers, squirmed on the couch: "I can't believe they're letting the Hornets back in the game."

He shouted at Kendall Gill, whose shooting had been off. "Go to the hole!" Gill took a jumper that missed. "Youth!"

When Larry Johnson celebrated after the Hornets closed the deficit to two points, Jordan said, "Too soon to do all that jumping up and down. You lose energy. You need that high emotion for later in the game. That's inexperience."

"The Knicks aren't like that anymore," said Jordan. "And a lot of that has to do with Patrick, and with Doc Rivers." Patrick Ewing took a shot that hung, hung on the rim, then fell in.

"That's amazing, man—what touch!" said Jordan. "And he's doing everything he can to win. Like he's getting better position so he doesn't go out on fouls as often. But one of the biggest things is how he kicks the ball out when he's double- and triple-teamed. Before, he thought he had to do it all himself. Now he has confidence in Starks and Blackman and Rivers to hit the outside shot—Doc especially has helped settle down the younger guys."

And Anthony?

"Not my favorite guy. It's one thing for a guy to come in the league and try to assert himself, but you can't antagonize people to the point of violence."

"Look, look there," said Jordan. "The Hornets have trouble shooting from outside because of the Knick defense. Look how close the Knick defenders are—they don't give you a foundation."

Jordan was particularly impressed with Pat Riley's handling of the rookie Hubert Davis: "He didn't let him die on the bench. And Hubert shoots just like his uncle." That is, Walter Davis, like Hubert and Jordan a former Tar Heel. "Walter was my idol. A great jump shot, and Hubert is a carbon copy."

Anthony Mason took a strong rebound. "He's one of the most valuable players. Very versatile. I didn't realize how good he was until this year. He and Oakley together—they'll beat you for the offensive rebound."

Jordan said he also likes Starks very much. "He's a guy who has bounced around in the CBA, and this league, and now he has stepped up.

He takes the responsibility when Patrick goes out. But if Patrick gets tired, and Starks isn't hitting—they're in trouble."

On Charles Smith: "He's been disappointing because they want him to be a tough guy, and he's a finesse player."

When Blackman hit the final basket, Jordan exclaimed, "That's a veteran! Under pressure, he wasn't going to be rushed. But where was the defense? Inexperience."

And Jordan's view of a Knicks-Bulls series?

"After our last game in New York, when they beat us," he said, "I saw Spike Lee at courtside and said, 'You think the Knicks are going to win this year, don't you?' He said, "Yeah, I do.' I said, 'Surprise, surprise, surprise.'"

A HUMBLED JORDAN
LEARNS NEW TRUTHS

April 11, 1994

EVERY MORNING WHEN HE wakes up, Michael Jordan was saying, he sees the face of his dead father, James. Every morning, as he did this morning when he rose from bed in his hotel room here, he has a conversation with his father, his greatest supporter, his regular companion, his dearest and most trusted friend.

"I talk to him more in the subconscious than actual words," said Jordan today, in front of his locker in the Birmingham Barons Class AA clubhouse. "'Keep doing what you're doing,' he'd tell me," said Jordan. "'Keep trying to make it happen. You can't be afraid to fail. Don't give a damn about the media.' Then he'd say something funny—or recall something about when I was a boy, when we'd be in the backyard playing catch together like we did all the time.

"It takes your mind away from what's happening. Lifts the load a little bit."

The memory and the pain of his father's murder are still very much alive in Michael. It has been less than a year since James Jordan was murdered last July, at age 56 after having pulled his car to the side of the road one night to take a nap in North Carolina. The police say his killers were two young men who chose at random to rob him.

The days since then have often been wrenching for Jordan, who retired from his exalted state as the world's greatest basketball player and decided to pursue a career as a baseball player. And while he still says his baseball experiment is fun, these days lately for Michael Jordan have not been strictly a fantasy camp. They have been difficult.

"For the last nine years," he said, "I lived in a situation where I had the world at my feet. Now I'm just another minor leaguer in the clubhouse here trying to make it to the major leagues."

He is a 31-year-old rookie right fielder for the Barons of the respectable Southern League, considered a "prospects league," and his debut has been less than auspicious.

"It's been embarrassing, it's been frustrating—it can make you mad," he said. "I don't remember the last time I had all those feelings at once. And I've been working too hard at this to make myself look like a fool."

In his first two games for the Barons, Air Jordan had hit little more than air, striking out five times in seven tries, along with a pop-out and groundout.

There has been much speculation about why Michael Jordan would walk away from basketball to subject himself to this new game, one he hasn't played since he was 17 years old, and had played in high school and the Babe Ruth league.

"It began as my father's idea," said Jordan, in the season of 1990 when the Bulls were seeking their first National Basketball Association title. "We had seen Bo Jackson and Deion Sanders try two sports and my father had said that he felt I could have made it in baseball, too. He said, 'You've got the skills.' He thought I had proved everything I could in basketball, and that I might want to give baseball a shot. I told him, 'No, I haven't done everything. I haven't won a championship.' Then I won it, and we talked about baseball on occasion, and then we won two more championships. And then he was killed."

On the night last October when Jordan announced to Jerry Reinsdorf, the owner of both the White Sox and Bulls, that he was going to quit basketball, they were sitting in Reinsdorf's box watching the White Sox–Toronto playoff game. Eddie Einhorn, a partner of Reinsdorf on the White Sox, was home recuperating from an illness when he got a phone call from Reinsdorf that night. Reinsdorf told him what had happened and then added, "And guess what he wants to do next. Play baseball!"

In December, Jordan was hitting in the basement batting cage at Comiskey Park. This spring, Reinsdorf allowed him to play with the White

Sox in Sarasota, Florida, and then permitted Jordan to try to realize his dream—and "the dream of my father, both our dreams"—by starting in Class AA ball.

"My father used to say that it's never too late to do anything you wanted to do," said Jordan. "And he said, 'You never know what you can accomplish until you try.'"

So Jordan is here trying, lifting the weights, shagging the fly balls, coming early to the park for extra batting practice, listening while another outfielder, Kerry Valrie, shows him how to throw from "the top," or over the head, and Jordan then practicing over and over by throwing an imaginary ball.

This morning, he sat among players who are as much as 12 years younger than he is. Black-and-silver uniforms hang in his locker with the No. 45, which he wore in high school, and not the No. 23 he made famous in Chicago. He had several bats stacked there, with the names of Steve Sax, Shawn Abner, and Sammy Sosa on them. He is still looking for a comfortable bat, the Michael Jordan model.

"It's been humbling," he said. And you could see that in his eyes. Gone is that confident sparkle they had at playoff time against Magic's Lakers, or Bird's Celtics, or Ewing's Knicks.

"I just lost confidence at the plate yesterday," he said about his three strikeouts on Saturday. "I didn't feel comfortable. I don't remember the last time I felt that way in an athletic situation. You come to realize that you're no better than the next guy in here."

The other day in Chicago, Einhorn offered a theory on Jordan's baseball pursuit.

"This is the most amateur form of psychology, but I wonder if Michael in some way is not trying to do penance for the murder of his father," said Einhorn. "I wonder if he's not seeking to suffer—to be with his father in this way."

"Seems to be true, doesn't it?" said Jordan, removing his designer bib overalls and reaching to put on his Barons uniform. "I mean, I have been suffering with the way I've been hitting—or not hitting."

He smiled wanly. "But I don't really want to subject myself to suffering. I can't see putting myself through suffering. I'd like to think I'm a strong enough person to deal with the consequences and the realities. That's not my personality. If I could do that—the suffering—to get my father back, I'd do it. But there's no way."

His eyes grew moist at the thought. "He was always such a positive force in my life," said Jordan. "He used to talk about the time my Little League team was going for the World Series and we were playing in Georgia and there was an offer that if anyone hit a homer they'd get a free steak. I hadn't had a steak in quite a while, and my father said, 'If you hit a homer, I'll buy you another steak.' It was a big ballfield, and in the fourth inning I hit that sucker over the center-field fence with two on to tie the game 3–3. We lost it anyway, 4–3, but I've never experienced anything in sports like hitting one out of the park."

He was reminded about the time his father, bald like Michael, was told that he has the same haircut as his son. "Same barber," said James Jordan. "That," said Michael, "was my father."

The effects of his father's death remain with Jordan in other ways. He has purchased a couple of guns that he keeps in his home in Highland Park, Illinois. He says he always looks out of the rearview mirror of his car and drives down streets he wouldn't normally take. "You never know, someone might be following you. I'm very aware of that. It's second nature now."

And his offer to lease a luxury bus for the Barons' road games had another motive beyond just giving his 6'6" frame more leg room. "I don't want to have a bus break down at 1:00 at night in the South," he said. "You don't know who's going to be following you. I don't want to be caught in a predicament like that. I think about what happened to my dad."

The people in the organization see progress. "When I first saw him hitting in the winter," said Mike Lum, Chicago's minor league batting instructor, "it was all upper body. He was dead from the waist down. I think that's been a big change." But Jordan still has not demonstrated power in a game, though in the Cubs–White Sox exhibition game in Wrigley Field last Thursday he hit a sharp double down the third-base line. "He's got to learn to hit before he hits with power," said Lum. "He's got to master the fundamentals."

Jordan has had so much advice that, he said, "I've got a headache." Before today's game, he said, "I was thinking too much. It's just got to flow."

He has played adequately in the field, catching all the fly balls hit to him and playing a carom off the "Western Supermarkets" sign in right field with grace and making a strong throw to second base that held the runner to a single. "My defense has kept me respectable," he said.

The players in the clubhouse, at first in awe of this personage, have come to treat him like a teammate. "And I can learn from his work ethic," said Mike Robertson, a three-year minor league outfielder. "He's good to be around."

One fellow who wasn't so happy was Charles Poe, who was sent down to Class A to make room for Jordan. Poe had said that he resented Jordan's having taken his position.

"I talked to Charlie about that," said Jordan. "The coaches told me that he was going to be sent down anyway, that he wasn't ready for Double A. But I said to Charlie, 'Sometimes in life, things don't go your way. You just have to use that as energy to move forward. Never give up.'

"I don't think he really meant to come down on me. But he has to learn that as much as he loves the game—as much as I love the game—it's a business. Charlie's a good kid. He had a tough life, growing up in South Central Los Angeles.

"I told him, 'Charlie, you and I are in the same boat. We're hoping to make it to the big leagues. If it's meant to be, we will. I had some bad days in basketball, and things improved. We just got to hang in, no matter what.'"

Jordan said he had planned to play all season, all 142 games, make all the bus rides—some as many as 10 and 12 hours long—and then see what happens. As for the NBA, the only reminder is a sticker on his locker that someone had put up. It reads: "Barkley for Gov."

Charles Barkley, an Alabama native, has spoken of his desire to run for governor of the state. "I told Charles," said Jordan, "that if that ever happened, you be like Huey Long in the movie *Blaze*, a total dictator. I told him to stick to TV commercials."

Jordan laughed, then grabbed a couple of bats and went out to the batting cage to try again, and again. After that, he trotted out to right field, a position his father's baseball hero, Roberto Clemente, played. Perhaps it is only coincidence.

•   •   •

Michael Jordan finished his minor league baseball career in 1995, with a batting average of .202, with three homers and 51 RBIs in 127 games and 497 plate appearances. He returned to the Bulls in March of that year.

JORDAN HITS GARDEN
AT CRUISING SPEED: 55

March 29, 1995

PEOPLE WERE SCOURING THE record books to find out when anyone had done in Madison Square Garden what Michael Jordan had done last night against the Knicks. Like most points in a half, or most points in a game, or most points in...

They were looking in the wrong place.

You don't find what Jordan did in the game in the record books. You check memories, like the time in the Garden that Ol' Blue Eyes had the joint swinging, or the Stones had it rocking, or Gunther Gebel-Williams tamed his lions and mesmerized the crowd, or the first Ali-Frazier fight.

The hype for this game was similar to that for the previous four Jordan had played in since he returned 10 days ago from his prodigal stint as a minor league fly chaser in the White Sox organization. That is, Michael Miracle is back. Over all, though, he had been simply a miracle waiting to happen.

The World's Greatest Hoopster scored 55 points, including a jump shot to put the Bulls ahead by two with 25 seconds left in the fourth quarter. And then, with the game tied, and with 3.1 seconds left, he went up for the shot that everyone knew he'd take and, with Knicks lunging after him, he passed to Bill Wennington under the basket for the stuff that won it for the Bulls 113–111.

The game opened about as spectacularly as it ended. Jordan hit a jump shot from the left to start the scoring. The next time down he hit a jump shot from the top of the key. He missed his next shot and then flew down the baseline and laid in the ball. He hit six of his first seven shots before Phil Jackson, the Bulls coach, removed his shooting star, presumably for a rest. But perhaps he was taking pity on John Starks and Anthony Bonner and Derek Harper and Greg Anthony who, individually and en masse, were taking futile turns trying to guard Jordan.

Jordan returned and wound up with 20 points in the first quarter. At this rate, he would score 80 for the game. Inevitably, he cooled down. He only scored 15 in the next period—including one delicious double-pump shot off Patrick Ewing—dropping the pro rata to 70 points for the game.

And thus he wound up one of the most preposterous first halves in the history of the Garden. Jordan hit on 14 of 19 shots, including your occasional three-pointer.

It was reminiscent of the first Ali-Frazier fight in which Muhammad Ali, so charismatic, with his red tassel white shoes and his dancing skills, dominated the spectators' attention. In the excitement, however, Joe Frazier was winning the fight. Similarly, at the half, the Bulls were losing 56–50.

But it was everything and more that the capacity crowd of 19,763 could have hoped for.

In Jordan's four previous games since his return to basketball, he had fairly lackluster games, for him, other than the last one, against Atlanta, in which he hit a jumper at the final buzzer for a 99–98 victory. He seemed not quite his old self, even somewhat nervous, since he hadn't played a National Basketball Association game since June 1993, when the Bulls beat Phoenix for their third straight NBA title.

His opener 10 days ago in Indianapolis saw him miss 21 of 28 shots. He appeared nervous, as he did last Friday night in his home opener in the new United Center in Chicago. When he was introduced to the crowd of 20,000, there followed a crashing, blinding, sound-and-light show that one might have expected for something else, like Moses receiving the Ten Commandments.

Both teams sought to make statements last night, the Knicks that they could whip the Bulls with Jordan, the Bulls that they were monsters once again.

And Jordan was eager to return as the great scorer he was when he left the game—he had averaged 32 points per game, the highest in history. But if there was a fault to his game last night, it was that he was looking for only one open man—Mr. Miracle. His first assist came with 50 seconds left in the game. He didn't get his second until—well, until it was time to win the game.

"When I was playing baseball, I still felt I could play this game," Jordan said with a smile in the interview room afterward. "I'm starting to get a little hang of it again."

In fact, for fans who came to see something memorable, a performance for the ages, they wound up in the right place. They hardly noticed that he had chilled from his hot start, and finished with only 55 points. For those scouring the record book, if they must, it was the most ever scored by an opponent in the new Garden. The previous mark was 50, by—who else?—Michael Jordan.

JORDAN HAS THE GAME, THE VALUES

November 5, 1997

MICHAEL JORDAN WAS CURIOUS about the recent HBO documentary on Joe DiMaggio. "I didn't know a lot about DiMaggio," said Jordan, "and some people have compared me to DiMaggio. I wanted to see it."

He was impressed, he said, because DiMaggio took his image seriously, not just performing on the field to the best of his ability—a leader by quiet demeanor and an explosive bat but also comporting himself as a gentleman.

DiMaggio recognized a responsibility to maintain dignity as, particularly, a symbol for the Italian Americans of the 1930s, the immigrants and sons and daughters of immigrants yearning to rise in American society. For many, those were causes enough.

And when Paul Simon wrote the lyrics in "Mrs. Robinson" about "Where have you gone, Joe DiMaggio?/The nation turns its lonely eyes to you," Jordan came to understand that DiMaggio was taken to embody a sense of values that transcended ethnic and racial lines. It is a sense that increasingly escapes this generation of people, especially athletes.

Jordan, like DiMaggio, remains a consummate performer in the arena and elegant away from it.

When Charles Barkley threw a man through a plate glass window for tossing ice cubes on him in a bar, Jordan told Barkley in a telephone conversation, "Charles, I love you like a brother, but you can't do that kind of thing. It's stupid. And you have to stay out of bars. They're only trouble."

Barkley protested. He said he wasn't going to allow people to "mess with my manhood."

Jordan felt that there were other ways to demonstrate "manhood"—one of which would be discretion.

Shaquille O'Neal exercised second thoughts in this regard. After his fine and suspension for slapping and knocking down Greg Ostertag of Utah in an argument before a recent game, O'Neal issued an apology in writing to the other large center and added: "I acknowledge my responsibility to set a good example for young people and I admit that in this instance, I did not do so. I ask those young people not to emulate my conduct here because there is no excuse to engage in physical confrontation."

While O'Neal seeks to reassert values, aberrant acts by high-profile athletes occur regularly. "It must be the money," Deion Sanders sang in a song he wrote a year ago that deserves the artistic anonymity it has found. One aspect may indeed be the money, the millions that accrue to young men barely out of high school.

The times have produced a remarkable chemical reaction in some players: it has fattened their wallets and bankrupted their wits. It seems that, like Barkley, who, in a commercial of all places, said he was no role model, too many athletes believe they can do whatever they want, whenever they want.

But this is beyond being simply a role model. It is about being a good citizen, period. About having a good work ethic, and about not abusing drugs or alcohol or one's spouse, among other items.

In most cases, the role models of the so-called role models have been found at home. And it is not news that a breakdown of family structure contributes to bad behavior. Jordan keeps perspective by recalling how his parents raised five children in Wilmington, North Carolina, his father "working two and three jobs" and his mother "managing the budget for the house and stretching a dollar as far as it could be stretched."

Jordan said, "I'm not kidding myself, I'm no Muhammad Ali," whom he said he admires. Nor, he said, is he Joe Louis or Jackie Robinson, people who stood for something beyond just sports. "They carried the burden of an entire race; I've never had to do that," said Jordan.

"I can only do what I'm comfortable doing, and working with kids in the inner city is one of them. But I try to do what I can in other areas. Like I'm keeping on top of how Nike treats workers in Asia"—he has a huge endorsement contract with Nike—"though I think some of that is misunderstood. And when my dad was killed, groups wanted me to campaign against handguns. I said I was opposed to private handguns, but I felt pressured, so I declined."

He said he believes that he will fade from popularity when he retires. "My lawyer doesn't think so," said Jordan. "But I disagreed. Look at Magic and Bird. They're already waning. I'll be the same."

Perhaps. But as with DiMaggio, many lonely eyes may properly turn to Jordan.

FOR JORDAN, LAST DRIVE
DOWN LANE AT GARDEN

March 9, 2003

WHEN THE CHICAGO BULLS featuring, sadly for the home team, the indomitable Michael Jordan, emerged on the court to play the Knicks in their numerous NBA playoff games during the 1990s, the wholesale racket in Madison Square Garden was ear-piercing as well as spine-tingling.

It was Ali versus Frazier, Pancho Gonzalez versus Rod Laver, and Marilyn Monroe, scooped into a sequined dress, singing "Happy Birthday" to President John F. Kennedy, all rolled into one. There was such electricity, such energy, that had the building been a spaceship, it would have taken flight.

On Sunday, Michael Jeffrey Jordan—now wearing a Washington Wizards uniform as well as assorted medicinal wraps to keep his 40-year-old, 6'6" body from coming unglued—will play in Madison Square Garden for, most likely, the last time. This time, it is a different mood from those playoff years. The Knicks and the Wizards are middle-of-the-pack teams, trying to reach the eighth and last playoff spot.

Recently, Jeff Van Gundy, who was an assistant and later became the coach of the Knicks during those playoff years against the Bulls, was asked about his memories of Jordan in Madison Square Garden. "Unfortunately, they are almost all bad," he said. "Every time we had a chance to advance in the playoffs, maybe get to the Finals, Michael Jordan primarily was there to stop us. We could never quite get over that hump."

On February 28, at Madison Square Garden, during the ceremony retiring Patrick Ewing's number, Jordan attended and was introduced to the crowd. He was booed.

"That was only because he broke their hearts so often," said Ewing, now an assistant coach for the Wizards. "They still love him."

Jordan smiled through it all, and a smile crept onto his face Friday morning as well.

"I don't ever remember being booed when I was playing there, but if those fans booed, it's because you did something well," Jordan recalled in the MCI Center after a Wizards workout, leaning against the wall outside his locker room, wearing a floppy tennis hat and warm-ups. "It's not because you played dirty. I consider the booing to be a point of respect. Especially at the Garden. Those people there really know basketball."

Jordan said he remembered hearing about Madison Square Garden when he was a boy, then playing there for the first time when he was in college at North Carolina. "It was the place to showcase your basketball talents," he said. "I remember the New York guys on the North Carolina team saying the Garden was the Big Show. And when I played there I was amazed at how knowledgeable the fans were.

"You'd hear them calling out, 'Box out,' or 'Screen and roll,' or 'Force him to his left; he can't go left.' You don't hear those kinds of things in too many places. Sure, it was always a special occasion to play in Madison Square Garden."

The fans had good reason to show respect, even if it came in baritone form. In the '90s, Jordan's Bulls won six titles in the last six full seasons he played—he retired after the 1992–93 season before returning late in the 1994–95 season, and retired again after the 1997–98 season. He has scored 40 or more points against the Knicks 19 times and has averaged 31.6 points against them in his career. In 1995, in one of his most memorable games at the Garden, or anywhere else, he scored 55 points in only his fifth game back from his one-and-a-half-year sojourn with baseball.

"That 55-point game was one of those times when I just couldn't miss a shot," Jordan said. "They kept throwing people at me, but it didn't make a difference."

Then it came down to the last seconds of the game. It was tied 111–111. The crowd was roaring. "I went up for the shot—I always plan to take the shot when the game's on the line—but I saw Wennington free," he said.

Bulls center Bill Wennington grabbed Jordan's pass and dunked to win the game 113–111.

On that scorching offensive night for Jordan, it was only his second assist. He shot 21-for-37 from the field, including 3-for-4 on three-pointers, and added 10 of 11 free throws.

It was a typical Jordan move: the Knicks stay close, have a chance to win, but then Jordan inserts the dagger to kill off all hope. He didn't do it in all the games—there were playoff games in which, for example, he shot 3-for-18. But he would shake that off and soar again.

And the memories come flooding back. The Wizards assistant Johnny Bach, who was an assistant with the Bulls when Jordan played for them, remembered a clutch moment in the final seconds when Jordan stepped to the foul line and sank two free throws—with his eyes closed.

Bach was sitting on the bench beside Phil Jackson, the Bulls coach. "I said, 'Oh my God, Phil, he's shooting them without looking!'" he said.

It was true. "Probably happened in '93, or maybe '96," Jordan said. "I wanted Patrick and Charles Oakley, especially, guys who were friends of mine, to know that I was in total control, that I had total confidence. I wanted them to think: 'He's toying with us. He's in total control.' It wasn't necessarily like I was trying to intimidate them, I was just trying to, what, discourage them."

Jordan said that shooting free throws without looking wasn't so unusual for him. "I did it many times, in practice," he said, "and even in games, so I was pretty confident."

In another playoff game at the Garden, with the game again on the line in the closing seconds, he stepped to the foul line and winked at Trent Tucker, a former teammate with the Bulls who was then retired and sitting behind the basket.

"What does that mean?" someone sitting in front of Tucker asked. "Oh, it means: 'No problem. Got everything under control,'" Tucker replied. And Jordan sank the shots.

During one period of the Knicks-Bulls rivalry in the Jordan years, Van Gundy said in a television interview that Jordan's friendship with Ewing was a con job, that he was trying to soften up Ewing.

"I believed that Michael was such a competitor, and so smart, that he would use everything he could to get an edge," Van Gundy said. "He knew how to talk to the players. He knew how to talk to the coaches. He knew how to talk to the referees."

Although Van Gundy's remarks have the ring of truth, Jordan denies trying to con anyone. "I almost never talked to other players," he said. "Oh, Patrick and I would go at it a little bit—he'd call me lucky, and I'd have some choice words for him—but we were friends. I mean, off the court. We'd talk shop. When guys like John Starks or Gerald Wilkins or Johnny Newman were guarding me, I never talked to them. I think it was Van Gundy who was doing the con job. I think he was trying to get into Patrick's head for his purposes, like coaches try to do."

Oakley, now a reserve forward with the Wizards, recalled frustrating games against the Bulls when he was with the Knicks. "They were always battles," Oakley said. "But did the referees favor Michael? Probably. I remember one game, I stole the ball from him, and then the next time down I stole it again—but they called a foul." Oakley laughed. "I thought maybe there was something shady going on."

Jordan credited Oakley with "quick hands." But, Jordan added, "Sometimes, they just weren't quick enough. But Oak to this day says I had the referees in my pocket."

Jordan has special memories of another former Knick, Starks. "I loved John Starks," he said. "He was really a competitor. He really tried to challenge me. But I think in his mind he knew when he was guarding me that he was overmatched."

Jordan was injured on numerous occasions before big games against the Knicks, and yet invariably played. Once, when his right shoulder was injured, he practiced shooting jump shots left-handed. He was going to play no matter what. He shot right-handed in the game, and lit up the arena. "I love the unknown," he said. "I've always felt, if I can walk, I can play. And I don't know what I'm capable of. So I push myself past what I thought I could do, and most times I do it."

Jordan, averaging 19 points per game, did it the other day. He had back spasms against Toronto and had to be helped off the court. The next morning he could barely walk. He had heat treatments and electrical stimulation and played that night against the Clippers.

Although Jordan's body does not allow him to fly through arenas as he once did, he remains a staunch and savvy competitor, good enough to make the All-Star team this season.

And his final appearance in the Garden will be one of great anticipation, for players, for fans, for Jordan himself. He plans to play as he always has, with tongue-wagging intensity.

"What I want to do," Jordan said, "is leave the game with no bullets left in my gun."

VI

THE BEST OF RIVALS

THE MAGIC OF JOHNSON

June 11, 1988

THE BEST CENTER IN the National Basketball Association plays guard for the Los Angeles Lakers, the best forward plays guard for the Lakers, and, needless to say, the best guard in the NBA plays guard for the Lakers. Maybe the best coach does, too. And team physician and ballboy and usher and popcorn vendor and whatever else it is with which Earvin "Magic" Johnson decides to occupy his time.

On Thursday night, in the second game of the NBA Finals, Johnson, rolling out of a sick bed in which for almost two days he had suffered from the flu, drove his team to victory over the Detroit Pistons in the Forum outside Los Angeles 108–96, in a game that was of paramount importance to the Lakers, and evened the series at one game apiece.

The series resumes with three games now on the opponents' court, in the Silverdome in Pontiac, Michigan.

It is difficult to conceive of either of these two clubs, wolfish for the championship, winning three straight games anywhere. And especially not Detroit against the Lakers, and not against Magic Johnson.

From the microphones of Billy Cunningham and Dick Stockton on CBS Thursday night, we heard the tale of Magic's illness, and how, now, with the cameras panning on him as he dribbled in his marionette-style, herky-jerky fashion up the court, "you can see," said Cunningham, "the fatigue on his face."

In the first quarter, he scored no points. And it's true that a scrunch-eyed grimace had covered his countenance. Was this, to paraphrase Edward G. Robinson's question in an earlier drama, the end of Magic? At least for the night?

Not at all. In the second quarter, Johnson scored nine points to lead the team.

Beyond that, he was doing his customary stuff all around the court: zipping adroit passes, and snagging rebounds, and driving through the rivals, making spin shots and making that hook shot that he learned a year ago from Kareem Abdul-Jabbar and that is now as deadly as Abdul-Jabbar's. And there is that outside shot that once he didn't have, but, well, with a little lower-case magic, and a goodly amount of sweat alone in a gym, he has made materialize.

And notice that when there's a moment in a game that calls for Merlin, Magic invariably answers. When the other guys have what they used to call in television land "momentum," and now call being "in the flow," it is Johnson who is instrumental when the aforementioned momentum is slowed, or the flow flustered.

And so Magic Johnson played not under the weather Thursday night, and, for him, not over the weather, either. But in his customary climate, which is torrid.

He played 42 minutes, this sorry, flu-ridden creature, and hit seven of 12 shots from the field, 9-of-9 from the free throw line, for 23 points, and had seven rebounds and 11 assists.

Nearly a carbon copy of what a sound Earvin accomplished in Game 1. Obviously, then, Magic, a virtual shell of his former self before Game 2, according to the electronics observers, has the best healers around, or he swiftly studied the art of Hippocrates himself, and applied it forthwith.

The last is conceivable for those who have followed the prestidigitation of Johnson. In Johnson's rookie season, in the Finals of the NBA of 1980, Abdul-Jabbar had sprained an ankle and so Magic was conscripted from the guard position to fill in for the great Laker center.

At 6'9", Johnson had revolutionized the guard position. Never had anyone that tall done anything like that. He played the position with the dexterity of a six-footer. Then he was called on to play center, and did it like a seven-footer.

It is the stuff now of both fairy tales and history tomes how Johnson scored 42 points in the pivot and the Lakers won the championship, four games to two, over the 76ers.

There was what seemed the lowest point in his career early in the 1981–82 season, when he argued with coach Paul Westhead. Westhead wanted a slower, local-stop game, Magic wanted the express. Magic issued an ultimatum to the owner of the team and said it's him or me.

It was Westhead. Magic was 22 years old and in his third season. He was criticized widely as a spoiled brat, a product of the new age of pampered athletes. But it turned out he was right.

The Lakers have played seven times in the Finals in the 1980s, winning four, and Johnson was three times named the Most Valuable Player of the playoffs.

Winning is many times beyond pure skill. There is a mind-set involved. A willing of the parts, not just of the body, but of the team. Johnson has mastered this aspect, with his passing, with his ebullience, with his perceptions not only of the movement of the ball but also of the men in the game.

In 1976–77, his last year in high school, he led the Everett team of Lansing to the Michigan state championship. Two years later, as a sophomore at Michigan State, he led the team to the NCAA championship.

The following year he was at guard and then center for the Lakers, the champions of the NBA. Perhaps no one else has ever accomplished such a feat of three championships on three such levels in three years.

His accomplishments have been amazing, and he's still at it.

A number of years ago, I had lunch with Blackstone the Magician. When the check came, I took it, noted the bottom line, and looked up.

"Blackstone," I said, "you're a magician, let's see you make this check disappear."

He smiled. "I'm not that good," he said.

The feeling here is that Blackstone was very good, but that Magic Johnson could have made that check go poof!

MAGIC JOHNSON'S LEGACY

November 8, 1991

MAYBE THERE'S NOT JUST one moment you remember about Magic Johnson, the basketball player and the man. Maybe it's a great and wonderful collection of moments, seen in the mind's eye like a film, of Magic's no-look passes; of that quirky, high dribble and then sliding to the hoop for a finger-roll layup; of his long, looping one-hander; and of his spirited professionalism, which could be seen with his unabashedly high-fivin' his mates or getting on the case of, say Vlade Divac, for blowing kisses to the crowd and not keeping his mind squarely on the game.

Coming through in each of the frames of that mental film, though, is the smile of Magic Johnson, who played basketball with so much joy. Even when things were low for him in the game, even, for example, after the Lakers fell behind in the last NBA Finals in a terrific series with the Bulls, he said, "This has been beautiful basketball." His smile was somewhat wan, but he smiled.

Yesterday, in a nationally televised news conference, he again smiled, though again wanly, and told the world that he has learned he has been infected with the AIDS virus. He stood at the microphone, ducking nothing, just as, after losing games, he never ducked the press and explained what had to be explained. He said now that he had been tested positive for human immunodeficiency virus.

He said that he was feeling fine, but that he would have to retire from basketball.

He reminded us that anyone may be susceptible to life's cruelties. "You think it can never happen to you," he said, "that it happens only to other people." He said he was going to be a spokesman on HIV, and tell people that, he said, "if it can happen to Magic Johnson, it can happen to anybody." The message was: everybody should be more careful, practice safe sex, and smile. He said that he was against the wall, but that he would be swinging. Though Magic Johnson led the Lakers to five NBA championships and has been the Most Valuable Player in the league three times, Magic Johnson hasn't always succeeded on the basketball court. And when he shot an air ball at the end of a game in 1981 to keep the Lakers from going past Houston in the playoffs, he was called "Tragic Johnson."

Yet the smile of Magic Johnson, more than anything else, appeared to typify the man. Anything else, including the inevitable questions that will arise about his sexual preferences, has nothing to do with this man. His infection may change for some how they perceive Magic Johnson. It should not. Magic Johnson is no less the special man than he ever was.

We hear a lot of talk that athletes are role models, and most of it is nonsense because we don't really know the people behind the basketballs, or baseball bats, or tennis racquets.

We don't really know about their private lives, and their public personas may be nothing more than mere masks. And so it may be with Magic.

But after all, after 12 years as a professional basketball player, of watching him charge around the court and sweating in his basketball shorts, we came to have a sense of him. Many of us doubted the sincerity of that smile, early on, but we came to comprehend that, in terms of his work, it was absolutely genuine. So we learn once again, sadly, that anyone is vulnerable to deep tragedy, no matter how wise or clever or rich or strong or brave. And no matter how beloved.

We learn—as we recall Magic Johnson play basketball—that we should enjoy what we have and when we have it, to make the most of our abilities. We should, as he has, devote everything within our power to whatever it is we felt is worthwhile.

Magic Johnson gained the respect of many because, among other things, he devoted much of his off-the-court time to raising money for charities. On the court, he kept making himself better in his profession, no matter how good he got. And that, too, seemed to indicate the heart and mind of the man.

In a game, Magic Johnson always gave you your money's worth. When you bought a ticket to see Magic Johnson play, you were in for a treat.

He may have been the best basketball player the game has ever known. But more than that, more than Magic Johnson the basketball player, we remember the smile of Magic Johnson, Magic Johnson the man.

"Now I'll just be like one of the old-timers, in a sense," he said at the news conference. "And I hope to lead a long life."

And he departed, with a smile, of course. The smile of a fine and courageous man. Magic Johnson's legacy.

THE COLORING OF BIRD

June 2 1987

ON THE EVE OF this championship series that makes the basketball fan tingle with expectation—another in the enduring, bruising Laker-Celtic series, the clash of Magic and Bird, the hobbling Parish and McHale who maybe should be in traction versus the quadragenarian Abdul-Jabbar, the numerous Coopers who seem to reproduce themselves on the court versus D.J., of whom there is only one, and who is rarely anywhere except in the right place at the right time—with all this, an unfortunate note has been raised.

It is the matter of racism, concerning the white star in a predominantly—75 percent—black league.

The controversy created here was lit after the seventh and final game of the Eastern Conference championship, in which the Celtics beat the Pistons 117–114 and earned the right to meet the Lakers in the Finals for the 10th time in NBA history.

In the visiting and losing team's locker room Saturday afternoon in Boston Garden, Isiah Thomas, the Detroit guard, said he didn't want it to sound like sour grapes, and that there was no question that his team got beat, and that they came up short, but he harbored a resentment.

In regard to Bird, he said, "I think Larry is a very, very good basketball player. An exceptional talent, but I'd have to agree with Rodman. If Bird was black, he'd be just another good guy."

Dennis Rodman, the teammate to whom Thomas had referred, had said that Bird was "overrated," and that the only reason he had won three straight league Most Valuable Player Awards (until this year, that is), "is because he's white. That's the only reason."

The nation, however, whether in the Garden or in their living rooms, observed the kind of player Bird is.

He led—no, drove—Boston to victory Saturday afternoon—scoring 37 points, more than anyone else in the game, adding nine rebounds and nine assists and playing all 48 minutes (the only one to do so) in an arena so hot it was more suitable for roasting chickens than playing basketball. It was also Bird who made the play in the fifth game that turned defeat for the Celtics into victory, by stealing an in-bounds pass from Thomas with five seconds left, then passing to Johnson, who made the layup. It provided the Celtics with the one-point margin of triumph.

If Bird hadn't made that play, the Pistons and not the Celtics would be here competing in the NBA Finals.

And it is Bird who has contributed mightily to three Celtic championships—and possibly a fourth—in the eight seasons he has been there.

"What I was referring to," said Thomas, by telephone yesterday, "was not so much Larry Bird, but the perpetuation of stereotypes about blacks.

"When Bird makes a great play, it's due to his thinking, and his work habits. It's all planned out by him. It's not the case for blacks. All we do is run and jump. We never practice or give a thought to how we play. It's like I came dribbling out of my mother's womb.

"You hear it on television, you see it in the papers. I remember watching the NCAA finals between Syracuse and Indiana. I listened to Billy Packer, who I like, and who I think likes me, and he said when Indiana was sending in Garrett and Smart, 'Well, here come the athletes into the game.' The word *athletes*. I think that that's an unconscious statement concerning race. I don't like it.

"Magic and Michael Jordan and me, for example, we're playing only on God-given talent, like we're animals, lions and tigers, who run around wild in a jungle, while Larry's success is due to intelligence and hard work.

"Blacks have been fighting that stereotype about playing on pure instinct for so long, and basically it still exists—regardless of whether people want to believe it or not.

"And maybe I noticed it more during this series. I listened to Tommy Heinsohn on tapes of the games, and he kept going over plays by Bird, like that left-handed bank shot, where he might not with someone else. And maybe I was more sensitive to it because Boston has more white players than any other pro team, and maybe because it's so hard to win in Boston

Garden. I feel that it's not so much the fouls that the referees call there, but the ones they don't call.

"Like the punches that Parish hit Laimbeer with. I guarantee you that if it was in Atlanta, and Tree Rollins did that to Laimbeer, Rollins is thrown out of the game so fast you wouldn't believe it." Parish, who was fined and suspended for one game after that game, was not even called for a foul at the time. About Bird's steal in Game 5, Thomas said, "It was a great basketball play. I didn't put enough zip on the ball, and Laimbeer didn't step up to get it. Meanwhile, this white guy on the other team who is supposed to be very slow, with little coordination, who can't jump, all of a sudden appears out of nowhere, jumps in, grabs the ball, leaps up in the air as he's falling out of bounds, looks over the court in the space of two or three seconds, picks out a player cutting for the basket, and hits him with a dead-bullet, picture-perfect pass to win the game. You tell me this white guy—Bird—did that with no God-given talent?"

Thomas is on-target in regard to his views of stereotyping blacks. When you hear "athlete" these days, it often means "black," and in the context Thomas stated. The referees' disappearance in the Parish incident was nothing but deplorable.

In the case of Larry Bird, though, his record—both personal and in regard to team performance—speaks with eloquence for him. Black, white, or fuchsia, Larry Bird must be considered not just "another good guy," but one of the best players to ever tuck in a jersey. It says here, the best.

BIRD FLIES TO ANOTHER LEVEL

June 13, 1987

MAYBE, AFTER THESE EIGHT years, mine were lying eyes after all.

Maybe, after all these years, the old cerebrum was distorting the images that were making their circuitous way through the lens and optic nerve and canal of Schlemm.

Maybe I only thought I saw Larry Bird playing basketball at least as well as it has ever been played. Maybe it wasn't happening at all. Could it be that William Sampson, a sociology professor at Northwestern University and a twice-a-week columnist on the opinion page of the *Chicago Sun-Times*, was correct in his column of last week?

"Mr. Bird is a great jump shooter. That is his only asset!" wrote Mr. Sampson. "He is slow, cannot jump, cannot play defense, and would never get his jump shot off if the referees didn't allow him to take three steps (as opposed to the legal one and a half steps) every time he touches the ball. Further, his teammates are allowed to set illegal picks for him all the time.

"What's more, a defender had better not think of playing Mr. Bird closely. The refs simply will not allow it. All this goes on while the fawning announcers dummy up and act as though Mr. Bird is the greatest thing since sliced bread.

"It's part of the plan. The plan to have a Great White Hope in a sport that is dominated by blacks. Indeed, even the players come to believe Mr. Bird's press clippings, and that stuff the announcers spout about how he is the best and smartest player in the game. He is nowhere near being either."

In a column in *Newsday* last week, Les Payne, also on the opinion page, wrote that Bird was "overrated." "Simply stated," Mr. Payne wrote, "Bird has been marketed, for reasons more psychological than commercial, as the Irreproachable White Hope." Mr. Payne added, though, that Bird, "who is a very fine forward, is not as great as sportswriters would have us believe."

No rational person can dispute that there is racism in this country, and that it ought to be condemned and obliterated. But these two writers, both black, picked the wrong target. Anyone who truly knows basketball—anyone who knows sports, for that matter, and is thinking and seeing clearly—can appreciate Bird.

Sugar Ray Leonard was in Boston Garden Thursday night after the Celtics beat the Lakers in Game 5 of the NBA Finals. "I look at Bird," he said, "and I see that special aura—again, that certain something—that gives everyone around him the impression, 'Damn, we can do it!'"

The columns of Sampson and Payne stemmed from remarks some two weeks ago by Isiah Thomas and Dennis Rodman of the Detroit Pistons after their team was eliminated by Boston in the seventh game. Rodman, a rookie, said that Bird was overrated and that the only reason he won three straight awards as Most Valuable Player was that he's white. Asked to comment right afterward, Thomas said he agreed, and that if Bird were black, "he'd be just another good guy."

Thomas later contended that he was kidding about Bird being just another "good guy" if he were black. "Larry is a magnificent player," Thomas said. Bird said he believed Thomas' initial remarks were made "in the heat of battle," under great frustation and disappointment.

The feeling here is that Bird was right. Thomas meant them just as he said them at that moment. But Bird also knew the respect that Thomas has for him. "I went out of my way last summer to seek out Larry and Bill Russell, to ask them how they win, and how I can help make the players around me better players," Thomas said privately.

Thomas has also discussed this topic with Magic Johnson, one of his best friends. It is Johnson, in fact, who Bird says "is the best right now."

Johnson is of like mind toward Bird. "When I play against Larry," Johnson said, "it takes my game to another level...It's so much fun. It's like, if he goes before I go, and retires, I'll probably leave right after that, because it's not the same with nobody else."

Magic Johnson and Larry Bird, both 6'9" tall, entered the National Basketball Association in the same year, 1979. Johnson is a guard, Bird a forward.

Both have meant an enormous amount to their teams, including their unselfish play, team leadership, "passion for winning," as Johnson calls it, along with their superb passing, shooting, ball-stealing, and rebounding.

Johnson joined one of the great players in the game, Kareem Abdul-Jabbar, and they've been in the Finals for six of the last eight years, winning three. Bird joined the Celtics, who had the second-worst record in the NBA the season before (29–53) and, with no other change in the starting lineup, he led them to the best record in the NBA in 1979–80 (61–21). The next season Boston won the league championship. They've since won two more.

Magic Johnson, this year's Most Valuable Player, is black. If he and Bird were turned into photographic negatives, it is conceivable that charges of "overrated" might, in a moment of frustration and disappointment, be leveled at Johnson.

After all, he has physical limitations, like Bird. He has never had a jump shot, for example, but, like Bird, has endeavored to improve. In this playoff series, Johnson has been deadly from outside. And the hook shot that he learned from Abdul-Jabbar this season won Game 4.

Bird, meanwhile, has labored to make his left hand so good that he's as quick to shoot with it around the hoop as he is with his right, his natural shooting hand.

Leaving Boston Garden after Game 5 and holding a cup of soda in his right hand, Bird was asked to sign autographs. He casually signed with his left hand.

"Do you always write left-handed?" he was asked.

"No," he said, shrugging, "but I've got something in my right hand."

THAT QUIET MOMENT
FOR LARRY BIRD

August 19, 1992

IF, AS HAS BEEN said, it is the quiet moments, the moments out of the spotlight, that most define character, then this was one of them.

It was a few years ago, when Larry Bird was still healthy, still untroubled by the back problems that forced him yesterday, at age 35, to untie his basketball sneakers for the last time. Bird, as usual, had come onto the court in Boston Garden two hours before the game, under the dim lights, to shoot alone for 45 minutes, working on his moves and priming his mind for the game ahead. His only audience was the working men who put up the baskets and lay down the parquet floor.

It was considered unusual then to spend so much time working out before a game, although many have since followed suit. And Bird didn't fool around. You could see the intensity in his face, his eyes narrowed at the hoop, the familiar and smooth Swiss-clock release and follow-through.

A team trainer fed him the ball. Bird now began his routine shooting from the right side of the court and swung around to the left. He made one shot, another, and another.

The working men, about eight or 10 of them, had stopped putting up tables at courtside, and watched, as they often did. They now counted among themselves: 10 in a row, 15, 18, 20, 22, 24. On the next shot, from the top of the key, Bird missed.

"Boo!" chimed the working men. "Boo!" Bird turned, looked at them, and began to laugh. So did they.

It saddened many when Larry Bird announced his retirement yesterday. Many will miss him very much, but it's my impression that few will miss him more than those laborers.

Larry Bird was first, like them, a working man, one who gave the paying customer and the paying boss and his coach their money's worth. And those working men at courtside understood and appreciated that, just as Bird understood what it meant to be a working man. He was a garbage collector who became a kind of Rembrandt as an artist and a craftsman and an athlete.

When Bird dropped out of Indiana University, he was employed for a while as a garbage collector in his hometown, French Lick, Indiana, part of the working class, if not the underclass.

But some special quality within made him strive to be different, to go beyond just being an athlete: Was it to prove something after the suicide of his father when Bird was in his teens? Or watching his mother work to support the family? Or some Midwestern ethic, or inborn pride?

And while he sometimes appeared plodding as he ran down the court and was less than the best jumper, his instincts, his zeal, his technique, and his killer will made up for whatever he lacked.

Bird became more than a great athlete, he became a champion. He became perhaps the best college basketball player in the country at Indiana State, and, for his 13 seasons with the Boston Celtics, one of the best pros ever.

It was said about Bird, just as it was about Bill Russell before him, and Magic Johnson his contemporary, that he made the other players around him better.

He did it by all the prescribed verities of team play: hitting the open man (remember how he stole the ball from the Pistons and hit the streaking Dennis Johnson for the winning basket in the playoff game?), hustling so hard that he seemed to be in two places at one time (remember the shot he missed from the top of the key and he got the rebound at the base line, and scored?), being absolutely reliable in the clutch (remember—oh, there were too many times to remember just one!).

Statistics, while impressive, never told the story of Larry Bird. He never had to score 50 points in a game to be sensational, although he did that, too. One no-look, chest-high touch pass to a man cutting behind him was enough.

There have been other great players, and there are other great players, and there will be other great players, but it is doubtful whether there will ever be another quite like Larry Bird. It's sad that he's going, but it was a deep pleasure to have had him. Just ask the guys who put up the baskets and lay down the parquet floor at Boston Garden.

Sir Charles Rumbles

December 19, 1987

"CHARLES," CALLED A MAN in the stands, "you're a blimp!"

Shortly after that man in the stands had exercised his right to free speech under the First Amendment on Thursday night, and early in the first quarter at Madison Square Garden, Charles Barkley of the Philadelphia 76ers, a personage of imposing physical dimension, faked, dribbled, then rose up and whirled through space and above the Knicks, who gaped in wonderment as if seeing something float in from another planet. He slammed the basketball through the hoop with a ferocity that could make grown men quake. And did.

"I wasn't going to get in his way," Gerald Wilkins of the Knicks said of that particular shot, "and I wasn't anywhere near him."

"Barkley Beats Knicks" would read a headline in the following morning's paper. That just about said it. One, virtually, against five, or 10, or 15, if you include all the Knick players, and coaches, and ballboys, and Mike Saunders, the trainer.

"I propose a trade," someone at courtside said. "Charles Barkley for the entire Knick team."

"Are you crazy?" said a companion. "The 76ers would never go for it."

Charles Barkley, known increasingly as Sir Charles, a Knight of the Round Ball, may still be a blimp to some—he has trimmed down from 265 pounds to 250—but he's some blimp.

He is good enough to be among the leaders in four of the National Basketball Association's eight regular statistical categories: he's second in scoring average, second in rebounding, first in field-goal percentage, and ninth in three-point-shot percentage. And with only limited assistance from his supporting cast, he has helped move the 76ers past the .500 mark in the standings.

Yet, in the not uncommon injustice of the fans' balloting for the All-Star Game on February 7, he is only the fourth-best vote-getter at forward in the Eastern Conference.

Does this bother him?

"Naw," he said, "I'm happy just to help my team win, make two million dollars a year, and live in a big house on a hill."

"Charles," the man in the stands shouted later in the game, "nice pants!"

The fan persisted in trying to dismay Sir Charles, focusing on Barkley's baggy, tomato-red basketball drawers.

Sir Charles smiled, or continued smiling, because he sometimes smiles on the court after he makes a steal or a three-pointer and throws up his arms as if to say, "Touchdown," or takes part in a sweet play, or, generally, is gumming up the works for the other guys.

He had good reason now to express contentment:

In the first half, as his team took a 50–38 lead, all Sir Charles did was score 27 points, snare nine rebounds, block shots, throw timely passes, steal others (more than a night's work for most), and pump up his team with his unselfishness, his needling ("C'mon, we've got the lead; we're playing like we're behind!"), his intelligence on the court (his coach, Matt Guokas, calls it "presence"), and his boylike joy of playing the game, from opening tap to final buzzer, with all his heart.

It's a treat to watch Sir Charles, at 6'6" and with considerable chest and thick thighs, who, when he entered the league three seasons ago from Auburn, was known as the Round Mound of Rebound.

Meanwhile, it is not always what Sir Charles does that is so terrific, but what he doesn't do.

In the second half Thursday night, he took only four shots until deep in the fourth quarter. He did all he normally does, except look for a shot.

"I like to get a lot more guys involved so they won't be left out there," he explained. "I'm gonna do whatever it takes to win. But when we need a basket, I'm going to the ball."

"Hey, Charles," called the man in the stands, "nice haircut!"

The close-cropped functional hair style (perfect for the man on the go since all you need is to look at it and it's the same as if you had spent hours coiffing it) is reflective of his playing style: all business.

When the Knicks closed the gap to five points in the fourth quarter, Sir Charles used his formidable and mobile bulk to nestle under the basket, seek a pass, get it, and crash past poor Sidney Green for an important basket. He scored nine straight points down the stretch to help ice the game, 106–96, and wound up with 40 points and 17 rebounds.

At courtside, the 76ers television commentator is Hubie Brown, formerly of the borough of Manhattan.

"He's up there with the Jordans and the Magics and the Birds and the Akeems," said Brown. "He does this night in and night out. He exemplifies taking the pressure. The greater the adversity, the better he plays."

It took a little while for Sir Charles to be fully appreciated. Bobby Knight, for example, didn't put him on his 1984 Olympic squad. In the pros, Barkley didn't make the All-Star team until his third year. He was superb back then, and has gotten better. Last summer, he felt a need to improve his jump shot, and he did, sharpening his three-point shot to boot.

No one that big moves as fast or rebounds as powerfully or shoots from so far out so precisely. "It's scary," said Rick Pitino, the Knicks coach.

"Charles," called the man in the stands, putting on his coat, his voice softer than before, "you cost me money tonight."

THE HEART OF PISTOL PETE

January 16, 1988

TOO MANY TIMES, SAID Atlanta Hawks coach Richie Guerin in 1970, Pete Maravich gets himself "stuck up there in the air." It's a great trait for a moon, but not necessarily for a basketball player.

Pistol Pete Maravich was then a rookie in the National Basketball Association, and finding that his $2 million contract and his All-America press clippings and his great one-man show replete with feathery touch, blind passes, and slick dribbling—all done with long hair flopping and gray socks sagging—did not entitle him to immediate success in the league.

At Louisiana State University, where he averaged 44.2 points per game during three seasons (he remains college basketball's scoring leader), Maravich could go up for a jump shot and remain for a while, taking his good time, until he decided to pass or pop the shot. But then, there weren't many other 6'5" guards.

When he soared in the NBA, he discovered he had company. The guards there could hang from a roof beam or a moonbeam with as much perseverance as Pete. He soon adjusted his game and generally soared only when it was most propitious. He went on to play a decade in the NBA, twice making first-team All-Pro, and eventually making the Basketball Hall of Fame.

This was recalled the other day when an autopsy of Maravich, who died last week, revealed that he suffered from a rare, natural heart defect that had gone undetected during his life. He had no left coronary artery. Normally, humans have two.

"All those years," noted Earl Ubell, the science reporter on CBS-TV, "his life hung by a thread."

Most people with the kind of heart condition Maravich had die before they are 20; a relative few may live to 30. Maravich, who had been retired as an athlete for seven years, died at 40.

"For a guy to go 10 years in the NBA and have a congenital anomaly like that is, to say the least, very unusual," said Dr. Paul Thompson of Brown University, an expert on sudden death who was quoted in an Associated Press story Wednesday. "How could a guy like that run up and down the court for 20 years?" The question is provocative. We often talk about someone having heart. That their heart was in it. Songs tell us we gotta have heart. Could it be that Maravich, although with less physical heart than most, metaphorically had more? Could it be that he actually strengthened his heart because of his passionate involvement in the game? And was it this fulfillment that possibly contributed to his living virtually twice the expected lifetime? What did Dr. Thompson think? "I often tell my patients, the heart bone is connected to the head bone," he said. "There is no scientific proof that emotions and feelings and desire affect how we feel, but I think most physicians believe there is a correlation. It's entirely possible that Maravich's drive to excel and love for the game kept him alive." Did Pistol Pete have heart? "Oh yes, oh sure," said Butch van Breda Kolff, who coached Maravich for two years with the New Orleans Jazz. "No one learns to handle the ball the way Pete did and not love the game. The hours that he spent on it. I remember one trick he did that I've never seen before. He would take a ball and slam it on the floor with two hands and have it bounce between his legs and he'd catch it behind him."

Maravich would recall that, as a boy, he dribbled a basketball wherever he went. In the movie theater, he once said, he'd sit on the aisle so he could keep bouncing the ball.

He played with a clear love of the game, sometimes even to his detriment, for as someone recently pointed out, he was an individual in a team sport. And early in his pro career, with two Southern franchises, Atlanta and New Orleans, he was also a "white hope," it was said, in a black-dominated sport.

When he was derided early on by fans, and even by teammates, Maravich persevered, just as he had in college, when he was the whole show, playing for his father, Press, which was a kind of burden as well.

He had dreams and strivings, perfectionist's dreams and strivings. "One of these nights," he said, after a game at LSU, "one of these nights

I'm going to hit all my shots. Forty shots, maybe. I'll hit 'em all. I don't know when that night will be. I just know it's coming."

It never came, not that kind of night, although he had many brilliant ones, like the February night in 1977 when he scored 68 points against the Knicks, on 26-for-43 from the field and 16-for-19 from the free throw line. Only four players have ever scored more in an NBA game. His heart never showed signs of weakness, although he proved physically vulnerable. He came down with mononucleosis, and separated his shoulder. In 1972, he suffered from Bell's palsy, a temporary nerve disorder that caused headaches and a partial paralysis of the right side of his face.

Heart may also mean conquering adversity. Maravich came back from illness and injury. He became a strong enough team player to twice make first-team All-NBA. He had problems with alcoholism during his playing days, but beat that, and became a health-food enthusiast. In retirement, he was active as a born-again Christian.

Then, 11 days ago, after not having played the game he loved for nearly a year, he entered a half-court pickup basketball game in Pasadena, California, with a chance to once again soar and hang in the air.

"I feel great," Maravich said, breaking a sweat. A few minutes later, the concealed thread from which his life had been hanging since birth, snapped. Pistol Pete Maravich collapsed and died on the basketball court, where, for so many years, his heart had been.

PAUL SILAS
WAS NO STEREOTYPE

June 2, 1992

THE QUESTION WAS ASKED of Paul Silas: "Could you jump?" Silas is a former rebounding ace in the National Basketball Association and a black man. "No, not really," he replied. "I could never really just sky—not like a Billy Cunningham or a Dave Cowens."

And then this black man who couldn't jump laughed, laughed at himself and laughed because of course the examples he used indicated that at least some white men can jump, despite the title of a current feature film, and despite such contemporary white skyers as Dan Majerle and Rex Chapman.

"Remember, Cunningham was called the Kangaroo Kid," said Silas. "And you always knew Cowens played above the rim." There was irony in Silas' remark, at the reversal, or the crack, in the stereotype.

Silas, though not a leaper, was the personification of a power forward. When he retired in 1980, he was the ninth-leading rebounder in NBA history, with 12,357 boards. He succeeded because he was relentless, and because, as he said, "I had to learn to use my wits." It was those qualities that, as an assistant coach with the Knicks last season, he taught to or revived in such talented people as Patrick Ewing, Xavier McDaniel, Charles Oakley, and Anthony Mason, and to which, in the playoffs, anyway, they seemed suddenly to respond.

And it is those attributes that he will seek to impart, now, to players like Derrick Coleman and Sam Bowie and Chris Dudley and Terry Mills, for last week Silas accepted an offer by the Nets' new coach, Chuck Daly, to join New Jersey.

"The tough play under the boards and that terrific pursuit for rebounds people saw in the Knicks in the playoffs was unquestionably an extension of Silas," said Ernie Grunfeld, the Knicks director of player personnel. "We'll miss him."

Silas left the Knicks primarily because Daly had promised him more input into the overall game plans—Knick coach Pat Riley had kept that aspect mostly between him and his top assistant, Dick Harter. Silas, once the head coach of the Clippers, felt that such added responsibilities with the Nets might be an important consideration in his quest to return as a head coach in the league.

"You know what made the difference in our rebounding in the play-offs?" said Silas. "It was Dennis Rodman. Somehow, it finally kicked in to the heads of our players that one way to beat the Pistons was to keep Rodman off the boards. And to do that we had to keep an eye on him and box him out wherever he was. We started doing that with Rodman—who isn't a great leaper, either, but has a knack for positioning—and then we began doing it with everybody else, in both the Detroit and the Chicago series."

As a player Silas had to figure out how to make the most of what he had. He was 6'7" and strong, but relatively bound to earth. So he improvised. He understood that rebounding wasn't just jumping, but positioning and timing, with a little intimidation thrown in. He devised the trick of getting good position by first going out of bounds—"there's a lot more room there," he said—and then pushing his way in under the basket. Wes Unseld observed this nuance and there were times when both players were fighting for position—out of bounds. "Jump," Silas told his players, "when the ball is at its peak. Think about that."

"I was a rookie and he was a veteran and he greeted me and smiled at me when I entered the game," said Grunfeld, who had played against Silas in the NBA. "And then under the basket he gave me an elbow to the chest that knocked me out of position and he got the rebound. He laughed all the way down the court, and the coach took me out of the game."

As a coach, just as a player, Silas used imagination. He told his players, "Go after those rebounds like they're pieces of chicken." "How many pieces of chicken you gonna get tonight, Oak?" he'd ask. The players would laugh with him, and maybe get a little hungrier, which was the point, after all.

A few years ago Isiah Thomas made news when he complained that television commentators in particular perpetrate racist stereotypes by invariably describing white players as "smart" while blacks are "athletic."

Silas demonstrated that there is more to basketball than sheer ability to sky. "You take any field," said Silas, "and to be a champ you have to exercise more than just talent."

He also believed a certain tough-minded resolve is essential.

"If I knock a guy down with one of my love taps—that's what I called those shots—I'd tell him I was sorry as he lay there," said Silas, with a gentle smile. "And if he got up, I'd knock him down again. Oh, absolutely."

THE GOSPEL
ACCORDING TO SHAQ

November 1, 1994

WHILE IN TORONTO LAST summer as a member of Dream Team II, Shaquille O'Neal was approached by people telling him they had seen his father on television talk shows. O'Neal called the man he considers his father. "Daddy," he said, "I heard you were on TV." His father said, "No, I wasn't."

The man appearing on those shows was in fact someone Shaquille knows but wants nothing to do with. "And that's when I got the idea to write that rap song," said O'Neal yesterday. This was just before practice in Orlando where the 7'1", 300-pound center was preparing to lead the Magic into the NBA season.

"Yo, yo, I want to dedicate this song to Phillip Arthur Harrison 'cause he was the one who took me from a boy to a man, 'Cause as far as I'm concerned, he is my father, 'cause my biological didn't bother." Thus begins the rap song, which appears on O'Neal's recently released album, *Shaq-Fu: The Return* (Jive Records), and is also being released as a single.

The song is both ardent autobiography and grateful tribute to Harrison. "It deals with responsibility," said O'Neal. "It deals with what being a real man is all about."

In the song, O'Neal tells how his "biological father left me in the cold, when a few months old" and "you brought me into this world but you're not my dad."

Now, according to O'Neal, the biological father, the one on the talk shows, is seeking to cash in. "Now that I have fame and fortune," said

O'Neal, "he's been coming around. My feeling is, if he wasn't around for the first 22 years, then I'm movin' on with my life the way I did before—without him."

In a time when the breakup of families causes so much turmoil in our society, O'Neal feels it is important to tell his story.

"What's going on is terrible, the way fathers desert families, and the way young girls have babies and the boy cuts out," he said. "Something's got to be done about it. If I can help even one person out of 10, or out of 100, that's good. I wish I could help everyone, but it doesn't work that way."

When abandoned, his mother, Lucille, worked by day in Newark and Jersey City and dropped off her child with aunts and uncles. She then met Harrison, who fell in love with her, but, intones O'Neal, "She said you want me, you gotta have my son, or else it's like the hot dog without the bun—guess what, he accepted, and the responsibility, he never left it."

Harrison raised O'Neal and his two siblings after joining the Army as a private and then sometimes working as many as three other jobs, from driving a truck to running a bowling alley to working in a gym. Phil Harrison took his paternal obligations seriously. "He disciplined me right from the git-go," said O'Neal. And Harrison put "clothes on my back" and, as the song says, "food on the table—he wasn't gone with the wind like Clark Gable."

And Harrison was there when O'Neal was cut from his high school basketball team. "He gave me confidence that I have to keep working at it, working at anything, to get good." he said. "And when I was a little kid, I was afraid of the ball. He said, 'You're tough. Don't be scared.'"

When Harrison was sent to a base in Wildflecken, West Germany, he took his adopted family with him. O'Neal, then about 15 years old, was 6'7" but frustrated because he couldn't jump high enough to dunk the ball. It happened that Dale Brown, the coach of Louisiana State, was giving a clinic there. Harrison suggested his son speak to the coach, and ask about leg exercises.

Brown did, and the two—no, three, including Harrison—kept in touch, which is how O'Neal wound up at LSU.

O'Neal's father encouraged him to stay in school and get good grades. "I wasn't a brainiac," raps O'Neal, "but I tried hard, got to watch the Knicks play if I had a good report card."

He discusses "father and son trials and tribulations back then." "That's when I was gettin' cool, bein' a follower and my grades started slipping," he said yesterday.

With his spectacular dunks, spin moves, blocked shots, and a prodigious charisma, O'Neal has become the hottest sports hero since Michael Jordan. And his rap message is significant.

If someone like Shaq doesn't deliver the message, then who else will? Answer: the Phillip Arthur Harrisons of the world.

DISGUSTED PIPPEN SITS DOWN
FOR GAME-WINNING PLAY

May 14, 1994

WHERE WAS SCOTTIE PIPPEN when the team needed him on the court in the waning seconds of Game 3? Why wasn't he on the court? Why was he having words with his coach?

The score was tied 102–102 after the Knicks' Patrick Ewing hit a three-foot hook shot. There was 1.8 seconds to go in the game in which the Knicks had staged another remarkable fourth-quarter comeback at Chicago Stadium. The Bulls, with possession of the ball and reeling because the Knicks had wiped out a 22-point deficit at the end of the third quarter, had called a timeout.

The crowd of 18,676 fans was roaring, as only those Chicago fans can roar.

Phil Jackson, the Bulls coach, designed a play in which Pippen took the ball out of bounds at mid-court and Toni Kukoc would take the last shot at the top of the circle.

According to Andrea Kramer, an ESPN reporter who was beside the Bulls bench at this time with a cameraman, quoted Pippen as issuing an expletive and then saying, "I'm tired of this." And Pippen then sat down.

Some of the other players said, "Pip, come on, get up, what are you doing?"

He refused to come back in the game. Since the Bulls only were sending four men on the court, Jackson had to call a second timeout.

Jackson sent in Pete Myers in place of Pippen. Myers passed the ball to Kukoc, who bounced off his man, Anthony Mason, and then sank a 22-foot shot at the buzzer to give the Bulls a stunning 104–102 victory.

It was the fourth time this season that Kukoc has made a long shot to win a game at the buzzer.

After the game, Jackson told reporters, "As far as the last play goes, Scottie Pippen was not involved in the play. He asked out of the play. That is all I'm going to say about it."

In the locker room, Pippen said, "Phil and I kind of exchanged some words. That was pretty much it. It wasn't Phil taking me out of the game, we pretty much exchanged words and I took a seat. I think it was frustration. We really blew this game as much as we possibly could. We were able to pull off the win. Toni made another outstanding shot and it was a well-called play by Phil."

As he got up to leave, Pippen added, "I wasn't doing anything, anyway. That's pretty much it."

Pippen, who scored 25 points, was just 1-for-4 in the fourth period.

Pippen and Kukoc have had a rivalry going back some three years, in which Jerry Krause, the Bulls general manager, had pursued Kukoc, a Croat who had been one of the European League's finest players.

The 6'11" Kukoc was perceived as a kind of annoyance if not a threat. Because while Kukoc was being pursued, Pippen, who had been a Bulls standout, was involved in sticky contract negotiations with Krause.

When the Dream Team played Croatia in the Barcelona Olympics, Pippen and Michael Jordan, his running mate with the Bulls, seemed to focus on Kukoc in their first game and stymied him, though he performed much better in his second appearance against the Dream Team.

Pippen has expressed dissatisfaction with Kukoc in some ways with the Bulls, and was known as giving him a difficult time in practice sessions. But some viewed that as simply the Bulls way, as learned from Jordan who gave many a difficult time in practice, including a younger Pippen, which was said to help steel him to the NBA wars.

In recent days, Pippen has also said that he believes he deserves to be the highest-paid Bull. He is earning $3 million per year, with two years remaining on his contract. But Kukoc, who is earning an estimated $2 million-plus, has a clause in his contract that may allow him to go above $3 million.

Pippen said he didn't mind if Horace Grant, the Bulls forward, was paid more than he was. Grant is an unrestricted free agent after this season—but he didn't want Kukoc to be.

Earlier in the season, Pippen also gave Bulls fans a nasty hand signal when they booed him. Later, he said he felt he was being booed because he is black. He apologized for his remarks the following day, saying he knew that some white players with the Bulls have been booed, too.

Jackson said he would address the Bulls' problem of wilting in the fourth quarter, for the third straight game, Saturday at practice.

"We got away with a game which we basically lost an 18-point lead," said the Bulls coach. "Patrick Ewing shouldered the game and he played great."

Jackson added, "It is not just our offense, but our defense, too. Our opponent has something to do with that."

Said Kukoc, "How did I do it? Easy, I shoot the ball and hope it goes in. The ball came in my hands and there was not much to think about. I had a pretty good look at the basket."

As Expected, Rodman
Does the Unexpected

May 30, 1998

DENNIS RODMAN, MADLY TATTOOED and polychromatically thatched, is often an eyeful, sometimes an earful, but always a handful. For the opponent as well as for his own team, the ever-patient, ever-prodigious Bulls. And in the Eastern Conference playoff finals against Indiana, Rodman has, as expected, been a significant factor, although not always in expected ways, which fits the image.

He has come late to practice, come late to games, been kept out of the starting lineup, returned to the starting lineup, given the Bulls energy when they needed it and sometimes endangered that energy with some outrageous play or move—from an egregious foul in a clutch moment in Game 4 to a technical foul, and fouling out, in Game 5.

But last night in Game 6, Rodman provided his customary vigor—diving for loose balls, slapping at balls he couldn't reach and snaring those he could, winding up with a game-high 12 rebounds. He contributed mightily in keeping the Bulls close in a furiously played game, one that they lost 92–89.

Rodman, the National Basketball Association's leading rebounder, has had reduced playing time and reduced rebounding statistics in this series. He has complained that officials are, in effect, watching him as vigilantly as a cat does a mouse hole, eager to blow the whistle against him at even the first appearance of an infraction.

Rodman has the capacity to torment opponents by what he does, and what he says. Sure, he holds, he elbows, he grabs, he puts a full nelson on an opponent after he has scrambled for a loose ball, to keep the other player from hurrying downcourt on a fast break. While other players use some untoward tactics, too, no one equals Rodman's quantity or quality. But he is in a league of his own in regard to, well, the gender gap.

"In the last game of the regular season," recalled Antonio Davis, the Pacers forward who is often guarded by Rodman, "we got tangled up. He held my hand up over my head, and then he started to waltz with me! I couldn't believe it. At first I thought it was funny. And then I thought, 'He's mocking me!' And I got mad. Suddenly I was thinking about him, and not my game anymore. He can do that. He's smart; he'll try everything he can to throw you off. But I was prepared for him this series. I've just tried to ignore him."

This is not easy to do. In the NBA Finals against Seattle two years ago, Frank Brickowski of the SuperSonics, sick of Rodman's physical tactics in the game and aware of such publicity stunts as the one in which Rodman married himself in a wedding dress, called Rodman a name that was meant to question his manhood.

Rodman smiled. "You've got nice-looking legs," he said to Brickowski. "Would you like to go out with me after the game?" Brickowski exploded, as did his game.

One of Rodman's favorite targets is Alonzo Mourning, the Miami Heat center. Mourning has also questioned Rodman's off-the-court preferences—although he might not have read Rodman's book about his love affair with Madonna—and Rodman knows this. When Mourning makes a nice play against the Bulls, Rodman will pat him on the backside. It makes Mourning uncomfortable. When there is a loose ball, Rodman might stay atop Mourning for an extra beat or two, making Mourning seethe.

"Mourning tries to contain himself," said Steve Kerr, a Bulls guard, smiling at the thought. "And he doesn't say anything. But you see it building and building, and finally he erupts." In one game, Mourning was soon whistled for two technical fouls in quick succession and was removed from the game.

"Guys suddenly forget their set patterns, they're out of position, the coaches are screaming at them but they don't hear—they got Dennis on the mind," said Isiah Thomas, a teammate of Rodman's with the Pistons. "Dennis knows there's this homophobia among a lot of players in the league. So he uses that and everything else he can. It's amazing how many guys fall for it."

Some don't. Karl Malone, for one, never responds to Rodman. And Charles Barkley gives it back to him.

"He has heart, and he's challenging and tough and very strong," Antonio Davis said of Rodman. "If he doesn't get you with his goofy stuff, then he pushes you down on the hips or pulls you by the shirt. I'll be physical in return, but I've avoided dancing with him again."

Whether or not Rodman's outrageous antics are done for the sake of marketability, as Michael Jordan believes, it is clear that image is important to him. After a team workout, for example, Rodman, a relatively poor shooter, is rarely seen practicing shooting. "I don't think he wants people to see him doing it," said Phil Jackson, the Bulls coach. "I'm not sure why. But one night I came to our practice facility to get some papers. I saw the light on in the gym. And there was Dennis practicing his shooting."

And last night, despite the loss, Rodman demonstrated once again that he is strange like a fox.

ISIAH THOMAS' INDOMITABLE MOTHER

December, 23, 2003

IT IS A MOMENT indelible in Isiah Thomas' memory, and it says a great deal about who Isiah Thomas is, where he came from, and the obstacles he had to hurdle to succeed. Thomas, now 42, is back in basketball as of yesterday, having accepted the position of general manager of the Knicks, replacing Scott Layden.

The story, as Thomas recounts it, took place on a night in the summer of 1966, when the Vice Lords, a notorious street gang in Chicago, stopped in front of the home of Mary Thomas, a single parent. She had nine children, seven of them boys, ranging in age from Lord Henry, 15, to the baby, Isiah, five. The Thomases lived on the first floor of a two-story, red-brick building on Congress Street, facing the Eisenhower Expressway.

One of the Lords rang the doorbell. Mary Thomas, wearing glasses, answered the door. She saw behind the gang leader the rest of his entourage, wearing tams and carrying guns.

"We want your boys," he told her. "They can't walk around here and not be in no gang."

She looked him in the eye. "There's only one gang around here, and that's the Thomas gang," she said. "And I lead that."

The gang leader said, "If you don't bring those boys out, we'll get 'em in the streets."

Mary Thomas has also talked about the incident. She said she shut the door, and the gang members waited. Isiah remembers cowering in a corner. She went to the bedroom and returned with a sawed-off shotgun. She opened the door.

She pointed the gun at the figure before her. "Get off my porch," she said, "or I'll blow you across the expressway." The gang leader and his associates disappeared.

Some of Isiah's brothers indeed succumbed to the ravages of inner-city life, but, protected by other brothers and influenced greatly by his mother, whom he calls his role model, he never got involved with gangs or drugs. On the strength of his basketball talent, he received a scholarship to a suburban high school and traveled daily by train and bus for over an hour in the early morning to get there. He received a scholarship to Indiana and won an NCAA championship in his sophomore year under Bob Knight.

Knight was infuriated that Thomas, the best player on his team, would consider turning pro; Knight has attempted to rewrite history and says he encouraged it. But Thomas was the No. 2 choice in the 1981 draft, and the Pistons signed him to a $1 million contract.

At 6'1", Isiah Lord Thomas III, in his 13 pro seasons, became one of the greatest players in NBA history. He spearheaded the Pistons to back-to-back championships in 1989 and 1990. Behind that boyish smile was a killer instinct.

He could shoot, drive, pass, leap, lead, play injured, and was as tough as a middleweight contender. He was Michael Jordan, only five inches shorter.

"I think I've had something to prove all my life since the day I was born," Thomas, wearing a dark blue suit, blue tie, and a striped blue-and-white handkerchief blooming from his breast pocket, said at his news conference yesterday. "The odds were stacked against you, it was the little guy fighting. And people were always doubting if you could do it."

When he was in jeopardy of losing his coaching job with the Indiana Pacers last season, he said, "I just keep fighting and I just keep competing."

But as willing and wise and wily as he is, he has gotten himself into hot water. When, for example, Dennis Rodman, then a rookie with the Pistons, said that the Boston Celtics' Larry Bird would be just another player if he were black, Thomas agreed.

Later, Thomas said that his remark came out of frustration, in the heat of a wrenching playoff loss. He said he had the highest regard for Bird the player, but blacks, he said, were always being looked at as just natural talents, not as having brains, as though "we came dribbling out of our mother's womb." He apologized to Bird on national television, and Bird, in a news conference, accepted without a smile.

In 1994, after Thomas' last season as a player, he was named vice president for basketball of the expansion Toronto Raptors. His first draft pick was controversial, Damon Stoudamire, a small point guard like himself. But Stoudamire became the Rookie Of The Year. Thomas also drafted Tracy McGrady. But two years later, Thomas was out, losing in a power struggle for team supremacy.

In 2000, Thomas was named coach of the Pacers, replacing Bird, who no longer wanted the job. Before this season, Bird became the team's president of basketball operations, and one of his first acts was to fire Thomas, whose team had lost in the first round of the playoffs in each of his three seasons.

With his deep pockets, Thomas became the majority owner of the Continental Basketball Association, which, after 55 years of existence, went out of business following two years of his leadership. There were surely extenuating circumstances, including his decision to take the Pacers job while he was still running the CBA, but, nonetheless, some of the CBA team owners held him responsible.

When he signed with the pros, he promised his mother he would graduate college. After seven years of summer school and correspondence courses, he did. He was playing a playoff game the day of the graduation, and Mary Thomas received her boy's diploma on stage at the Bloomington, Indiana, commencement.

It is only speculation what Thomas can, or cannot do, with a foundering, despairing, and salary-cap-strained Knicks team.

But if he can take command of the situation, exhibit the kind of acumen and courage in his dealings as his mother did against such as the Vice Lords, the Knicks are in for some good and exciting times.

FOR CALVIN MURPHY, LIFE IS ALWAYS LOOKING UP

November 2, 1972

"MAY I TAKE YOUR coat, Timmy?" asked Calvin Murphy.

Timmy, who is 11 years old and one of the few basketball players in the world shorter than Calvin Murphy, stiffly shrugged out of his coat at the door of Murphy's midtown hotel room.

Timmy had pulled strings with a sportswriter (who doubles as his father) to meet Murphy, the Houston Rockets' 5'9" guard. Now the meeting had come to pass and Timmy was somewhat scared. ("What will I talk to him about?" he asked often on the way over. Timmy was already learning the conflict between dreams and realities.)

"Hey, man, you're wearing Cons," exclaimed Murphy, as the three sat down. "Oh ye-ah. Cool."

Timmy proudly lifted his feet with the white sneakers and purple laces.

"You know, a lot of guys now, they're into Adidas or Pumas," said Murphy. "But I'll never change from Converse. They mean too much to me. When I was a kid in Norwalk, Connecticut, I was too poor to buy anything except those buck-ninety-five specials. You know the ones. You run for two minutes and the bottoms start flappin' out.

"I didn't get my first pair of Cons until I was in the ninth grade. My coach said, 'Uh, Cal, let's go downtown and get you some decent sneakers.' We did, and it almost ruined my game. I stopped movin' for awhile. I mean, I became real dainty because I didn't want to bruise my Cons."

Laughter melted the ice.

"Yeah, and Cons got so big in the neighborhood," Murphy continued, "that we wore those black low-cuts for dress. You could be wearin' a suit and tie, but if you didn't have on those black Cons, you couldn't really strut."

The photograph inside Timmy's notebook had come warmly alive. Timmy is one of many boys who has latched on to Murphy as the symbol of hope for the small man. Murphy, the littlest player in the National Basketball Association by at least three inches, says he gets hundreds of letters during the season from boys asking how he did it.

Timmy—who one night before going to bed asked, for personal reasons, how the NBA draft works—now asked Murphy if he had ever wished he would grow when he was 11 years old.

"Sure," said Murphy, "and I thought I would since my whole family is big. I've got two brothers who are now 6'3" and 6'4". But by the time I reached the ninth grade I knew I wasn't going to grow. So I stopped worrying. I just tried to do the best I could with what I had."

Timmy asked about discrimination. "Never for color," said Murphy. "But my height, yes. I remember once I went to a schoolyard in Brooklyn and Connie Hawkins was king there and I asked to get in a game. I never got in the game. I kid Connie about that now.

"My friends, of all people, used to discourage me. Like when I went to high school, my friends said I was too small to make the basketball team. I tried out anyway. I made all-state my sophomore year.

"Same thing when I went to college. They said high school was small time, college was the big boys. I made All-America three straight years. So then people said that was college. The pros, those are the big boys. Well, this is my third year in the pros, and I'm still getting a lot of PT—playin' time."

Murphy said he did have troubles adjusting to the pros. He was so aggressive at first that he was even battling Wilt Chamberlain for rebounds ("pretty foolish, huh?") until he resolved to stay a little farther outside, play good defense, take a jump shot when he had one, and mostly "pass the seed."

Murphy said that he does have a lot of natural ability, but was clumsy when he was young, played all day every day for years, developed his jumping ability by playing in heavy work boots.

He now believes that the small man has a greater chance of playing basketball than ever because he can fit easily into the modern fast-break game.

After almost an hour, it was time to go. Murphy helped Timmy on with his coat. At the door the sportswriter suggested that Timmy demonstrate his jump shot. Timmy was ready.

"Wow, a lefty, and look at that wrist snap on the follow-through," said Murphy. "To-o-o strong."

Timmy and the sportswriter walked to the elevator. Timmy was frowning. "I should have taken my coat off when I shot," he said. "Then I could have really soared."

A GIRL'S CRY FOR HELP
TO MUGGSY BOGUES

May 31, 1995

An unusual letter arrived early this month with a Newburg, Missouri, return address:

> "Hi, I go to Newburg Elementary. On May 23 I am going to graduate from 6th Grade. I would like Muggsy Bogues to be a speaker. Why I am writing this is I read your article about how Muggsy was shot when he was 5. I was hoping you would help me because of the gun violence in Rolla, a town close to us. I am scared of it spreading to our town.
>
> April 9th there was a gun shooting, two kids were shot and one died, the other in critical condition. There are some kids in Newburg who want to be like gang members.
>
> Can you please tell how I can get ahold of Muggsy to talk at my graduation?
>
> Thanks for your help,
> Kerri Russ

Newburg, Missouri? Threat of gang violence? Upon reflection, why not? Why should it stop at the city limits of New York? Or New Orleans? Or Beaumont, Texas? And obviously, as the cry from the heart by this young girl indicates, it hasn't.

Newburg, it turns out, is about 100 miles west of St. Louis, has a population of about 800, and Rolla, the Phelps County seat, about 13,000.

Muggsy Bogues, meanwhile, is a hero and inspiration to many because not only is he a star National Basketball Association point guard for the Charlotte Hornets, but he stands just 5'3", in a league where the average player is 6'7". He also grew up in the projects in Baltimore, had a father who was sent to prison for dealing drugs, and was indeed shot by an irate storekeeper in his Baltimore neighborhood when he was five.

Kerri's letter was forwarded to David Falk, head of the sports agency of which Bogues is a client. Sometime afterward, Kerri received the following from the agency:

> Thank you for your letter…Muggsy appreciates your enthusiasm and the fact that you recognize him as someone who could have an impact on you and your classmates.

But, it went on to say, Muggsy had other commitments and couldn't appear at her graduation. The letter congratulated her on her graduation and there was enclosed an autographed picture of Muggsy.

Kerri hadn't asked for an autographed picture (though now, she says, she carries the picture with her "wherever I go."). She had pleaded for help, hoping that someone with influence could talk sense to the young would-be toughs in her town. And, like many young people in this country, she looked first to a national sports hero, one whose legitimate triumphs are regularly visible. This, too, is a comment on our society.

Was Bogues aware of the letters? Would it even matter to him? Bogues has a reputation for taking seriously his standing as a role model, and is called upon often and responds positively to charities and youth groups.

A phone call was placed to Bogues. He seemed vague about the letters. It was understandable that he might not speak at the school's graduation—he said he had other commitments—but did he have any words at all for Kerri and her community?

"My heart goes out to Kerri," Bogues said. "I know violence is everywhere in America, and it's hard to escape it. But everyone has to try to get involved to help. Even Kerri can help. She can talk to her parents and other parents about talking with the kids who might cause trouble. She has to talk to her teachers, and community leaders, too.

"These other kids have to know that one incident, one shooting can change their lives forever. Not everybody walks away. I was lucky. But these kids who deal with gangs and drugs have to know that there are only two ends for them: jail or death.

"The community has to help kids develop self-esteem apart from doing wrong. I was fortunate in having my mother and other people in my community instill principles in me. I know some people say, 'Yeah, Muggsy, it's easy for you to say. Look where you are now.' But I wasn't always here. It didn't just happen all of a sudden. There is always a struggle. I'd tell Kerri, don't be afraid to go for your dreams, to keep doing what she thinks is right. She has to try to keep her head above water because there are a lot of good things ahead for her."

Last Tuesday, as scheduled, 12-year-old, 5'0" Kerri Russ, in blue satin dress and a wrist corsage, graduated from the sixth grade. There were no incidents from any of the "mean kids," as she described them.

"It's the end of school, so everybody's happy about that and kind of quiet," she said. Then she was off to the park to shoot hoops. "I want to be a basketball player," she said.

WHEN SOME WONDERED
IF LEW HAD IT

April 22, 1989

BACK THEN, BACK 20 years ago, he was not yet His Royal Baldness, or the Ancient Mariner, and not yet Kareem Abdul-Jabbar, and with hardly a notion that one day he would become a six-time Most Valuable Player, a member of six NBA championship teams, and the highest scorer, the most prolific shot-blocker, and the man who would play more minutes, and more games, and more years, and play to an older age than anyone else in pro basketball history.

Back then, Lewis Ferdinand Alcindor Jr. was 22 years old, with a full head of hair, a sweeping shot that would later be dubbed the Sky Hook, and, also, something to prove.

Back then, in 1969, he could hardly have dreamed that tomorrow, at age 42, when the Los Angeles Lakers engage the Seattle SuperSonics, he would be playing in the last regular season game of the season, and of his career—he has announced his retirement—and that CBS-TV would switch its previously scheduled game, Atlanta-Detroit, to let the country see it.

But two decades ago he had to demonstrate that he was truly more than just a hot-shot college star.

He had been drafted out of UCLA by the Milwaukee Bucks, who signed him to a $1 million contract—enormous in those days—and his first competition, his pro debut, in effect, was in late August at the annual Maurice Stokes benefit game at Kutsher's Country Club in the Catskills.

Lew Alcindor—it would be two years before he would change his name to Kareem Abdul-Jabbar—would be playing against some of the league's best players, and going head to head with Wilt Chamberlain, who'd been around.

That night, mixed with the smell of balsam and blintzes, there was an air of expectation. Fans and players alike wondered how he would fare.

And the owner of the Bucks, Wes Pavalon, who had invested so much money on this 7'2" rookie, was flying in in a private plane to see for himself.

Pavalon arrived just in time to be met by the departing crowd. The plane had run into some trouble. At the gym, finally, Pavalon saw Jack Twyman, a former NBA player.

"What happened?" Pavalon asked. "How'd Lew do?"

"Wes," replied Twyman, "your boy made some moves you just wouldn't believe." "Good moves or bad ones?" asked Pavalon. Twyman laughed, and told him about how Alcindor got the ball in the corner, and gracefully drove and slammed the ball through the hoop. He'd done that before, of course, but he had never done it over the arms of Wilt Chamberlain.

Alcindor played 25 minutes, mostly against Wilt, and made six of 11 shots from the field, took 10 rebounds, and blocked four shots. Chamberlain hit 6-of-8 from the field, pulled down 16 rebounds, and blocked six shots; he was also voted the Most Valuable Player in the game.

Afterward, Alcindor said no, he didn't feel pressure, that he had played too many pressure games in his life to be upset now. "Besides," he said, "I was out there to learn."

He would not only learn more about Alcindor the basketball player, but also about Alcindor the man, too.

Pavalon, however, didn't buy the business of no pressure. He said that the pressure had to be tremendous: "He's got such an image to live up to." Pavalon recalled that he had spent a day with the young Alcindor and "everywhere we went people were asking him, 'How's the weather up there?' and stuff like that."

"We were in an elevator," he said, "and Lew made the best comeback I think I've ever heard. This guy looks at him and says, 'How's basketball?' And Lew says, 'I don't know. Ask basketball.'

"You can imagine what Lew is up against."

Alcindor would change his name in the summer of 1971 when he converted from Catholicism to Islam. And maybe because of the pressures that Pavalon noted, Kareem, a bright and sensitive man, developed a reputation for being aloof, if not in fact curt with new people.

After he had won his first MVP award, in 1971, and still Alcindor, he was talking with reporters, and said he was planning a trip to West Africa to learn something about himself.

"Exactly what?" he was asked by one in the group of reporters, all of whom were white. "I don't think you'd understand," said Alcindor. "Try me," said the reporter.

"It's sort of like going back to find your roots," he said. "Maybe I can find some answers to myself there. I'm still searching."

Whether he has found what and whom he was looking for, only he knows. But the concerns and questions that he and Pavalon and others may have had about him as a pro basketball player 20 years ago, those are now answered in the record book, again and again and again.

THE NIGHT WILT SCORED 100

March 1, 1987

HE WAS SO LARGE and so strong and his feats were so outlandish that he wouldn't be nicknamed for anything so mundane as a mere world, or planet, or star. He was named for an entire constellation. He was the Big Dipper.

When someone without an ounce of creativity tried to tag him with Wilt the Stilt, he scorned it—the rhyme too obvious, the symbolism too limiting. Big Dipper, however, was acceptable.

Wilton Norman Chamberlain would be to basketball what Paul Bunyan was to logging, Hercules to stables, and King Kong to assorted skyscrapers.

Chamberlain once recalled driving across Arizona or New Mexico and pulling his car momentarily to the side of the road, when he was attacked by a mountain lion. He said the mountain lion jumped on his shoulder, and he grabbed it by the tail and flung it into the bushes.

"Well, I wasn't there," Cal Ramsey, the former Knick announcer, once said, "but Wilt says it happened, and I'm not about to say it didn't. Besides, he showed me these huge scratch marks on one shoulder. I don't know any other way he could have gotten them."

When Frank McGuire became Chamberlain's coach with the Philadelphia Warriors before the 1961–62 season, he called all his players individually into his office to chat with them. "When Wilt came in," said McGuire, "I asked him how long he'd like to play. He said, 'Forever.' I almost fell off my chair. I said, 'No, Wilt, in a game.' He said, 'I don't ever have to come out of a game.' And he didn't."

That season, Chamberlain averaged 50.4 points and 48.5 minutes per game, in a 48-minute game (the overlapping percentage point in minutes played was caused by overtimes).

In his first season in the National Basketball Association, with the Warriors, the 7'1", 275-pound Chamberlain, the swift Chamberlain (he had been an outstanding high school quarter-miler in Philadelphia), the agile Chamberlain (he had been a superb high-jumper for the University of Kansas), the unbounded Chamberlain (he would one day seek and come close to fighting for the heavyweight championship against Muhammad Ali), and now this rookie Chamberlain broke the record for most points averaged in an NBA season, 37.6. He broke that record the next season, with 38.4. In his third season, he averaged a Babe the Blue Ox figure of 50.4 points per game. This was 1961–62, and in a triple-overtime game against the Lakers early in the season, he broke Elgin Baylor's single-game scoring record with 78 points. Baylor had scored 71 a year earlier.

"One day," Al Attles, a teammate, told a friend in mid-February, "Wilt's going to score 100 points. Wait and see."

Neither Attles nor the friend had to wait long. On March 2, 1962—25 years ago tomorrow—Chamberlain scored 100 points.

Chamberlain, then 25 years old, established the mark against the Knicks, in the Hershey Arena in Hershey, Pennsylvania, and did it, in the mold of the fabled, despite having had no sleep the night before.

Chamberlain was too huge for just one city, and so he played for Philadelphia but lived in New York, on Central Park West.

"He was always on time, and never missed a practice, or a bus, or was late for a game," said McGuire.

On the night before the night of the game in Hershey, Pennsylvania—a site at which the Warriors would play a handful of "home games"—Chamberlain was out on a late date in New York and never did get to sleep.

When he walked into the dressing room in Hershey, McGuire came over and showed Chamberlain two New York newspapers with quotes from some Knicks about how they were going to "run me ragged," Chamberlain recalled, because, the players said, they "know" he is pretty slow and doesn't have stamina.

"Coach McGuire knows that's ridiculous, but he doesn't know I haven't had any sleep yet," said Chamberlain, "so he just grins slyly and says, 'Let's run 'em tonight, Wilt.'"

"We ran, all right—and ran and ran and ran."

Chamberlain now lives in the exclusive area of Bel Air in Los Angeles, in a $1.5 million mansion he had built about 15 years ago. Now 50 years old, he seems to have aged little. Occasionally, there is still a report that some NBA team wants to sign him for part of a season. He laughs about this, and graciously declines. When last seen in Manhattan, over the summer, Chamberlain was still a well-chiseled specimen, with a slim waist and biceps the size of, well, not quite watermelons, but cantaloupes, anyway. He is still busy in sports, and is an avid volleyball player, and retains ambitions of playing for the 1988 United States Olympic team.

But now he was looking back instead of forward, back to that Friday night 25 years ago in Hershey. It was a rather small arena, seating 7,200, and a crowd of 4,124 showed up.

"It's amazing," Chamberlain recalled in a telephone interview recently, "but I'll bet I've had 25,000 come up to me and say they saw the game. What's more amazing is, most of them say they saw it at Madison Square Garden. That's some feat. Can you imagine how good their eyes were?"

One person who was not at the game was Phil Jordan, the Knicks starting center, who was ill. Eddie Donovan, the coach of the last-place Knicks, started his second-string center, Darrall Imhoff. It was Imhoff's assignment to guard Chamberlain with, of course, help from the forwards when possible, as was the case with all the centers in the NBA who played Wilt. "You're all I've got tonight," Donovan told Imhoff. "Try not to foul out."

Imhoff tried, but didn't succeed. "He was getting down the court so fast I couldn't keep up with him," recalled Imhoff, who played a total of 20 minutes and fouled out in the fourth quarter. "We tried collapsing three guys around him, but it didn't help."

Chamberlain recalled that he hit his first six jump shots from the outside, and at the end of the first quarter the Warriors were ahead 42–26. Chamberlain had 23 points, including nine straight free throws.

"Remember, I was a notoriously bad free throw shooter in games," said Chamberlain. "But now I thought I might break a record, but it was for consecutive free throws. Breaking the single-game record for total points didn't enter my head—not even at the half."

At halftime, Chamberlain had 41 points, on 14-of-26 from the field, and 13-of-14 from the free throw line.

"I'd often come into the dressing room at halftime with 30 or 35 points," said Chamberlain. "So 41 was not a particularly big deal."

Everything was going in for him from the foul line and from the field: his fade-away jumper off the backboard, his jump shot from in front of the basket, his finger-roll, and, of course, his periodic dunks.

He recalled that there were few dunks, although Richie Guerin, the Knick guard who scored 39 points that night, remembers that there were more than a few.

No one will ever be certain. It was a simpler age, an age in which sports were considerably less inundated with technology than they are today, and not all games were televised. This one, unfortunately, was not. So all we have are the memories of eyewitness accounts, some of which differ in small detail.

In the third quarter, Chamberlain scored another 28 points, and now had 69. "It looked like I had a good chance to break my record of 78," he said. "I didn't even think of 100."

On the Warrior bench McGuire was coaching, as he recalls it, just another game. "But somewhere in the fourth quarter, one of the players woke me up and said, 'Coach, do you realize Wilt has 86 points?' Or some number like that. And I really hadn't been aware of it."

David Zinkoff, the public address announcer at the Warrior home games, started calling out how many points Chamberlain had every time he scored in the fourth quarter. And the fans began screaming, "Give it to Wilt! Give it to Wilt!" And the Philadelphia players were. "We did for two reasons," said Attles. "One was, our style of play as designed by Coach McGuire was to get the ball as close to the basket as possible for a shot, and that meant getting it to Wilt in the low post. The other was, we wanted Wilt to break the record. We all liked Wilt a lot. He's got a reputation by some as being kind of tough, or whatever. But he's really a wonderful guy. We were happy to get him the ball."

Earlier in the season, McGuire recalled, he had informed the team of his philosophy to get the ball to Wilt. "And they said fine, no problem," said McGuire. "But they asked me one thing. When the season was over, and their personal statistics might be a little barren, would I go to management at contract time and talk for them. I said, 'Absolutely.'"

Now Wilt had about 90 points with a few minutes to go. McGuire, a New Yorker, said he felt a little sheepish about having Wilt go for the record, "I never want to embarrass anyone on the basketball court," he said, especially a New York team.

The New York team wasn't happy about it either.

"We began to foul their players," recalled Guerin, "and sometimes even foul Wilt. And they began to foul us to get the ball for Wilt because we began to stall. It turned into a travesty. It's not what basketball is supposed to be all about."

Bill Campbell, doing the radio play-by-play, made an audio tape of Chamberlain's final eight points of the game: Chamberlain made a 12-foot bank shot to give the Warriors a 161–139 lead, and Chamberlain 94 points. He made another basket moments later: 96 points. With 1:27 left, Chamberlain had 98 points. He then stole an inbounds pass and shot for 100, and missed.

"The Knicks are eating up time and the Warriors foul Guerin deliberately," said Campbell. Guerin made two free throws.

Then Zinkoff told the crowd, many of whom had left their seats and were now surrounding the court, "He's going for 100, sit back and relax."

The crowd screamed, "Give it to Wilt! Give it to Wilt!"

The Knicks pressed, and Guy Rodgers threw a long pass to Chamberlain, who shot and missed. A reserve forward, Ted Luckenbill, rebounded the shot, passed it back to Chamberlain, who missed again, and Luckenbill rebounded again, and passed to Joe Ruklick, another reserve, who passed the ball to Chamberlain, who shot again, and scored! Finally!

"What a relief," Chamberlain would recall.

Suddenly the invisible wall that kept the fans on the outside of the rectangle of the court broke, and they came flooding wildly onto the court.

"I remember Wilt was carrying four or five kids on his back," said McGuire. "It was quite a scene."

There were 46 seconds to play, but the game would not be resumed, and the Warriors won 169–147. "It was just as well," recalled Attles. "That round number of 100 is magical. It wouldn't be quite the same if Wilt came back and scored a total of, say, 103."

In the dressing room afterward, Wilt checked the statistics sheet and noted that he had shot 36-for-63. "My God!" he said. "That's terrible. I never thought I'd take that many shots in a game." He was pleased, though, with his foul-shooting: 28-for-32, the most free throws scored in a regular season NBA game and one of the best nights from the foul line in his career. (His career foul-shooting percentage was only .511.) Others had had good games that night, as well, although they were overlooked. Attles, not known as a good shooter, had a perfect shooting night: 8-for-8 from the floor, and 1-for-1 from the foul line.

"For years afterward, I'd kid Wilt that I took the pressure off him so that they couldn't sink back and guard him," Attles said.

"Not true," Chamberlain recalled recently. "He scored so well because no one was guarding him. He was crying so much about no one ever knowing he'd had a great shooting night, that about three years ago I gave him the damn game ball from that night."

It was also a symbol of Chamberlain's appreciation to his teammates. "Without them I could never have broken the record," he said. "They went way beyond the call of duty."

For all of Chamberlain's athletic achievements, that 100-point game stands out in the minds of many.

"Even today when I'm an airplane terminal, or hotel lobby, I hear people saying, 'He's the guy who scored a hundred points,'" Chamberlain said.

They also say something else, according to Chamberlain. "They say, 'Yeah, but his team lost the game.' We didn't, though we did lose the one where I scored 78 points. But I always said, 'Nobody roots for Goliath.' But now, I don't know, maybe people are beginning to appreciate some of the things I did."

On the bus ride back to New York after that night 25 years ago tomorrow, Imhoff sat alone in deep thought. Finally, he looked up and shook his head. "I can't have a nightmare tonight," he said. "I just lived through one."

Chamberlain also went back to New York. He remembers driving back with Willie Naulls and a few other Knick players.

"We talked about the record, and they said it might never be broken, and I thought it would—records are always broken," said Chamberlain. "Even though I had just scored 100 points against these guys, it was a nice ride back. I was extremely tired—remember, I hadn't slept in about a day and a half—but I was still on a high, and it would be hours before I finally got some sleep."

MAE WEST, WILT, AND THE HALF-COURT KING

December 2, 1989

ALTHOUGH KAREEM ABDUL-JABBAR IS now gone from the sports scene, having retired last season after his 20th year in the National Basketball Association, his career scoring record of 38,387 points still lives, and, many believe, may live forever.

"It's nothing," said Charles Miron. "It's minor league."

Minor league? "Certainly," said Charles. "I've scored more than 175,000 points, and I'm still going strong. I'm the highest scorer in the history of half-court basketball." Charles looks you right in the eye and says, "Name another."

After playing a few games several days a week for at least five decades, Charles said his self-figured total comes, in round numbers, to better than 175,000.

Charles Miron is a New Yorker of an indeterminate age; that is, he won't determine for anyone how old he is. "What's the difference?" he asks. He says he was poppin' 'em in on the Rockaway Beach courts in the 1940s with players like the Cooz—Bob Cousy, who "started as a center in the parks, and if he hadn't gone into full-court might have broken my record"—and Dick McGuire.

"Games were tough there," Charles said. "In other places, a defensive ace would say, 'I held my man to two shots.' At Rockaway, someone like Tricky Dick could say, 'I held my man to two passes!'"

A few years ago, Charles said he played in Manhattan Beach with Chris Mullin. "He was scoring like crazy," said Charles. "But yours truly had a few, too."

Charles stands 6'2", and his hair is somewhat longer, grayer, and thinner than in the Cooz–Tricky Dick days. He was recently met wearing a Tyrolean hat with a red feather, a brown leather jacket, slacks, and, of course, sneakers.

"You never know," he said, "when you might run across a basketball game."

He still plays basketball—mostly half-court and generally the three-on-three version—on various indoor and outdoor courts around New York, and other points domestic as well as foreign. "I played in Sweden not long ago," he said, "and they're funny there. No one speaks. I play in New York, and no one shuts up."

Charles' record has been achieved by an undiminished love for the game of basketball, a looping left-handed set shot (he never went much to his right, or drove to the hoop, or rebounded—all of which has helped avoid wear and tear on the legs), and, he said, "I don't drink. I don't smoke. I don't do drugs." He smiled. "But of course that's not my complete dossier."

Charles' dossier, beyond intimate details, contains a variety of careers, including art dealer, magazine writer, novelist, and devotee of animals. He once owned a pet ocelot (visitors were taken aback to find in his apartment a jungle animal that he had described as a pet cat) and nurtured a greyhound named Misty ("a bag of bones when I found her in a pet store") into a show champion. Also, Charles was an actor. In the late 1950s he sought a role in the road show of *Diamond Lil*, starring Mae West. He auditioned for the part of her Latin lover. "You know her line, 'Why don't you come up and see me sometime?'" said Charles. "Well, I did. She held auditions in her penthouse at the Wellington Hotel. I was young and nervous. She was lying on a couch in a green satin dressing gown. She was twirling her hair—golden blonde—with her finger. It was about 100 degrees that day. She said, in that sexy way, 'Most people's hair gets flat when it's this hot. Mine gets cur-ly.' Oh, man! I got so weak in the knees I almost fell over." Charles read, Mae West listened, and she hired him, not as the lover, but for a smaller part.

Basketball, though, and a half-court were never far from Charles' heart, or feet. "You never get your name in the paper playing half-court," he said, "and I've never seen a great half-courter who played for the girls, either, like a lot do in college. You play for within yourself."

He said that he just might "get 200,000 points before I rack it up."

One day not long ago, just before boarding a plane, he noticed a fellow passenger, a very tall man. "Dipper!" said Charles to Wilt Chamberlain, meeting him for the first time, but knowing that he likes the nickname Big Dipper and hates the Stilt.

Charles told him that he looked in great shape. "I play a lot of volleyball," explained Wilt. "I still play ball, too—hoops," said Charles. "I'm the king of half-court basketball." "No kidding," said Wilt. "Over 170,000 points, Dip." "Congratulations," said Wilt.

Chamberlain, recalled Charles, was sitting in two seats, in order to spread out. "I'm sitting in half a seat," said Charles. "For half-court," said Wilt.

"Precisely," said Charles.

JERRY WEST
AT CHILDHOOD'S END

April 12, 1974

LOS ANGELES—"IF YOU'D GO into an office and see a man my age, a 35-year-old businessman, doing some of the things I do with my co-workers, you'd think he was a madman," said Jerry West recently.

"We act like kids, rasslin' and bumping a guy into a door and throwing a ball at him, and the constant riding that goes on in the locker room. You've got to have a lot of kid in you to be an athlete. And, frankly, I've loved it. I feel like I'm the luckiest fella in the world. It's been an incredible life. Incredible. But I don't feel much like a kid anymore. I feel now I should do something more constructive with my life.

"That's why I think that this will be my last season."

Now at the end of his 14th season in the National Basketball Association, Jerry West suits up for Los Angeles Lakers games but sits on the bench. It is a strange and frustrating posture for one of the finest guards—one of the finest players, period—to ever lace on a professional sneaker.

West has played little this season because of a severe groin muscle pull. It causes him pain when he runs, even trots. He can, however, jump. "Yes I could shoot but I couldn't get open," he says, with a wry upturn of his thin lips.

The Lakers, champions two years ago and runners-up last season, have been struggling to make the playoffs this season. The departure of Wilt Chamberlain to San Diego in September took much of the wind out of the Lakers' championship chase. West's injury deflated the team further.

"What hurts so much," said West, "is you don't feel like you're earning your pay." (Which is estimated at $300,000.)

Some of this pain is relieved in places like New York's Madison Square Garden, where West was introduced before the game and received a long, farewell standing ovation from not only the 20,000 fans, but from the Knicks players, too. West's blue eyes dampened.

He says he is an emotional man; he is also prideful. He says that this will probably be the last time he will ever be in a basketball uniform of any kind. He is not one, he says, to begin playing in YMCAs for the fun of it.

"I've set such high standards for myself that I couldn't enjoy playing the game on any lesser level," he said. "But I'm still very competitive. I'll play golf to satisfy that part of me, and I may go into business or coaching, and I'll set the same high standards for myself in those areas as I did playing basketball."

He says he would like to get away from basketball entirely for a few years; in fact, he'd like to get away from work for a few years.

"I'd like to be on my own for awhile," he said. "You know, I've had a coach telling me what to do for the last 24 years of my life." He began his basketball life as a skinny kid in Cabin Creek, West Virginia. Later he became an All-American at the University of West Virginia. In 1960 he joined the pros.

"You begin as a kid and you stay a kid in many ways if you are a basketball player," he said. "I took the game very seriously. And the pressures were tremendous. But a lot of the enthusiasm you have to have is childlike. And then you horse around to relieve some of that pressure.

"But I sit on the bench now, and I realize that when you can't do it physically, it changes your mental outlook. You begin to see that you have to do something else with your life. Something more constructive. By that I mean, I want to use my mind. I think I have a good one. I don't want some job where I just sit and do nothing. There's more to me than that, there's more to me than Jerry West, basketball player."

West said that he has been preparing for the end for some time. "I've watched a lot of ballplayers come and go," he said. "And I saw a lot who never thought this athlete's life would end. I didn't want to suffer the kind of crash they did when it was over. And so I think I'm pretty well adjusted in that respect. My ego, my view of myself as a man, was never dependent on how well I played basketball.

"And I've always felt lucky. I don't know why I was never booed. Can you imagine that? Never booed. And I don't know why I've had the success I've had. I mean, take any two guys. They're built alike, look alike, and yet one guy is a better ballplayer than the other. A lot of guys thought about the game as much as I did, had as much desire, and practiced as hard—even harder. I guess someone up there was looking after me.

"And what an indescribable feeling to be cheered. How many men in their lifetimes are applauded the way an athlete is?

"I've enjoyed the camaraderie of teammates. I'll miss that a lot. But right now I feel like just going somewhere where there is no basketball and there is no coach running my life. But I'll probably miss the hell out of that, too, after about a week."

BILL RUSSELL'S AGELESS LAUGH

March 27, 1976

THERE IS THE SLIGHTEST pause before Bill Russell laughs that laugh. In a twinkling, he knots his forehead, squinches his eyes—as if waiting for the ripples of joy to rise within his 6'11" body—tosses back his head, and laughs. Explodes.

Some say that laugh is a kind of cackle. It is no cackle. It may be high-pitched like a cackle and staccato like a cackle, but it possesses a grandeur and gusto emphatically unlike a cackle. And to be within earshot of this remarkable sound is to be unequivocally tickled.

The nation got a dose of it for a few years, back when Russell was a television commentator for the National Basketball Association games.

When a jivey black dude named Dancin' Harry did an odd little jig at courtside during a timeout, Russell and the cameras watched for a while before Russell broke the spell. "Contrary to popular belief," he said, "not all of us have rhythm." And Russell laughed deeply. A good line is to be appreciated—even if it's his own.

Russell is now the coach of the Seattle SuperSonics of the NBA. It is a team that in the few years he has been coach has gotten better and better. He seems able to make his world the best and most joyous possible.

He rid himself of some players he inherited who would not contribute to the unselfish style of play he demands; it is the unselfish style that so characterized him as a player with the Boston Celtics and helped make him the most dominant athlete in any team sport in American history. The Celtics won 11 world championships in the 13 years he played with them.

And this from a guy who could not make his high school team until his senior year.

After a loss, Russell does not punch lockers, as do some of his colleagues. He is worldly enough to elicit a laugh if it suits, even in a gallows situation.

In reply to a question recently, he said, "Hell no, I've never been embarrassed about my laugh. Not everybody can laugh."

He is widely respected—if not necessarily widely admired—for his staunch individualism. For example, he does not sign autographs. "It's the most impersonal thing I could possibly do," he explains.

He quotes Gandhi as saying, "I am only concerned with the truth as it reveals itself to me." Russell adds, "When I was young, I soaked up information like a sponge. Then I got to the point where I felt capable of making my own value judgments on the life around me. And I learned it is better to understand than to be understood.

"For example, take the busing issue in south Boston. People say it involves racism. Well, I know that the whites in that area are primarily Irish Catholic. And I think about the war in Northern Ireland. And there are no blacks there.

"And I think about the fighting in Angola, between the blacks. Is it racism? I think it is a fear of the unknown. The whole world suffers from it."

Russell says his ruling philosophy is to give people room. "I don't want to put a bummer on anybody," he said. "But if it's between you putting a bummer on me, or me putting a bummer on you, I opt for you."

And he laughed his lusty laugh.

He was asked if athletes should be models for youth. "Depends on the athlete," he said. "Generally, I think a father should be the model."

He is the father of three; the eldest is a son 18. What can he tell the world about being a father? "Who knows anything about being a father?" he asked. "It's all hit-and-miss. I'll be 104 years old and won't know."

A few scraggles of white have appeared in the black beard of the 40-year-old Russell. Does it bother him?

"Oh, no," he said. "I've never been a young lover."

"Does that mean you've always been a middle-aged lover?"

Russell paused, tossed back his head, and laughed that whopping laugh, that vital laugh, that ageless laugh.

VII.

A COTERIE
OF COACHES

PAT RILEY
TAKES THE REINS

June 1, 1991

PAT RILEY GOT A bit steamed, in his cool-cat way, when someone asked if just about anyone could have coached the Lakers to championships, given such players as Magic Johnson and Kareem Abdul-Jabbar.

"That's a question that I get all the time," said Riley, without a smile. His reply to the question was that he loved having such great players, but he also gave the impression that he was pretty good at what he did, too.

This occurred yesterday at a news conference at Madison Square Garden in which, to the shock and amazement of no one, Riley was named the new coach of the Knicks.

Introducing Riley was the Knicks president, David Checketts, who said that magic will return to the Garden, "not in the form of the player, but with the team."

Riley would be assured success, in fact, if he could bring the upper-case Magic with him. It happens that said person is otherwise occupied, and so Riley must look elsewhere for help.

Magic is in Chicago, seeking his sixth NBA championship ring, which he will obtain only over Michael Jordan's airborne body.

Riley, as previous coach of the Lakers, succeeded at the bottom line: he won. Four times in nine years. Only Red Auerbach has done better as a pro coach.

It doesn't take a basketball genius, meanwhile, to understand that Riley needs more than Patrick Ewing to straighten out the Knicks, which is what the last five Knick coaches discovered. After all, Ewing has been a member, and the star, of the Knicks for the past six seasons, only two of which were winning seasons.

So Ewing without question needs help, and it won't come strictly from the coach. Ewing is not the center that Kareem was, and Kareem didn't win a title in Milwaukee until he was teamed with Oscar Robertson, and was without a title in L.A. until a smiling, spinning, dazzling rookie named Earvin Johnson Jr. of Lansing, Michigan, appeared on the scene.

Now, a coach can be a tail and wag the horse, and a coach may be a head and plan for the horse, but he can't be the whole horse. So no matter how well he coaches, no matter how well he manipulates and cajoles and threatens and shouts and runs a rake through his moist coiffure, he must still have the ponies.

Getting them will be the job of Knick executives Checketts and Ernie Grunfeld, with considerable input from Riley, certainly. Beyond that, what else can a coach do?

A coach can exert authority, even over high-priced players. He can have them sit on the bench when they don't follow instructions, or lose concentration, a particular sickness of the Knicks. But a coach can only do this if the players understand that the coach has the confidence of management, and that he is secure in his job.

Few Knicks coaches have had that. With Riley having signed a contract believed to be for many millions and for five years, it provides leverage.

"What is essential," said Jerry West, the general manger of the Lakers and Riley's former boss, "is stability at the top."

For that reason especially, he said, "they need a person like Pat Riley in New York."

"You can't have a new coach coming in every year," he said.

"Pat likes what he does," continued West, "he believes in himself, and he's been in a good situation, so he knows how that works."

As far as being a motivator is concerned, something many say is Riley's forte, West said, "Being a motivator is a very, very overrated thing. The players understand what they have to do, and it is up to the coach to devise a correct system for their talents."

For all that, however, some in the Laker organization were unhappy with Riley, and when he left the Lakers after last season, some people thought he did not jump, but was pushed. Some players thought he was too overbearing, that his ego had got out of control, and, according to one person, there was great discontent among the players—particularly James Worthy, Michael Cooper, and Byron Scott (not Magic Johnson, though, who got along with him)—as they lost to the Phoenix Suns in the first round of the playoffs, four games to one.

"Pat Riley left on his own accord," said West. "He did a tremendous job for us."

"Some players will always be upset," said Riley, who is currently a television analyst. "But I left the Lakers because I wanted to try something else." He returns, he said, because he misses the action on the floor.

So Pat Riley is now in New York, with basketball pump and hair dryer, and with a terrific scrapbook. All he needs now are some players. Resumes are accepted, especially from anyone named Earvin.

MO CHEEKS
SAVES THE GIRL

May 11, 2003

EVEN BILLY CUNNINGHAM'S MOTHER wrote to Maurice Cheeks, expressing her admiration for his rescue of 13-year-old Natalie Gilbert from the most profound embarrassment before the Portland-Dallas NBA playoff game on April 25. Helen Cunningham, the mother of the former NBA star forward and coach of the 1983 champion Philadelphia 76ers, is one of the more than 1,700 people who in the last two weeks sent e-mail messages or wrote letters of appreciation to Cheeks, the Trail Blazers' reserved but effective coach.

Letters are still arriving.

But on that night, as Natalie stood near half-court before more than 20,000 fans in the Rose Garden in Portland and in front of national television cameras, the words to the national anthem stuck in her throat. Cheeks made the extraordinary gesture of suddenly appearing like a dream at her side and slipping a paternal arm around her shoulder while he began a duet. He then raised his right hand, as though conducting the Mormon Tabernacle Choir, and urged the crowd to join in, which it did, vigorously, out of relief and a shared sense of humanity.

Cheeks' moment of chivalry, replayed numerous times on television news and sports shows, touched the heart of some Americans in a most welcome and unexpected way. Ministers have written that Cheeks demonstrated the embodiment of the Good Samaritan, and spoke of him in their sermons. Coaches expressed sentiments that it was the kind of message in sports they hope to convey—as opposed to the anger and rage and self-promotion that are so prevalent.

Many have asked for tapes of the incident. Parents and teachers felt compelled to write. Billy Cunningham, having tuned in to the game at his home in a Philadelphia suburb, saw Natalie, an eighth grader, suddenly grow paralyzed with fear. Like virtually everyone else watching, he desperately hoped that she would quickly recover.

"What Maurice did," Cunningham said, "brought tears to my eyes. I was so proud of him. But that was typical Maurice, to spontaneously do the right thing at the right time and generally without any fanfare. And so smart."

Cunningham was the coach of the 76ers when Cheeks joined the team in 1978 as a relatively unheralded rookie out of unheralded West Texas State. The lean, 6'1" Cheeks quickly earned a starting job as point guard—and quiet leader—on a team with standout veterans like Julius Erving, Bobby Jones, and Doug Collins.

"Shortly after Maurice rescued that girl," said Cunningham, who coached Cheeks for seven seasons, "my mother called me. She said, 'I'm writing Maurice a letter. It was one of the most beautiful things I've ever seen.' I called Maurice and told him to be expecting a letter from my mother. He laughed, and promised to write her back."

Cheeks, reached recently by telephone, said of that moment with Natalie Gilbert, "I never thought about doing it before I did it. I just saw a little girl in trouble and I went to help her. I'm a father. I have two kids myself. I'd have wanted someone to help them if they could."

About the warm and voluminous response to Cheeks, Cunningham said, "Maurice deserves the recognition." It is true. While Cheeks was honored as a player—his 15-year NBA career was highlighted when he led the 76ers to an NBA championship in 1983, and five times he was named to the NBA's all-defensive teams—he never called attention to himself. He preferred to go about his business as a reserved, but fiercely competitive, professional. When Cheeks was traded to the Knicks in 1990, near the end of his career, I wrote that his game had class, but it was more like the shine of velvet than the glitter of gold.

Cheeks was named coach of the Trail Blazers before the 2001–02 season, after seven years as an assistant coach with Philadelphia. He inherited a team that seemed the polar opposite of him: several of his players have had recent problems regarding drug possession, domestic violence, speeding, and other violations.

Oddly enough, the players on the court responded to Cheeks as a coach. "He has the unusual ability to be friendly with the players, but also to discipline them in such a way that he doesn't lose them," said Jason Quick, who covers the Trail Blazers for *The Oregonian*.

"When some of the guys got into some of those off-the-court problems this season," Cheeks said, "I told them, 'You're grown men. You have to be in control, and be accountable.'"

But it shook him. "I'm the coach," he added. "A team is supposed to reflect the coach."

But no one thought the players' poor behavior in any way reflected Cheeks. How they responded in the playoffs did. In Portland's recent opening playoff series against Dallas, the Trail Blazers fell behind by three games to none in the four-of-seven-game series. "A team has to win four games to win the series," Cheeks told his team. "And Dallas hasn't done that."

Portland won the next three games before losing Game 7.

"To have his team hang in like that was amazing," Cunningham said. "I've never heard of another team in the history of the NBA that had more turmoil."

What he did with his team pales in regard to the heartstrings with his deliverance of young Natalie Gilbert. And were it not for another woman, Cheeks might never have been in a position to help, or, as he said, sing in public for the first time.

When Cheeks was a freshman at West Texas State in Canyon, Texas, a long, long way from the Robert Taylor housing projects on the South Side of Chicago where he was raised, he called his mother. He told her he was lonely and unhappy and wanted to come home.

"I had a scholarship there, one of the few colleges to offer me one," Cheeks said, "and my mother tried to reason with me to stay. I said, 'No, I'm leaving.'"

"She said, 'Maurice, you quit school and you better not come home,'" he recalled with a chuckle. "I stayed in school. I don't know what would have happened to me if I hadn't."

.   .   .

Maurice Cheeks was released as head coach of Portland after four seasons there and, following that, was head coach of the 76ers for four years. He currently is the head coach for the Detroit Pistons.

PITINO AND THAT RICH TRADITION

May 27, 1989

LIKE A GOOD FIVE-CENT cigar, a good million-dollar teacher is very hard to get these days.

Which is what the University of Kentucky is discovering.

That bluegrass institution of higher learning has been entreating a New Yorker named Rick Pitino to come teach its youngsters how to pick-and-roll, handle the low post, and press an opponent like a dry cleaner. But Pitino ponders.

The amount of money being offered him would make a chemistry professor (who averages $47,470 per school year at Kentucky) slaver. That's because in many colleges, basketball is second only to godliness, and chemistry runs far back in the field.

And unless the chemistry professor moonlights as an alchemist, transmuting class notes into C-notes, then it is still the basketball coach who helps the college earn millions every year from gate receipts and television contracts.

Reports, meanwhile, maintain that for Pitino to coach some 15 Alpine undergraduates each season, the commonwealth of Kentucky is prepared to stuff around $5 million for seven years into his well-tailored trousers.

Now, in academic circles, Pitino's deal would be pretty good work if you can get it. The class is small, the students are usually attentive, and you can attend the daily seminars in shorts.

Not only that, but the learned pedagogue doesn't have to do all the labor himself. He has a handful of assistants to help him along when he's got to be across town doing his TV show, or out of town to see somebody about a shoe endorsement.

His is a heavy tutorial load.

In the past, an extra perk for the students was to pick up a few extra bucks—a thousand here, a thousand there—by shaking hands with a prominent Wildcat fan, or looking into your sneaker after a winning game.

The NCAA investigated and found that it didn't approve of this stuff and last week hit the university basketball program with some of its stiffest penalties. Meanwhile, the university had already dumped its basketball coach, Eddie Sutton, eased out Cliff Hagan, its athletic director—this machine almost wrote "general manager," which is what pro teams have—and gone looking for a guy with no stains on his coaching vest.

Pitino, after a visit to the campus this week, said he remained uncertain. He has a nice gig in Manhattan, and is paid handsomely. He says he'll announce his decision next week.

It is beyond question that he is a superb coach. He teaches. He motivates. He enriches. He built winning teams and packed the stands at Boston University, at Providence College, at Madison Square Garden.

The Kentucky president, David Roselle, who has been on the job for two years, has insisted he wants a program so clean you could eat off its basketball floor. And it seemed that Pitino was a perfect guy to go after. Then something odd happened.

It was recently revealed that as a graduate assistant at the University of Hawaii, Pitino had been among those cited by the NCAA for 60 violations by the school's basketball department.

This was not widely known. Afterward, Pitino had no such problems at BU or Providence.

Pitino has been evasive about Hawaii, seeming to say that he had done nothing wrong but that it was 15 years ago and he had learned from his transgressions.

He also said he had never broken a contract: he meant acrimoniously, because he left BU with two years remaining on his contract, and at Providence he had just signed a new five-year deal before going to the Knicks. He has three years to go on his Knick contract, which was recently extended.

Though Pitino may occasionally speak in hazy phrases, he has generally been a pretty good citizen.

At Kentucky, C.M. Newton, the athletic director, said, "We're going to have some tough times—we've had some tough times before—but we're going to rebuild. And when we rebuild, it's going to be a program that wins, because that's the Kentucky tradition."

True, it has been some tradition. Kentucky has won more basketball games than any other college. But its players shaved points in the early '50s, and the school was penalized for other infractions by the NCAA later in the '50s, in the '70s, and in the '80s. And cheating was demonstrated by a Pulitzer Prize–winning series of articles by the *Lexington Herald-Leader* in 1984 to have been an integral part of the program for years.

If Pitino chooses to head for Kentucky, it would be getting a man who might, for perhaps the first time, balance the academic and basketball interests of the school.

Of course, at $1 million-plus per year to learn 'em hoops, the chemistry professor might still be wondering what is balance at a university, anyway.

•   •   •

Rick Pitino accepted the offer from Kentucky and departed the Knicks.

How Lenny Learned
to Stay Cool

January 18, 2004

HE HAS BEEN ACKNOWLEDGED for possessing a special trait: grace under pressure. The image of Lenny Wilkens, the old (at 66) new Knicks coach, is just that: stoic as a statue. On the sideline during a game, his seemingly calm but mindful eyes and expressionless face above his knotted tie and natty suit are unchanging whether the whistle is for or against his team, whether the scoreboard shows his team losing or winning.

He's up on his feet, prowling the alley in front of the bench, sometimes crossing his arms to indicate his mood has changed—once in a blue mood, as it were. But scream, bellow, kick a chair, or pound a scorer's table? Never. Not Cool Hand Lenny.

But from where, one wonders, is this apparently placid persona derived?

It might have been that day at the basketball court at P.S. 35 in Bedford-Stuyvesant, Brooklyn. Little Lenny Wilkens, not yet grown to 6'1" and so skinny he might have fitted through a picket fence, was playing ball with some friends. The game was abruptly interrupted by a gang wielding zip guns, knives, and tire irons.

"I realized I couldn't panic," Wilkens said Friday morning, hours before his debut as the Knicks coach at Madison Square Garden against Seattle. "If I ran or even tried to fight back, I knew one of two things would probably happen: I'd get a good butt-whuppin', or I'd get killed. I thought, 'If I stay calm, maybe I'll find a way out.'"

It turned out that one of the gang recognized Wilkens as another gang member's cousin. They departed, leaving Lenny and his pals shaken but in one piece.

"You remember things like that; those things help," Wilkens said. "I found that it was better to keep your composure than lose it. As a player it helped, and as a coach it's helped for me to be in control of me."

In his first year in the National Basketball Association, however, as a first-round draft pick by the St. Louis Hawks in 1960, Wilkens remembers disputing a referee's call and throwing the ball into the air.

"'Rookie,'" he recalled the referee, Bob Duffy, telling him, "'if that ball comes down, you'll get a technical and a fine.'"

Wilkens said, "The fine for a technical in those days was $25. I tried to catch the ball before it landed, but didn't."

He said he learned two things: "Why blow $25 when I didn't have to, and I hurt the team with the technical."

But Cool Hand Lenny still had something to learn about temperament. In the 1978–79 season, when he guided Seattle to the NBA title, Wilkens recalls getting about eight technical fouls. "But one resulted in me being thrown out of a game," he said, "and we won that one."

Despite the cheerful result, Wilkens has not duplicated it. That is the only time he has been tossed from a game in his 30-year coaching career with Seattle, Portland, Cleveland, Atlanta, and Toronto, and two games with the Knicks. He has won—and lost—more games than any other coach in NBA history, and was inducted into the Hall of Fame as both a coach and a player.

What you don't see but can almost hear as Wilkens paces the sideline is the whirring of his brain. Someone in the NBA has said that Wilkens runs only eight or nine plays, and always has. If that's true, it's reminiscent of something Einstein said: "Everything should be made as simple as possible, but not simpler."

Wilkens said, "I run plays that I have to run depending on the personnel. I don't fit them to my style. I fit my style to them."

Some have been critical of the Knicks' hiring of Wilkens, saying his manner is too mild to light a fire under the players. The sense here is that Wilkens understands clearly, as always, what it takes to get his points across to a player unequivocally, and that the Knicks' main man, Stephon

Marbury, hungry to prove himself a winner in his hometown and a point guard like Wilkens, will embrace him. And as Marbury goes, so go the Knicks.

Wilkens surely knows that little will happen overnight. Some 20 years ago, I was with him in Los Angeles when he ran into his old friend Rodney from Brooklyn.

"Lots of teams going good this year: L.A., Philly, Boston, Phoenix," his friend said. "Won't be easy."

"Rodney," Wilkens replied, "when was it ever?"

PHIL JACKSON
AND THE LONG ARMS

April 29, 1991

THE CHICAGO BULLS ARE a team of long arms; hardly the shortest pair of them is that attached to their coach, Phil Jackson. Long and angular at 6'9", Jackson, moving at times like an ambulatory Tinker Toy, may be seen in front of the Bulls bench, striding or standing, sometimes crossing his lengthy arms in contemplation, sometimes unfolding them to demonstrate a point to a player, or remonstrate to a referee.

If a team may be said to resemble its coach, this one does so in ways that suggest the uncanny. The wingspans of Michael Jordan and Scottie Pippen and Bill Cartwright and B.J. Armstrong and Horace Grant are considerable, too, and have recently been put to good and bothersome use, which is the same thing as far as Chicago is concerned.

These arms suddenly materialize, like great tentacles, at the most inconvenient moments for the opposition, and they commence to block shots, steal balls, and knock a pass away just when someone on the other team is turning, say, to look for someone to pass to, and discover they are empty-handed.

Yesterday, all those arms were at their mischievous best again as they helped the Bulls beat the Knicks 89–79 to provide a 2–0 lead in their three-of-five first-round National Basketball Association playoff series.

It was a well-rounded use of arms, which is important to the Bulls, since for too long they relied on that exquisite couple belonging to one Michael Jordan.

"We don't need Michael to be superhuman," Jackson said, "we just need him to be Superman, which would be enough for us."

Which is what he got yesterday afternoon in that clamorous, gamy old basketball palace on the West Side of Chicago. Jordan scored 26 points, not 46 as he has often done in the past, as the Bulls spread the scoring wealth, as well as the defensive and rebounding chores.

Jackson himself was known as a man with not only long arms, but with sharp elbows, too. No one ever derived pleasure from guarding Jackson. The Bulls are a chip off the granite. As if to underline this historical note, Cartwright, in the first half yesterday, hammered Mark Jackson, which resulted in the Knick guard's being carted off to the locker room where seven stitches were spun above his left eye. Then Jerrod Mustaf, the Knick forward, suffered a broken nose in the second quarter when he was whacked by Grant.

"If you have enough time for the input," said Phil Jackson, "a team pretty soon begins to resemble the coach."

Did he see himself in the Bulls? "In some ways," he said. "There's a reliance on defense, and aggressiveness, and you set a tone that you don't beat yourself. The other team has to execute well and take care of the ball in order to beat us."

Mostly, though, you understand your limitations, he said. "And Phil did," said Walt Frazier, a former teammate. "That's because Red was always reminding him of them."

Jackson recalled that when he was a player with the Knicks, his coach, Red Holzman, had him play under the one-dribble rule.

"Yeah, Willis and me were told that we could do anything we wanted to on offense, but we could only take one dribble," Jackson said, referring to Willis Reed. "We were two big guys who maybe didn't handle the ball all that well."

He laughed. And a smile would come to the lips of most fans of the Knicks (lips that nowadays are generally pursed) who remember those superb teams of 20 years ago when Jackson would come onto the basketball floor, appearing as if he had just removed himself from a closet rack. Because his shoulders were so wide and straight, he was called the Human Coat Hanger.

Jerry Krause, the Bulls general manager, reached out for his long-limbed coach two seasons ago. Jackson was an assistant to Doug Collins when the Bulls decided that a change was in order. In other words, they were going to fire Collins. Not necessarily because his arms were short, but because his temper was. That was only one of several problems, such as, from the front office's view, maintaining too tight a rein on the players. He was calling plays almost every time the team came down the floor, restricting, some felt, their movements.

Jackson is looser, by design, and, though the team is structured, there is a broader sense of laissez faire. When he was a player, Jackson was loose, as well, but it came without forethought.

And it started when he was young. To illustrate, he recalls a time when he was a baseball player in high school in Williston, North Dakota, in 1963 and was on a team that one night faced the Satchel Paige All-Stars, a black barnstorming team.

"I was the opposing pitcher," recalled Jackson. "I heard a lot of jokes about me because of the way I looked. The length of my arms, being so lanky and gangly, and my hat fell of when I threw a pitch. I remember the catcher on the team saying to me when I came up to bat, 'You got such a relaxed attitude, you look like a brother, white boy.' I said to him, 'I look relaxed only because I'm so uncoordinated. I can't help myself.'"

That wasn't the end of that, however. "Satchel was having fun and he laid something up there for me that looked like a grapefruit," said Jackson. "I teed it up and hit it and it skipped off the wall. His team beat me, but I did get a hit off Satchel Paige. He was a wiry kind of guy. He didn't look like he was 65 years old to me."

Yesterday the long-armed Bulls, like their coach, were a hit, and were also aging the Knickerbockers.

.   .   .

The Bulls swept the Knicks in that series and went on to win the NBA championship.

THE CASE OF THE
MISSING SEVEN-FOOTERS

May 10, 1994

THE INSCRIBED LINES BEGIN, "Give me your tired, your poor, your huddled masses yearning to breathe free..."

And so Phil Jackson, the coach of the Chicago Bulls, figured where better to take his tempest-tossed team yesterday than to the Statue of Liberty?

On the morning after a disheartening 90–86 loss to the Knicks in Madison Square Garden, in which the Bulls had built a 15-point lead late in the third quarter, Jackson looked at his group on the team bus, dressed in their basketball togs and ready to go to the announced practice, and decided otherwise. Without telling his players, he instructed the bus driver to skip the practice site, the Downtown Athletic Club, and head for the Staten Island Ferry.

And while reporters waited at the club, the defending National Basketball Association champions disappeared. For a time, it was the Case of the Missing Seven-Footers.

Jackson, who occasionally gives his players books to read that smack of culture, had thought a day off would do them more good than a practice. He told the team about the history of the ferry and the significance of the statue. Jackson understands that, after a nine-month season, his players probably know all the plays. They probably know how they should rotate on defense, and spread the court, and hit the open man.

Pat Riley, too, took the Knicks on a diversion this year. During a miserable road trip, he surprised the team by detouring one night to that oasis of culture, Reno, Nevada.

Perhaps Jackson was taking a page out of Riley's book, and recalling that one can suffer from "paralysis by analysis."

Or did Jackson, in his quest to ease the pain of defeat, recall how cheering Edna St. Vincent Millay had found the Staten Island Ferry? In *Recuerdo*, she wrote, "We were very tired, we were very merry—We had gone back and forth all night on the ferry."

Or he may have taken a page from John Masefield, who, in *Sea Fever*, understood that, to clear his head, "I must go down to the seas again, to the lonely sea and the sky—And all I ask is a tall ship, and a star to steer her by..."

The Bulls star Scottie Pippen didn't steer anything yesterday morning, as it turned out, but as the boat cruised across Upper New York Bay, he first lay on his back on the bench, soaking up rays, and later stood as the boat passed the Statue of Liberty and wondered if there was an elevator that takes you to the top, or can you reach it only by stairs?

Pippen was wearing the same black-white-and-red basketball sneakers, size 15, that he wore during the game. They are Nike Air, named for the founder of the line, one Michael Jordan, or Air Jordan, who has departed the Bulls for greener pastures, the outfields of various minor league baseball parks.

Pippen's sneakers are custom made for him, but it is curious that it is, in effect, a Michael Jordan shoe, and Pippen has the dubious legacy of having to fill those shoes.

He didn't quite live up to that in the eyes of some, but memories may be short. While it is true that Pippen didn't lead the Bulls to victory in the first game, neither did Jordan, last year.

In last season's opening playoff game between these teams in the Garden, the Knicks won 98–90, and Jordan scored 27 points. Pippen scored 24 points in that game, just as he did Sunday.

And while some have criticized Pippen for not being Air Jordan, it must be remembered that sometimes Air Jordan wasn't even Air Jordan. The Bulls' problem Sunday was that they had no one to fill the shoes Pippen wore while playing with Jordan.

On the side of Pippen's sneaker, he has written, "4-Peat," a reminder that the Bulls want a fourth straight NBA title. "He's carrying the burden of three championships on his shoulders," said Pat Riley.

"I thought Scottie at times tried to do too much," said Phil Jackson after the game.

"Maybe I did try to push it a little too much," Pippen said. Pippen, however, has proved to be resilient despite past criticisms that he was "soft." "He's one of the toughest players in the league," said Riley, "and maybe the most complete player."

Jackson's intention, surely, of taking Pippen and Associates to the Statue of Liberty was not only to give them a respite, but also to light a torch under them. "It was good," said Jo Jo English, a Bulls guard. "It took our minds off a game we threw away."

Jordan didn't have such a great weekend, either. He went hitless in four at-bats for the Birmingham Barons.

Has he ever been to the top of the Empire State Building?

.   .   .

The Knicks beat the Bulls in that series and went on to the NBA Finals, where they lost to Houston in seven games.

VAN GUNDY'S LOVE LIFE, SO TO SPEAK

March 13, 1996

THE KNICKS WERE IN the soup, and management, partway through the season, decided to change coaches. After all, a number of players were disgruntled, and a few more were gruntled. Several preferred choices for coach weren't available at this time, so the Knicks reluctantly dipped into their own organization for what they termed an interim coach.

This was 1967, and the interim coach was one William Holzman, then a scout for the team, and he replaced Dick McGuire. When management approached Holzman it was made clear that a) it would most likely seek a more high-profile coach at season's end, and b) Holzman, who liked what he was doing, would be well served to accept the new job.

"No one said it directly," Red Holzman recalled recently, "but I got the feeling if I didn't take that job I'd get fired."

The Knicks lost their first two games under Holzman, and then responded to the coach, caught fire, and made the playoffs. Knick management kept the interim coach. Two seasons later, the Knicks won the National Basketball Association title, the first in team history, and three seasons after that won it again, for their second and last championship.

Nearly 30 years later, the Knicks again dismissed a coach and again plucked someone in the organization, this time an assistant coach, as an interim coach. Jeff Van Gundy, a small-boned, baldish, bright young man of 34, surely knows that one of the biggest problems facing him is how to handle the players, something at which Don Nelson, his predecessor, admitted he failed.

"I don't like the word *handle*," Van Gundy said yesterday after practice, and before the team left for Minneapolis to play the Timberwolves tonight. "It sounds too much like trying to manipulate them. That's not what I try to do. They're veteran players, and they know consistency has been a problem. And we have to improve on that. But look, I'm no great orator. And the best way for me to coach them is to be direct and honest and open to suggestions."

Van Gundy was an assistant with the Knicks under the mandarin-stern Pat Riley and assistant under the relatively more laissez-faire Don Nelson, and watched the Knicks prosper under Riley and crumble under Nelson with about the same nucleus of players.

If Van Gundy is as capable as some think he is, he will take the best each coach had to offer, and avoid the worst. Most recently, from Nelson, he has been made aware that stark honesty, or unvarnished directness, may not be the best carrot for some of these players.

For example, when Nelson first sat Patrick Ewing down and told him that he liked him as a player but hoped he would be a better passer, Ewing was shocked. "Better passer?" rejoined Ewing. "I think I'm a very good passer!" Patrick might be the only one who thinks so, and while Nelson was on the right track intellectually, he tripped diplomatically. "Patrick," a slicker tongue might have crooned, "you're one sweet passer, dude. Do you think we could see more of it—for the highlight films?"

And then Nelson not only replaced John Starks in the starting lineup with Hubert Davis, but added insult to injury by saying Davis was the better player. And while that may have been true, too, it was needlessly demoralizing.

That other interim coach, meanwhile, was the master of disciplining, or making a point, and at the same time allowing the player his dignity. Phil Jackson, the Bulls coach, who was a Knick player when Holzman took over the team, learned how to do that.

"One of Red's rules was everyone must ride the team bus," said Jackson. "But shortly after Red took over, Cazzie Russell decided to drive his car to Philadelphia for a game. When he came into the locker room, Red said, 'Cazzie, those highway tolls must be expensive.' Cazzie said, 'Oh, yeah, Coach.' Red said, 'How much were they?' Cazzie said, 'Eight dollars.' Red said, 'Well, Cazzie, I'll take that off the hundred-dollar fine.' Cazzie thanked him. I never saw a guy get fined and thank the coach for it."

The Knicks said they would analyze Van Gundy's performance and decide at season's end whether to retain him.

"That's all I can ask," said Van Gundy.

Did he know that Red Holzman, the winningest coach in Knick history, also began as an interim coach?

"No, I didn't," said Van Gundy. "That's a great story."

Young Van Gundy dreams of writing another.

VIII.

YOUNGBLOODS

HITTING THE LOTTERY AS A JUNIOR?

July 9, 2001

A STELLAR ARRAY OF basketball cognoscenti that included scouts from almost every NBA team and college coaches—pads and pencils at the ready, projected mental insights awhirl—flocked yesterday to see some 220 of the best high school players in the world showcased at Fairleigh Dickinson's Rothman Athletic Center. One player in particular, however, caught much of their attention.

He is a 16-year-old from St. Vincent–St. Mary High School in Akron, Ohio, who will be a junior in the fall. Many of the gathered connoisseurs believed that the lad, LeBron James, a 6'7", 210-pound point guard, shooting guard, and small forward—sometimes he plays as if he is all three in one, a kind of hoops Swiss Army knife—would have been taken in the first round of the most recent NBA draft, possibly a lottery pick.

Hey, it was one thing for three of the first four picks in the draft to be high school seniors, for the first time ever, and four of the first eight—but a high school sophomore potentially going pro? "And next year," said Sonny Vaccaro, founder and director of the Adidas ABCD four-day camp, which began yesterday, "LeBron could surely go in the lottery. He'll be bigger, stronger, and smarter."

Okay, still, a high school junior making the jump? Got to be kidding? No?

Tom Konchalski, who evaluates high school players for his respected *H.S.B.I. Report*, said, "LeBron isn't an extraterrestrial athlete, but he has a tremendous feel for the game. He sees situations two passes ahead of the play. He's been compared to Vince Carter and Tracy McGrady. But I think he has a better feel for the game than they do."

He meant than they did when they were James' age, right? "No, I mean right now," Konchalski said. "I doubt seriously if he's going to college."

So LeBron James, in a yellow uniform and wearing No. 155, his hair tufted out and his pants baggy, began one of the four games going on at once, after the first round of four games had been completed. There were marvelous players on the courts, including 6'6" Lenny Cooke of Old Tappan, New Jersey, and 6'8" Carmelo Anthony of Baltimore, but none except James made first team All-America last season as chosen by *USA Today*, the first underclassman named to the first team in the 18 years that such authoritative selections have been made.

He tried his first shot, a three-pointer from the top of the key, and it swished. His next shot was a three-pointer from the corner. Swish. There was a fast-break dunk, a clever pass for a basket, a missed jump shot, then he snared a rebound and stuffed it with both hands behind his head.

"Wow," one of the other players in the stands said. "Wow," said nearly everyone else.

James' mother, Gloria, watched her only child play. She is an enthusiastic fan of LeBron.

"What I want for LeBron is his happiness," said Gloria, who has worked in accounting and sales but is now unemployed. "He loves basketball. But I would like to see him graduate with his class from high school, at least. But we'll make a decision when the time comes. He's a level-headed boy. He's never given me a lick of problems. He's mannerable and respectful."

LeBron James, a solid B student, said that he wasn't sure what he planned to do. "College is important," he said, "you can't play basketball all your life. You should prepare for something else, too." To be safe, his mother said she was taking out an insurance policy on him.

Kwame Brown, the No. 1 pick by the Washington Wizards last month, received a $12 million contract for three years. "That's a lot of money," James said. "But we've struggled this long, a couple more years won't make that much difference."

Billy Donovan, head coach at Florida, had signed Brown to attend his university. "And he wanted to go to college," Donovan said. "But he made a decision that he thought was best for him, and his family. I can't fault him for that."

Ernie Grunfeld, general manager of the Milwaukee Bucks, was in attendance, primarily, he said, because his 6'6" son, Danny, who will be a senior, was playing—he's a good player but not a pro prospect, yet. "I wish all the kids would go to college first," Grunfeld said. "But I also don't think you should prevent someone from trying to earn a living. I just hope the kids who do skip college have the emotional and physical maturity to succeed."

Among the players, 6'7" Demetris Nichols from Barrington, Rhode Island, who will be a junior, dreams about an NBA future, like many of his peers, but is also realistic. "We talk more about college than the pros," he said. He also thought there was substance in the talk that Kobe Bryant gave to the group Saturday night. Bryant, the Lakers star, jumped from high school to the pros. "Kobe said, 'Go to college. You have something to fall back on. If you break a leg, then where are you?'" Nichols said.

But Kobe—who, like Brown, is an alumnus of this camp—didn't go to college. "He's good," Nichols replied, with emphasis. He added that he has to be careful: "Everybody wants a piece of you. If somebody tells me I should go pro, I'm going to make sure he knows basketball."

From appearances, that could be somebody like LeBron James, counsel also to himself.

KOBE THE HIGH SCHOOL PHENOM

February 27, 1996

THE SIGN IN FRONT of the high school in this small town some 30 miles north of Philadelphia stated that the game was sold out and that no tickets were available. People outside the double doors and in the packed parking lot on this crisp Friday night last week were asking whether anyone had tickets to sell. And no one did, clutching them like passes for entry through the Pearly Gates.

Taken in perspective, this was a Pennsylvania high school basketball equivalent. It wasn't just excitement for Lower Merion versus Norristown in the District 1 Class AAAA boys' final, a step from the state tournament. Much of the anticipation was for a slender, 6'6", 17-year-old senior for Lower Merion, Kobe Bryant.

With a shaved head, the graceful Bryant is considered by many scouts to be the best high school player in the country. He plays point guard, shooting guard, small forward, power forward, and center—not all at once, although it may seem so at times, but depending on the team's needs at the moment.

Bryant is the highest scorer in the history of southeastern Pennsylvania preps, recently passing Overbrook's Wilt Chamberlain, among others; a player whose coach said could become the next Michael Jordan, and one who, the school's athletic director said, has attracted as many pro scouts to his games as college scouts.

"Will he go pro or will he go college?" his father, Joe Bryant, said. "That's the big question."

Put another way, will he become the next Kevin Garnett? Last season Garnett, a 6'11" forward, went directly from Farragut High School in Chicago to the Minnesota Timberwolves of the National Basketball Association, one of only a handful of players to make such a leap over the past 20 years.

Garnett, who starts for the Wolves, followed in the footsteps of players like Moses Malone, Bill Willoughby, and Darryl Dawkins. More recently, Shawn Kemp jumped to Seattle after sitting out a year after high school.

Now, Kobe Bryant and others are receiving consideration. In the New York area, there has been speculation about whether Tim Thomas, the 6'10" forward for Paterson Catholic, in Paterson, New Jersey, might opt to turn pro.

Clearly, as the NBA has expanded to 29 teams, more players are needed to fill the rosters. And as more college players are leaving school early to join the pros, the high schools are the next logical place for scouts to look for talent.

Earlier last week, Lower Merion won a district semifinal before another capacity crowd after some 2,500 fans were turned away at the school entrance. Bryant scored 50 points on an assortment of drives, tips, and jump shots, including seven three-pointers, and collected his usual handfuls of rebounds, assists, steals, and blocked shots.

Kobe Bryant is the son of Joe "Jellybean" Bryant, a 6'9" journeyman forward for eight years in the NBA starting in 1975, then eight more years playing in Italy and Switzerland. He grew up overseas and became fluent in not only basketball, but also Italian, and "can dabble," his father said, in French, Spanish, and German. The elder Bryant is now an assistant basketball coach at La Salle University, where he was a standout player.

"Kobe's going to make the decision to do what he wants to do," Joe Bryant said while sitting in the bleachers before the game last Friday. "He'll decide after the season. But he's fortunate that he doesn't have to be pressured for money. We're hardly rich, but we're comfortable. And he's never wanted for anything.

"He's not a stereotypical black kid from an urban setting. We live in a five-bedroom house in a Philadelphia suburb. He's got both parents together, and both sets of grandparents, too. He's got two older sisters in college. And he has a kind of sophistication. He's a solid three-point student in a good suburban school, and got 1,100 on his SATs as a junior."

The money, to be sure, is intriguing. Standard three-year contracts for first-round draft choices range from $1.7 million, for the 29th pick in the first round, to $8.5 million for the top selection.

"Do I think he could make it in the NBA right now?" said Hal Wissel, head of player personnel for the Nets, and one who has scouted Bryant. "Yes. I think he has the skills." But Wissel cautioned that he thought Bryant should stay in school, for at least a year or two more, "to hone the skills, to mature physically and emotionally."

Wissel said he thought that Bryant could be a lottery pick, and might be drafted no lower than 15th, which would earn the player about $3 million for three years.

Garnett, who was the fifth pick overall in last year's draft, failed to make the requisite 700 score on the Scholastic Assessment Test and would have been forced to sit out a year if he had decided to go to college. That, he said, was the reason he turned pro. And now, at age 19, and after some uneasy early going, he is averaging 23 minutes per game and appears to be adjusting nicely in the pros.

Not all players do. Wissel was an assistant coach with the Hawks when Willoughby jumped from high school to the pros.

"I remember how lonely he was," Wissel said. "He was just a kid and had nothing in common with the men on the team. I remember seeing him once sitting in his Lincoln Continental and just playing with the windows."

David Stern, commissioner of the NBA, said that if it were up to him, there would be an age minimum for players in the NBA.

"We should have the right to have a policy to prevent teams from signing players out of high school," he said. "But the courts have not made it possible for us to have any age limits. But our system is to discourage very young men from opting for the pros. I would hate for our league to be in a position of encouraging young men to forgo their education. But legally we can't prevent them from trying to earn a living with us, when they wish to try."

Once a player turns pro, he becomes ineligible for college ball. Some players who leave school early, like Julius Erving and Isiah Thomas, take courses in summer school and by correspondence, eventually earning their degrees.

"I don't know if I'm ready yet for the pros, physically or mentally." Bryant said. "I mean, there are some pretty big boys in the pros. And you get a physical punishment night after night. And then there's the aspect of playing night in and night out. I mean, it's really a job!"

He said that college would be fun, even with the understanding that he would have to hit the books. "But that's something I've always done," he said. He added that his major would be communications.

Last summer, Bryant played at St. Joseph's University against a number of 76ers, including Jerry Stackhouse, the third pick overall in last season's draft and one of the leading candidates for Rookie Of The Year in the NBA. Stackhouse left North Carolina after his sophomore year. In those games, Bryant more than held his own and even beat Stackhouse in a one-on-one game.

"The next day, Dean Smith called me from North Carolina to recruit Kobe," Joe Bryant said with a wide smile. Smith was Stackhouse's college coach, as he was Michael Jordan's. And Smith is hardly alone in showing profound interest in Kobe Bryant. But of the hundreds of schools that have contacted the player, he says he has narrowed the list to North Carolina, Kentucky, Duke, Michigan, and, not unexpectedly, La Salle.

In the game against Norristown last Friday, Bryant struggled with his shooting, but midway through the fourth quarter hit a pair of dazzling drives that gave Lower Merion the lead. He scored 21 points—including 10 of 11 free throws—but made only 5-of-23 from the floor. And with 1:10 left in the game, and Lower Merion ahead by six points, Bryant fouled out.

"It was the worst shooting game I've ever seen Kobe play," the Lower Merion coach, Greg Downer, said later. "But remember, their defense was pretty good, too."

On the bench, Bryant, jumping to his feet, cheered his team on, sometimes pumping his fist, sometimes with palms down, bidding his teammates to be calm. The team preserved the victory and advanced to the state tournament, which begins tonight for Lower Merion with a game at the Palestra in Philadelphia.

"The thing the scouts like so much about him, besides his talent, is his mentality," Wissel said. "He's a very confident, very centered young man. And I guess you have to credit his dad, and his family environment, for a lot of that."

In the locker room after the game, Bryant's attitude was upbeat. "Yes, I would like to have shot better, but my dad always told me to be an all-around player," Bryant said. "And if I can't be on in shooting, then I can rebound, set up the other guys with passes, and play defense. And I think I did that."

Joe Bryant entered the locker room and he and his son threw their arms around each other and hugged.

"You guys won, that was the important thing," Joe Bryant said.

"And we go on," his son said.

They spoke quietly for a few moments, then the father left. Bryant, with equipment bag slung over his shoulder, hurried to catch a team bus, laughing and joking with teammates; the young man, even on a lackluster shooting night, properly confident of his talent and full of the pleasures of life.

KWAME BROWN GOES
THE FRENCH ROUTE

July 19, 2001

THE $12 MILLION MAN, the 6'11", 250-pound, $12 million teenager, to be more specific, found himself in Brasserie Jo, one of the better French restaurants in Boston and the first French restaurant he had ever knowingly patronized.

It was convenient for the 19-year-old Kwame Brown, being the dining establishment in the hotel where he was staying this week, and he was famished, having just come from a basketball workout. He knew he could also use the fuel, because he was making his professional debut that evening in the pro summer league here.

When Brown entered the eatery, he received some stares, since he is a rather large person. But it did not seem that the lunchtime patrons were aware that this young man in T-shirt, sweatpants, and sandals was the first pick overall by the Washington Wizards in the recent National Basketball Association draft, the first high school player ever selected first, and chosen by none other than the team's director of player personnel, Michael Jeffrey Jordan, the Bald One himself.

Brown, who is from Brunswick, Georgia, a town of about 14,000 on the Atlantic coast, perused the menu. "What's 'steak tartare'?" he asked the waiter.

"It's very good," the waiter said.

"It's uncooked," said Brown's companion, trying to be helpful.

"I don't eat raw anything," Brown said. "It'll kill you."

"Something to start?" the waiter asked, moving on.

"House salad," Brown said, "with French dressing."

"I know it's odd, this being a French restaurant," the waiter said, "but we don't serve French dressing."

"No French dressing?" Brown repeated. "Bennie's Red Barn has the best French dressing. Unbelievable."

"Bennie's Red Barn?" the companion said. The waiter's eyes widened. "It's the best restaurant in the Brunswick area," Brown said. "You've got to go there sometime. And the steaks. They've got this T-bone, it's this thick, and it's bigger than this plate. I like mine medium well, just this side of burnt."

He ordered the house salad with a balsamic vinaigrette dressing, and the classic Parisian steak frites, the house specialty. He also checked the prices, with some disdain. "In cities I'm visiting now," he said, "the prices in restaurants go up and the quality of food goes down."

This entire conversation was done in a most pleasant manner, handled with absolute aplomb by the young man. It was obvious that it would take a lot to intimidate him. His confidence is such that it was easy to picture him telling Jordan, when Brown worked out for him and the coaches in Washington before the draft, "If you pick me, you won't be sorry."

Brown's cell phone, which he had placed on the table, rang. He answered, but cut the conversation short, apparently not wishing to be rude to his lunch companion.

He said he had been working out with some new Wizard teammates in Washington, including a potential teammate, Jordan. "Still looks quick," Brown said. "And he's always outsmarting you. On defense, he knows where you're going even before you do. And you turn your back on him and he's stolen the ball. He beats you to the spot.

"When I got a little discouraged, he said, 'Keep your head up. Don't lose confidence. Remember, this is a marathon, it's not a race.' I've got a lot to learn, and I'm looking forward to trying to learn it."

The house salad arrived. "Hmmm," Brown said, "this is grass."

"There's some mesclun and shredded Boston lettuce and cucumbers," the waiter explained.

"Could I get another salad, with regular lettuce?" he asked the nodding waiter.

There was another call on Brown's cell phone. "Hi Mom," he said. "Can't talk now. I'll call soon as I'm done." He closed the phone and put it in his pocket. "That was the call I was waiting for. Okay, I don't have to answer any others."

Brown is the seventh of Joyce Brown's eight children. She brought them up alone for the past 15 years, after her husband, Willie, was sent to prison with a life sentence for murder. Kwame was four years old at the time. To support her family, Joyce Brown worked as a hotel maid in Brunswick, until her back gave out and she went on disability. She has had other physical problems, including heart trouble and the loss of a kidney. The family had few luxuries, not even a car. They got around by bicycle.

"What my mother taught us was, never give up, no matter what," Brown said. "It's one thing for a single mother to raise one child. She raised eight. She's home now looking for a house. It's a dream of mine, to buy my mom a house."

About his father, Brown said, "He's satanic. I learned by example from him. I mean, I want the opposite of what he got. I want to be free. We've never had a relationship. I believe that everyone has two options in life. To choose right, or to choose wrong. It's not hard. I've had temptations, but I'm lucky that overall I've chosen right."

He said he plans to be thrifty with his money, and save most of it. "I don't wear jewelry," he said. "For what? So people can be jealous of what you're wearing and kill you for it? I've seen that. Happens every day. Doesn't interest me."

Brown, who signed a three-year, $11.9 million contract with the Wizards last week, was asked if people had come out of the woodwork looking for handouts now that he is rich. "And still coming," he said.

He gave several examples. "I've had a bunch of friends come to me, and say they have a record deal to make rap albums, but they need financing," he said. "I tell 'em, 'Good luck, but elsewhere.' One of my aunts asked me to buy her a house. I said, 'Sorry.' If I did, it'd be like a revolving door. I've got a lot of aunts."

He said his mother had thought about moving to Washington, and he had no problems with that. "But I told her I wasn't going to live with her," he said. "I've got to grow up on my own."

Just two months ago, he was attending his senior prom at Glynn Academy in Brunswick. He went with his girlfriend "at the time." What about girls? "I've seen guys shot and it's most often over girls. I don't think anyone is worth risking life and death over."

In his debut pro game on Tuesday night, the same day as his first French meal, Brown's team of young would-be Wizards played a similar group of Celtics players in the Clark Athletic Center at the University of Massachusetts–Boston. Brown admitted to being "scared to death" before the game, but as Jordan had told him, "All eyes will be on you, but just have fun. Play like you know how to play."

Indeed, he was impressive in his debut, though not spellbinding. He scored 15 points, shot 6-for-15, on smooth jump shots and strong drives to the hoop, both lefty and righty, took down six rebounds, and handled the ball well in 32 minutes.

"I thought Kwame played well," said Brian James, a Wizards assistant coach who is coaching the summer team. "He's got to improve his conditioning, and we have to work on his low-post skills. But it's like when I was with Toronto and we had Tracy McGrady right out of high school. You can't expect too many things too soon. But we were pleased with Kwame tonight."

Tom Heinsohn, the former great Celtics player and coach, watched Brown at the game. "I can see why Washington is so enthralled with him," he said. "He's physically mature and can put the ball on the floor for a big man. He gets to where he wants to go."

Stan Van Gundy, an assistant coach with the Miami Heat, said, "He's going to be a terrific player. For our sake, I hope it's not right away."

Brown said of his performance, "I had a great time. But we lost tonight. I'm looking forward to winning tomorrow."

Oh, but about Brown's entree at lunch, the Parisian steak frites.

"What is that on there?" Brown asked, when the waiter placed the dish in front of him.

"Garlic butter," the waiter said.

Brown stared at the yellow substance puddled on his meat. The waiter, well, waited. Perhaps he wondered if it was anything like the steak at Bennie's Red Barn.

After a moment, Brown cleared his throat and looked up. "Have any A-1 sauce?" he asked politely.

MEL DAVIS'
ESCAPE ROUTE

February 14, 1973

IN THE WINTER SUNLIGHT, broken bits of glass sparkle on the sidewalk and on the bare patches that pass for lawns on Fulton St. here in the Bedford-Stuyvesant neighborhoods.

Across the street from the project building where St. John's University All-American basketball player Mel Davis lives is a funeral parlor which is heavily patronized. There seems to be a black funeral a minute.

A common belief in the neighborhood is that the funeral director does a brisker business than anyone on the street, which includes the prostitutes, pimps, numbers runners, dope peddlers, contract "hit men," gamblers, the corner tavern which is the focal point for the garish nightly "carnival," and (a block away) the Psychedelic wig salon. A gallows joke has it that the funeral director gives great discounts for "O.D." deaths.

"In the summertime especially there must be 20 deaths a month on the street from drug overdoses," said Davis, looking out the window from the sixth-floor, six-room apartment where he lives with his mother, grandfather, and five younger brothers and sisters.

"And there's the knifings and shootings. You go in a hallway and you step over a dead body. Sometimes you go up the stairs and you step over a dead body. You go on the roof, more dead bodies.

"This is why I wanted to sign with the pros. I wanted to buy my family a house and get them out of here. I feel it's my responsibility. My parents are separated and I had to take the father role."

A moment of incredible bad luck has caused the Davis family to remain in that neighborhood.

March 21, 1972, had begun as one of the most exciting days in the life of Mel Davis, then a 21-year-old, 6'6" junior forward for St. John's.

That day the April issue of *Black Sports* magazine had come out and Davis' mustache-and-goateed face was on the cover. That night he was to play in a National Invitational Tournament game against Oral Roberts in Madison Square Garden, the dream place for New York ballplayers. His family and neighborhood friends would be there. Davis was already his school's single-game and season rebounding record holder and seemed certain of becoming the school's highest single-season scorer. And, best of all, on this day, an agreement with a National Basketball Association team had been reached. Davis, considered a "hardship case," would sign a contract for over half a million dollars at tournament's end. The Davises would soon be departing the Bed-Stuy.

Davis was so up for the game, he recalls, because he wanted to show everyone that he was worth the acclaim, worthy of the records, and a worthwhile recipient of the big bonus. His youngish mother recalls, to Davis' embarrassed "Oh ma, you're exaggerating," that on that night Mel went up so high for a rebound that his hip hit the rim.

In the first 10 minutes of the Oral Roberts game, Davis scored 12 points, pulled down 12 rebounds. The 12th rebound would be the last one he'd grab for at least one year. He crashed to the floor, writhing and gripping his right knee. In the stands his mother screamed.

Davis had torn up his cartilage. The pros tore up his contract.

Hope remained, however. Davis could play next season, surely, and nothing would be changed. Except one year. Davis underwent an operation on August 30. It was performed by Dr. James Nicholas, who has mended two of the most notorious knees in sport, those of Joe Namath.

Davis' knee was healing nicely. He had been jumping rope and doing light sprints and was prepared to join the St. John's basketball team in two weeks, in late November. But more incredible bad luck.

One afternoon he heard screaming on Fulton St. Nothing new, except this time the voices were familiar. He looked across at the funeral parlor, then to the adjoining building, St. Benedict's church. His seven-year-old twin sisters, Stacy and Tracy, go to school there. They were in trouble. Davis saw two junkies grabbing at the girls. Davis raced down the six flights of stairs, stumbling and falling on the last flight. He got up, ran across the street, and caught the junkies. And he got back the 30 cents lunch money the junkies had snatched from the girls.

The fall on the stairs again messed up his knee. Dr. Nicholas thought it best that Davis not try to play at all this season. So Davis remained on the sideline, still attending class, still receiving a living stipend which helps pay the rent and family food bills (along with his mother's salary as subway token seller).

The pro draft comes up in March. Teams are not sure what the status of Davis' knee is. Davis says it is nearly 100 percent healed, and all that he needs is a little work to get it to full strength.

Perhaps no pro team will take a gamble on him until he proves his knee is good again, which would mean using his final year of eligibility at St. John's.

Many people are pulling for Davis, including the people on Fulton St.

"I'm sort of looked up to around here," said Davis. "The junkies, the prostitutes, the numbers runners, they all talk to me. They know I've got a chance to get out of here, and they hope I make it. They respect me because I was strong enough to resist going the way they went."

And Davis had his opportunities: at Boys High, drugs were all over the place, he says. A basketball teammate gave Davis cocaine when he was a sophomore. Davis sniffed it and immediately went cold turkey. "My body felt like a toothache," he recalls. He says he never tried hard drugs again but remains concerned that his brothers and sisters might be enticed.

Davis also has experienced the violence of the ghetto. The worst example was when he was in the ninth grade. He had just played the final game of a basketball tournament in which he led his team to victory. He scored 71 points in the game.

As he walked out carrying his trophies, the player who had guarded him stepped from behind a door and slashed Davis' face with a straight razor. The gash took 65 stitches and the scar runs from Davis' jawbone to his lower lip.

"The other day," said Davis, "I ran into a dope pusher I knew on the street. He said, 'Melvin, when you get big time, don't forget us.'

"I told him I won't. Told him I never could forget."

•   •   •

Mel Davis went on to play four seasons with the Knicks and one with the Nets. He also went on to earn a marketing degree from St. John's, a master's degree in psychology and counseling from Fordham, and a master's degree in career planning from New York University.

KEVIN GARNETT COMES OF AGE

December 11, 1995

THE LIGHTS WERE BRIGHT in the Target Center arena here, the crowd was cheering, and the game had been stopped to let Kevin Garnett enter the contest last month for the Minnesota Timberwolves.

Garnett is the remarkable 19-year-old, 6'11" rookie who, just a few months ago, was in a tuxedo and size 13½ black shoes and attending his high school prom in Chicago.

Now he is in the National Basketball Association, the fifth player picked in the 1995 draft. He is the first player in 20 years to go from high school to the pros and was competing against, among others, David Robinson of the San Antonio Spurs, the league's Most Valuable Player last season. This was all a dream come true for Garnett, who, earlier in the year, had been playing in small gyms for the Farragut High School Admirals on the West Side of Chicago against Marshall High, or Collins High, or DuSable High.

Garnett reported to the scorer's table, ripped off his green-and-white Wolves warmup jacket, and was about to run into the game when an official halted him. "Where's your jersey?" he asked. "You can't play without a jersey."

Garnett was wearing a warmup shirt.

"My jersey?" Garnett said. He checked beneath the warmup shirt. His chest was bare. He looked toward his team's bench. "Anyone seen my jersey?" he asked.

He hurried over and with his long arms started searching under the chairs where his team sat. His teammates were laughing.

"Kevin," said his coach, Bill Blair. "It wouldn't be under there. Try the locker room."

Which was indeed where he found the jersey, which he had forgotten to put on. Within minutes, he was back on the floor and in the game, with jersey No. 21, and wearing his shorts in his customarily and stylishly hip-hop manner, so baggy, in fact, it appeared he needed suspenders or risked losing the shorts, too.

Beyond that, though, he has been comporting himself not like a wide-eyed rookie, but like a confident and willing-to-improve pro.

He is the first or second or third substitute in the game for the Timberwolves, who are bringing him along at a cautious but steady pace. He plays about 19 minutes per game and has demonstrated an ability to rebound, to block shots, to handle the ball and pass like a point guard, to run the fast break, and to shoot posting up like a center or shoot accurately from three-point range.

In the Wolves' 114–108 loss to the Charlotte Hornets on Saturday night, Garnett played 14 minutes and sank all four of his shots. But he also had two turnovers in that relatively brief appearance. He makes mistakes, to be sure, but his ability and his enthusiasm give the Wolves high hopes, and the warm feeling that they didn't make a mistake in signing him to a three-year, $5.6 million contract.

While there are times when he hangs his head after a mistake, there are the other times when, say, after he rams home a monster dunk, that he will belly-bump with a teammate like Isaiah Rider. And when he encouraged Terry Porter, the veteran guard, with a whack on the rear when Porter was reporting in to the game, he hit him so hard that Porter almost toppled over the scorer's table.

"He's a phenom," said his mother, Shirley Irby. "He's a once-in-a-lifetime, someone who is truly blessed."

A mother's pride is one thing. But someone like Kevin McHale's, the former Boston Celtic great and the vice president of basketball operations for the Timberwolves, is another. McHale was primarily responsible for drafting Garnett.

McHale observed him in high school. "I saw a young man with exceptional quickness for his size," said McHale, who is the same height as Garnett. "And I saw he loved to play ball, he was not afraid of a challenge, and when I looked in his eyes, I felt this was someone with a good sense of himself, and a sense of purpose. I put a lot of credence in the look in someone's eyes.

"But despite all that, you never know how someone's going to react. I've seen a lot of guys with talent who couldn't take the pressure or the challenge in our league."

When Garnett went to training camp with the Timberwolves, he didn't seem to be overawed, or overwhelmed. The big problem was his feet. And the rest of his body. The two-hour, two-a-day workouts were wearing him out.

"How did you do this for 13 years?" he asked McHale.

"I just closed my eyes," said McHale, laughing.

But Garnett also asked him another question, which made McHale see more to Garnett.

"What's it like to win a championship?" Garnett wanted to know.

McHale had won three NBA titles with the Celtics. "It's the best feeling in the world," he replied. Then he corrected himself. "It's the best basketball feeling in the world."

Garnett is thin, at 220 pounds, and needs to lift more weights, so he doesn't get pushed around under the basket by such world-class musclemen as Karl Malone and Charles Oakley.

But he listens and he learns. "One thing I told him about going to the pros," said his mother, "was to have respect, and to listen."

"Aw, mom," Garnett said at one point, "what do you know about the NBA?"

He said it with a smile, as she recalled, but he was also serious. "He wants to be on his own, to make it on his own," she said. "He's still a mama's boy—he'll murder me if he hears that—but he's a good boy."

Two years ago, however, an incident occurred that changed Garnett's life. He was a junior in high school in his hometown of Mauldin, South Carolina, a middle-class suburban community outside Greenville. There was a fight with racial overtones in a school corridor in which a group of black students badly beat up a white student. Garnett was part of the group charged with assault. He participated in a pretrial diversion program for first-time offenders, and his record was cleared. But there was a possibility that he would not be allowed to play on the school basketball team in his senior year—that after he had been named the best prep player in South Carolina.

What was he going to do? That summer he had met a Chicago high school basketball coach, William "Wolf" Nelson of Farragut, at the Nike

All-American camp. And he also became friendly with Ronnie Fields, an exceedingly talented guard for Farragut. Garnett found that he could relocate to Chicago and attend and play for Farragut.

Garnett moved with his mother to the Lawndale district in Chicago which, as Irby recalled, "was very, very hard."

"And yes, I was scared for Kevin," she said.

"There were gangs, drugs, shootings," Garnett said. "It was the ghetto. I was from a quiet, neat and clean town in South Carolina. This was like hell."

One of the people he had to contend with at Farragut was a gang leader known as Seven-gun Marcello.

Did Marcello actually have seven guns, Garnett was asked.

"I don't know," Garnett said. "I never wanted to find out."

Garnett made his way through the thicket of problems there—after a few months he and his mother moved to a better neighborhood—and he led his high school team to the city championship. He was named "Mr. Basketball" in Illinois, averaging 25 points per game, seven assists, 17 rebounds, and seven blocked shots.

He had thought about going to college, but he was unable to score high enough on the American College Test—he got a 16 on his second try, but it takes a 17 to be eligible for an athletic scholarship and play as a freshman. When he learned that he would be a certain lottery pick, and that millions would be available to him, he opted for the pros.

"He's not a dumb kid by any means," said Frank Valadez, an administrator at Farragut High School. "He just lives and breathes basketball."

There are adjustments to be made for life in the NBA, though.

"One thing I know is to be careful, not to hang around places I shouldn't," he said. "I've had one experience in being somewhere that caused me trouble, and that was that problem in high school in Mauldin. I'm in a high level now in the NBA, and I'm going to watch myself."

He has heard the talk that high school stars such as Fields, his former teammate at Farragut, and Tim Thomas of Paterson, New Jersey, might be tempted to follow his lead and jump to the NBA. "If they feel that this is the right thing for them, they should go after their dreams," he said. "But I would tell them that the NBA is no cakewalk."

His agent, Eric Fleisher, who is based in New York, says that Garnett has been conservative with his money. "His head is screwed on right,"

Fleisher said. Garnett says he has an appreciation for money because he remembers his handful of jobs as a kid in Mauldin, from bagging groceries to stock boy to working night and day in summertime flipping burgers in a Burger King for $100 a week.

With his millions, though, he has bought himself a Lexus and a Toyota Land Cruiser, to get around, he said, in the Minnesota snow. His clothes are of the casual high school variety, and his lone piece of jewelry is a gold chain with a peace emblem. On the court, he wears a rubber band around his wrist for luck.

He lives in a three-bedroom luxury condominium in Minnetonka, a suburb of Minneapolis, with his longtime friend from Mauldin, Jaime "Bug" Peters. The highlight of their decor, said Corliss Strong, Garnett's high school girlfriend from Chicago who comes up for regular visits, "is the television set, and the video games."

His mother has moved back to their house in Mauldin, and continues in the Mi Salon hair boutique she owns. "I don't need anything from Kevin," she said. "But he has been very generous to his mom."

At home, Garnett also cooks and makes his bed. The other night he made steamed shrimp and wild rice. "My mother will come up and fuss about this and that," he said, "but I think she's pretty pleased."

"I am proud of how he's living," she said, "but I don't think he's eating enough greenery. That's when he asks me to leave the kitchen."

The other day he and teammate Christian Laettner visited the St. Paul Children's Hospital. One of the youngsters they saw was a terminally ill boy named Arnold. Arnold did not know Garnett was coming there, and in his Make-A-Wish program, one of his wishes was to meet the young basketball player.

The boy, in bed, his head bald from radiation treatments, looked stunned when the two huge basketball players walked into his room. He was even wearing a Wolves jersey.

Garnett, who wore a black baseball cap turned backward in teenage fashion, shook the boy's hand. The players gave the boy a Wolves T-shirt and signed it.

"How old are you?" Garnett asked.

"Thirteen," said the amazed boy.

"I only got six years on you, can you believe that?"

The boy shook his head. They chatted some more.

"You gonna be rootin' for us?" Garnett asked.

"Yeah," Arnold said.

"That's good," Garnett said.

Later, Garnett, who had clearly been moved by the experience, told his roommate, Peters, and girlfriend, Strong, about it at dinner.

He talked about being lucky. He didn't have to say how lucky. And soon his thoughts would return to his new life, to the focus he had placed on games, so narrowly focused, in fact, that his mother knows not to call him on game days because his concentration is so intense.

"Like he told me not long ago, 'I've got things under control, Mom,'" she recalled. "It's like he's saying, 'Let me have wings, so I can fly.'"

IX.

FROM THE KNICKS' FIRST DECADE

A HANDFUL OF THROWBACKS

January 12, 1997

WITH A SILENT HULLABALOO of balloons and a rollicking blast from a brass band, a cluster of former Knicks and Celtics stars were given a send-off as they boarded a train at South Station in Boston yesterday morning. They were headed to New York and to a remembrance of times past.

Here were, among others, Dave DeBusschere and Earl "the Pearl" Monroe and Bernard King and Harry "the Horse" Gallatin, along with Bill Russell and Bob Cousy and Sam Jones and "Easy" Ed McCauley, all participants in this National Basketball Association promotion called Throwback Weekend. It was, in the 50th anniversary year of the NBA, a homage to the only two charter franchises still operating in their original cities, and to one of the most intense and enduring rivalries in sports.

"This is good," Red Holzman, the former coach of the Knicks, had said earlier to Dick McGuire, about the train trip. "You might be able to make a few bucks."

Tricky Dick smiled a knavish smile. Both legends understood that McGuire was not only a wizard with a basketball, but also adept at games of chance, particularly poker. Such amusements on train trips with teammates were available for McGuire to augment his basketball salary (which was in the low five figures, as opposed to today's high six- and seven-figure contracts).

"I loved playing cards with guys like Walter Dukes and Ray Felix," McGuire said. "They wouldn't fold even if they knew you were holding four aces."

Teams don't take trains anymore, and often players sit on airplanes with headphones and fall asleep to pounding tunes. It is a different world from the 1940s, '50s, '60s, '70s, and even '80s in which these players played. And much of this was recalled at festivities around the present-day Knicks-Celtics back-to-back games Friday night in Boston's Fleet Center and last night in Madison Square Garden.

At halftime, five players from each time shot free throws, and Gallatin, at age 69, graying, who retired in 1958 when teams were beginning to take planes instead of trains, was the only one there to still shoot them underhanded. He made his first one, as the crowd cheered.

"I don't understand why guys don't shoot that way anymore," he said later. "The last was Rick Barry, and he consistently led the league in foul shooting."

Gallatin mentioned that even Wilt Chamberlain had tried to shoot that way, but he failed, as he had at every other foul-shooting technique. "I had heard that he went to a psychiatrist," Gallatin recalled. "And the only result was that the psychiatrist became a better foul shooter."

Tom Heinsohn shook his head over the virtual elimination of the hook shot, his staple. "The players today are into the jump hook, and it's too easily defended," he said.

Jones said only Scottie Pippen, of the Chicago Bulls, shoots bank shots today, as he had done so magnificently in the '60s. Jones says he still plays full-court pickup games with high school kids.

"They can't understand how I get rebounds from them when I don't jump anymore," he said.

He was asked his secret. "I push," he explained.

Some of King's most vivid memories against the Celtics focused on Larry Bird, who did not take part in this weekend's festivities. "Playing against him, I learned that one reason he was so great was that he could get his space for his shot," King said. "You need room to shoot comfortably and some guys push off their defender with a forearm, but Bird did it with his shoulder—it's a nuance, but it made a huge difference."

King also recalled the first Knicks playoff game in 1984 against the Celtics in the old Boston Garden. Red Auerbach, the onetime coach and still president of the Celtics, was known for slippery strategies.

"I remember that the heat was turned on high in our locker room," King said. "And it was a warm spring day!"

Had this been a ploy by the wily Auerbach to enervate the opponent?

"That stuff is ridiculous," Auerbach countered. "If it was warm for them, it was warm for us. We had only one heating system. What did they think I did, air-condition half the court?"

Holzman recalled the seventh game of the 1973 Eastern Conference Finals in which they beat the Celtics and went on to the NBA title. "It was the first time Boston lost a seventh game of a playoffs at home," Holzman said.

But Auerbach, who said he loved beating the Knicks because he considered New York teams and fans arrogant, could still be an irritant to the Knicks, even at age 79. At halftime of the game in which the Knicks were leading, he spoke to the crowd with the assembled legends from both teams on the court.

"The Knicks were always our archrivals," said the acerbic Auerbach, "and I hope that the current Celtics can do to them was we used to do to them."

DeBusschere remembered the terrific battles with the Celtics and had mixed memories of Boston Garden. "It was exciting playing there, but it was depressing, too," he said. "It would start when you arrived at the Garden, with the elevated train tracks on the street overhead. There was never any sunlight. The locker rooms were dreary, and the parquet floors had those soft spots. You were never sure whether the ball on a dribble would bounce back up."

John "Hondo" Havlicek remembered the 1973 playoff series when he played all but one game despite having a separated right shoulder.

"I had to shoot left-handed and took some weird shots," he said. "But in the fourth game, I think it was, I didn't play. And as I walked to our bench in my street clothes before the game, the fans in Madison Square Garden gave me a standing ovation. I had always believed that the fans there, while they never wanted the opponent to win, were knowledgeable about basketball, that they would give credit to rival players they respected. That ovation was one of the great thrills of my life."

When the train arrived in Penn Station yesterday, the players were greeted with another blaring band, and cheering from the Knick City Dancers. This brought them all back to the present, but only momentarily. There were still memories to catch up with at the Garden last night.

SWEETWATER RETURNS
AFTER A LONG HIATUS

October 23, 1968

FOR THE FIRST TIME in their 43-year history, the Harlem Globetrotters played in Harlem. They took a day off from practice to stage a clinic at a junior high school, I.S. 201.

In the small gymnasium, Cal Ramsey, former NYU All-American and pro with the Knicks and Hawks, spoke into a microphone. Ramsey, now the dean of boys at 201, said, "Before we get on with the show, I'd like to introduce someone who's in the audience. My only boyhood idol and one of the greatest basketball players of all time, Sweetwater Clifton."

With a shy smile on his long, mustachioed face, Sweetwater Clifton rose slowly and waved his very huge hands. The 500 or so black kids who filled the gym applauded politely. Few had ever heard of Sweetwater Clifton.

Ramsey went on. "They have played in 87 countries and hold the record for playing before the most people, 75,000 in Olympic Stadium in Berlin, Germany, and right now we'll have the Globies come out and do their thing..." The spangled Trotters were greeted with such shrieks that the roofbeams rose 10 feet.

(Why hadn't the Trotters ever been to Harlem before? First of all, of course, they didn't originate from here. Al Saperstein organized the group in Chicago, and used "Harlem" to identify the club as Negro. "We should have been here before," said Meadowlark Lemon. "We've been goodwill ambassadors all over the world. It's about time we became goodwill ambassadors right here in America. All the Trotters have worked with ghetto kids. We want to do more. We asked to come here.")

Along the wall, seated in a fold-up chair, Nat "Sweetwater" Clifton watched in his sprawling, sleepy way, sometimes smiling as the crowd roared at the Globies' antics. "Sweets" was one of the all-time-best Globetrotters, and was a star in the glory days when they beat the powerful Minneapolis Lakers with George Mikan, in the late '40s. He was also one of the first black men to play in the National Basketball Association. He broke in with the Knicks in 1951. "Sweets" now drives a cab in Chicago, but was invited to New York by the Globetrotters for a reunion of sorts. ("I came into the NBA a little too early," he said, "before they started paying all that big money.")

The Globies' "opponents" for the day were five kids who wore yellow T-shirts with I.S. 201 printed on them, and street pants. On one of the first plays, Meadowlark Lemon got the ball in a pivot and in one slippery-fingered moment tucked the ball under his jersey and flung his arms around like a flipped-out windmill. The defending youngster was still searching for the ball when Meadowlark took a long step toward the basket and tossed in a bank shot. The boy exposed all his fillings and cavities and stared blankly. The crowd squealed. So did the lad, upon recovery. Sweetwater Clifton grinned.

On the wall near Sweetwater's seat was a bulletin board. Clippings from a year-old *Ebony* magazine were tacked to it. One article told of the handful of $100,000-and-over NBA players, including blacks like Wilt Chamberlain, Oscar Robertson, and Bill Russell. Part of another article described NBA team prospects with photos of all Negro players on seven teams: the Knicks had eight, Royals six, Pistons six, Bullets eight, Bulls six, SuperSonics six, and San Diego five.

When Sweetwater first began playing pro basketball, the Globetrotters were one of the few teams a Negro could play for. Now, about one-half of the NBA and ABA are black. And Globies no longer get the cream of the black crop. ("But they're still a good show," said Clifton.)

On the court, one of the yellow-shirted athletes dribbled up the middle. He was clear! He started to raise one leg as he went in for a layup. But he looked up to see a Globie on the shoulders of another, hands outstretched above the basket. The lad froze in midair, absolutely dumbfounded. One of his teammates fell down at half-court, he was laughing so hard.

Basketball is the game of the ghetto. All that is needed is a basket, homemade or citymade, a patch of dirt or pavement, a ball, and a mass of arms and legs and lungs. And it is from just such a ghetto as this, and with just such boys as those in yellow T-shirts, that Oscars and Wilts and Russells and Lew Alcindors and Cliftons and Lemons come from.

And sitting alongside the wall, with his long, mustachioed face, blue sweater, and white tab-collar shirt open at the throat, and, of course, those very huge hands, Sweetwater Clifton seems, in a most physical sense, to span an era.

"GEO. MIKAN VS. KNICKS"

March 11, 2001

ON DECEMBER 14, 1949, George Mikan, alone, played against an entire professional basketball team, or so read the Madison Square Garden marquee. In big, bold letters, the marquee announced: "GEO MIKAN VS. KNICKS."

In those days, Mikan, the rugged 6'10", 250-pound center for the Minneapolis Lakers, was the dominant player in the National Basketball Association, and the biggest draw.

Unquestionably, he was the league's first superstar, and in an Associated Press poll was named the greatest basketball player in the first half of the 20th century. (He would also be chosen as among the 50 best NBA players in history.)

Year after year he generally led the league in scoring or rebounding or both, and his team to the championship—he starred on seven pro championship teams in two leagues from 1947 to 1954.

But as good as he was, playing solo against the Knicks was still a stretch, even though, some nights, three and four opponents threw themselves at him as if he'd snatched their wallets.

"Before the game against the Knicks that night, something odd happened," Mikan recalled last week from his home in Scottsdale, Arizona, about that "marquee" game. "I had a habit of when I dressed before a game to place my eyeglasses on a locker shelf for safety. I'm very nearsighted and can hardly see without my glasses. So after I put on my uniform and then put on my glasses, I turned around. All of my teammates were still in street clothes.

"I said, 'What's going on?' Slater Martin, our great guard, said, 'George, didn't you see the marquee? It says you're playing the Knicks— go on out and play 'em.'

"Slater was the instigator of them giving me the rib. Well, I gave them a few choice words, and we all broke out laughing."

Mikan retired from basketball in 1956, became a lawyer, was commissioner of the American Basketball Association, and is now retired, but hardly forgotten. On April 8, at halftime of the nationally televised Minnesota Timberwolves–Los Angeles Lakers game, a life-size bronze sculpture of Mikan shooting his famed hook shot will be unveiled, and will be on permanent display in front of the Target Center in Minneapolis.

Mikan, 76, hopes to be there, but nothing is certain. He has not been well. Last March, his right leg was amputated just below the knee because of complications from diabetes. He wears a prosthesis. For a kidney ailment he must undergo dialysis four hours a day, three times a week.

On the day of the unveiling of the statue, a silent auction will be held in the concourse of the Target Center and the proceeds will go toward the Max McGee Research Center for Diabetes (McGee, the former Green Bay Packer receiver and a Minneapolis resident, has a 12-year-old son with diabetes).

Mikan's presence in basketball did more than stimulate attendance. It also influenced rule changes.

Mikan was one of the few players in his era to rise above the rim to block shots. So goaltending was entered into the rulebooks. To try to thwart Mikan's effectiveness, the free throw lane was widened from six feet to 12.

"It just forced me to be a better playmaker," Mikan said, "and I had some great teammates to pass to, like Vern Mikkelsen and Jim Pollard and Slater."

When Fort Wayne once held the ball and beat Mikan and the Lakers 19–18, the soporific slowdown eventually triggered the shot clock.

"Mikan was a giant among men," said Red Auerbach, who coached against him with the Celtics. "He was as overpowering around the basket as Shaquille O'Neal is today. George knew how to get position, and he was such a fierce competitor. He would certainly be a standout in today's game."

When Mikan entered DePaul University in 1941, he was awkward. Coach Ray Meyer worked diligently to develop his dexterity and a left-handed hook shot. Mikan became a three-time All-American.

"I had a right-handed hook and everyone had been overplaying me," Mikan said. "One summer Coach Meyer had me shoot 1,000 hook shots a day, 500 from each side.

"My lefty hook became better than my right, and it was hard for anyone to stop me."

In eight pro seasons, Mikan missed just two games, because of a viral infection. He broke numerous bones and sustained fractured elbows, arms, and fingers, and was sewn with 166 stitches. He once played in the playoffs with a broken ankle. "I just gritted my teeth," he said, "and hop-hopped up and down the floor."

Mikan credits advice from his father, who ran a bar and restaurant in Joliet, Illinois, for his drive to achieve. "My dad told me, 'Do the best you can. And so be judged.'"

RICHIE GUERIN SHOOTS THE
LAST TWO-HANDED SET SHOT

April 21, 1990

RICHIE GUERIN HAS BEEN in the news lately for something someone was about to do to him.

On Thursday night, April 19, Patrick Ewing came within four points of breaking Guerin's season scoring record for the Knicks of 2,303 points, a record that has held up for 28 years. It happened that Ewing became a little testy in the third quarter against Milwaukee, and was thrown out of the game. So the Knicks' seven-foot center had to wait until last night to do Guerin in.

But April 19 was the anniversary, the 20th, of a historic occasion of another kind in regard to Guerin, the 6'4" guard.

Return now to the night of April 19, 1970, when Tom McCollister, the publicity director for the Atlanta Hawks, called in to the National Basketball Association office the score of the Hawks–Los Angeles Lakers' fourth and last semifinal playoff game.

The Lakers had swept the series. McCollister, in a lugubrious tone, ran down the details. He came to "Guerin." Guerin, who would be 37 the next month, was the coach of the Hawks, and had somewhat retired as a player two seasons earlier. He would suit up now and then, however, when his troops were depleted because of injury or exhaustion, but during the 1969–70 regular season he had played in only eight games, and then only briefly.

In that last game against Los Angeles, two of his guards, Don Ohl and Walt Hazzard, were ailing, and another, Butch Beard, was a rookie. So, in the first quarter, with the Hawks behind 12–2, Guerin inserted himself into the lineup in the backcourt alongside Lou Hudson.

"Guerin played 35 minutes," reported McCollister, quietly, "made 12 of 17 field goal attempts, 7-for-7 free throws, had five rebounds, three assists, and four personal fouls. Thirty-one points." Pause. "They are burying him tomorrow morning at 10:00."

That was only a little hyperbole because they didn't bury Guerin, though he never played another NBA game. He lives and thrives today at age 56 as a managing director of the Bear, Stearns brokerage firm in Manhattan. "I didn't die after that game," Guerin recalled, "but I was so sore I felt like I wanted to."

What they did bury that night, though, was, sadly, the two-handed set shot, that beautiful, looping antique, of which Guerin said he hit "five or six that night." And of which he sank surely thousands in his 13-year pro career, and perhaps hundreds during his record-making 1961–62 season.

Guerin was the last player in the NBA to shoot the two-handed set, a shot as old as basketball. It was born with Dr. James Naismith's peach-basket invention in the Springfield, Massachusetts, YMCA in 1891. It was shot underhanded from between the legs and, through the years, from the waist, the chest, the eyes, and, like Guerin, from over the head.

The shot began feeling its age in the 1930s when Hank Luisetti of Stanford threw the one-handed set shot, at first considered "a hot-dog shot," into national prominence. In the '50s, particularly, the jump shot became commonplace and the two-handed set was headed for extinction.

There were pro hangers-on with the shot, like Carl Braun, Dolph Schayes, Dick McGuire, Larry Costello, Gene Shue, Al Bianchi, and Sam Jones. "And Kiki's dad," said Guerin, of Ernie Vandeweghe. But all had retired by the time Guerin played in his last game in the Forum in Los Angeles.

"That was the swan song of the two-hander," Guerin said. "I'm sorry to see it go. It added something, something very nice to the game."

In the swift pace of the game today, with its premium on jump shots and fast breaks, there is little in the play to remind one of the roots of the game, unlike almost every other sport we have.

"The jump shot is more glamorous, I suppose," Guerin said, "but the two-hander had an advantage in that late in the game the motion of the jump shot takes its toll on the body. There's no real exertion to the two-hander."

Guerin could shoot from long distances, and though it took a moment to set for the shot, he was dangerous because he was a strong, swift driver. He could also, if necessary, shoot the jump shot. But the two-hander, with that quick fixing of the feet, the flick of the wrists, and that lovely, rainbow arc, was the shot that Guerin had grown up with—"All of us in the East did in those days," he said—and relied on.

"I was of the jump shot era, and Richie tried to teach me the two-hander in practice," said Butch Beard, now a coach with the Nets. "My thumbs always got in the way. I never knew where the ball was going."

Guerin recalled that against Phoenix in 1969 he also had to reactivate himself. He hit six straight two-handers from about 30 feet out.

"Bill Bridges, our forward, was on the bench," Guerin said, "and he heard one of the ballboys say, 'What is that?' He never saw a two-hander before. To him I was a freak."

THE MURDER OF SID TANENBAUM

September 21, 1993

HE HADN'T COME HOME after work, and he hadn't called. This was not like him. For the 39 years of their marriage, Bobbie Tanenbaum could count on her husband, Sid, informing her of his whereabouts. A feeling of dread swept over her. She called at his office, the Able Metal Spinning and Stamping, in Far Rockaway, Queens.

He was the president of the company, having gone into the business started by her father. He had joined Able after retiring as a professional basketball player in 1949, following two years as a 6'0" guard with the Knicks and the Baltimore Bullets.

The Tanenbaums had met in 1945, when Sid was the star and leading scorer of the New York University team, a junior who would lead the Violets to the National Collegiate Athletic Association final, where they lost to Oklahoma 49–45. He was voted the Haggerty Award as the best player in the metropolitan area and was named to All-America teams.

Bobbie Wolfson was a freshman at NYU and knew nothing about basketball. Sid told her he was on the "j.v.".

"He was always unassuming," she said recently, laughing about their first meeting.

On the day Sid Tanenbaum did not call, Thursday, September 4, 1986, there was no answer to the phone at his office. Bobbie called a few other places. She phoned her two adult sons, their only children. In time, two police officers arrived at the Tannebaums' house in Woodmere, Long Island. A rabbi accompanied them. Her worst fears had been realized.

Sid Tanenbaum was dead, at age 60. He had been stabbed in the back with a steak knife by a woman who had tried to borrow $25 from him at work.

Tanenbaum, as Bobbie recalls, "always let everyone in the door."

"He was always doing things for people," she said. "If the mortgage was due and they didn't have money, he helped them out. If their kids needed money for school, Sid went into his pocket. I begged him not to let people in. He said he could take care of himself, that no one would hurt him and that I shouldn't worry."

His son, Michael, an optometrist in Northport, Long Island, said that his father had grown up poor in the Brownsville section of Brooklyn, sometimes sleeping on cold floors, and never forgot what that was like.

"The factory was in a poor neighborhood, and my dad sympathized with the people," he said of his father's business. "His heart went out to them. His dream, when he retired from the business, was to become a social worker."

Molly Dotsun, a 37-year-old woman, was arrested shortly after the stabbing. She is currently serving a seven-to-21-year prison sentence for manslaughter.

Tanenbaum is in the news because this evening, at a dinner at the Downtown Athletic Club, he will be inducted into the New York City Basketball Hall of Fame, along with five other players: Roger Brown, Tony Jackson, Nancy Lieberman, Jim McMillian and Max Zaslofksy; two coaches, Lou Carnesecca and Jammy Moskowitz; a contributor, John Nucatola; a sportswriter, Lenny Lewin; and a team, the 1938–39 James Madison team that won the Public Schools Athletic League title.

Tanenbaum left the shaky, early world of pro basketball because he didn't like the travel and he didn't feel there was a stable future.

But Tanenbaum remained in good shape and never stopped playing basketball. Even at age 60, he played every Sunday in regular half-court games at the North Woodmere Park.

"He was still amazing on the court," said Sherman Smith, who played against Tanenbaum as a member of the Brooklyn College team, and who played with him in those pickup games. "He was a fragile-looking guy, but he was awesome. His ball-handling was still great and he had the right- and left-handed hooks. And his two-handed set shot—the shot he was famous for—never left him. We played with the younger guys and some had never seen that shot."

When the slight, graying man lofted the shot, Smith recalled, "the young guys said, 'What's that? What's he doing?' And by the time they found out, the ball was dropping through the basket."

At the North Woodmere Park where Tanenbaum played in his last years, there is now a half-court tournament played in memory of him. It takes place one Sunday every summer, and this year there were 85 teams participating. Next year there will be a girls' segment and one for wheelchair players. Friends of Tanenbaum also instituted a foundation in his name and award $400 each year to a scholar-athlete in each of two neighborhood Long Island high schools, Hewlett and Lawrence, and in Thomas Jefferson in Brooklyn, where Tanenbaum had graduated.

On the tall wire fence at the entrance to the court, a plaque has been erected. There is a drawn likeness of Tanenbaum on it, and an inscription: "Sid Tanenbaum Memorial Courts. N.Y.U. All-American, New York Knicks. He touched us all."

X.

ON A PERSONAL NOTE

To Hoops on Its 100th

December 25, 1991

SENT A CHRISTMAS GIFT recently to the Springfield, Massachusetts, YMCA. It was a basketball. This doesn't exactly make me Kris Kringle, but it was the least I could do.

I've been playing basketball ever since grammar school, ever since high school, ever since college, and still haven't stopped. I understood Isiah Thomas when he mentioned in an interview why he had built a basketball court in his house. "Do you play anything else? Golf, say, or tennis?" he was asked. "No," he said. "Maybe one day. But, really, any chance I get, I play basketball. I'm still a hooper at heart." There are many levels of hoopers, from Isiah on down to—well, just on down.

Not long ago I was in Springfield on assignment and, knowing that the 100th anniversary of the game would soon be commemorated there at the Basketball Hall of Fame, I brought my hoop gear (somehow, I usually manage to find room in my bags for it) to the Springfield Y.

It was my first trip to that modest mecca where basketball originated, on or about December 21, 1891. Dr. James Naismith had been charged by his boss at the Springfield Y training school to develop an indoor game so students could get exercise during wintertime. Doc twitched his mustache with disdain, for he had other things to tend to, but then did as ordered. Up went a pair of peach baskets on the balcony, which happened to be 10 feet above the gym floor there. The next thing we know—100 years later—basketballs are bouncing all over the world.

Basketball may be played and seen and agonized over (note all the newspaper photos of tearful cheerleaders when their teams have lost) and loved by more people in more places than any other sport in history.

I paid a $10 fee at the Y and asked for a basketball. The woman behind the counter handed me a rubber ball with a bump in it. I asked for a ball without a bump, and a leather one. Rubber is for outdoor use, as everyone knows, leather for indoor. She had about six other balls. "They're all rubber, except for this one," she said, holding a worn leather ball in both hands. "But this has a flap on it." In fact, there was a loose tear in one of the strips on the ball.

"I'll take the one with the flap," I said, with a shrug.

How nice, I thought, that after 100 years the Springfield Y still has all the same balls that Naismith invented the game with.

Some things had changed, however. For one, this was a new building. And Naismith would never recognize the gym. No balcony, no peach baskets. Instead, glass backboards and a large wooden floor with colorful lines gleamed in the well-lighted room. Two young men were shooting at one basket. They invited me to play. I said yes. "Hey," said a guy who had just come in, "can I run wichyoo." Sure, I said.

We played with the ball with the flap, which was the best ball we had. We picked, we screened, we tried to hit a cutter, we took a bad shot, we made a surprising one—and heard the sweet snap of the net—we stole a ball, we lost one. There was a dispute. It was resolved. Play resumed.

The half-court game was reminiscent of basketball games I've played and watched, mostly with pleasure, for years. It is a lesson in human nature. It is not just who passes how, for example, but when—from playground to pro. It is beyond skill. It has to do with character, and characters, and I've personally known many, from one called Junior Jive (or just J.J.), a fancy young player who threw behind-the-back passes into the wall, to one named Monster, for his lummox game (and if you called his home and asked one of his kids for their father, they'd holler, "Monster—telephone!").

One is also known by the calls he makes in a pickup game—or doesn't make. Once, at a Y in Manhattan, two jerks—pals—argued for a dumb call and then quit in a huff. "There goes flotsam and jetsam," said one of the remaining players. Perfect.

Hoopers know that the best indoor ball is a leather one without a flap, and with a good grainy feel and grooves. That's why I had to send one to the Springfield Y. In appreciation.

Merry Christmas, Basketball, and Happy 100th.

HOOPS, CHICAGO STYLE

February 7, 1988

I INFORMED MARK AGUIRRE, the Dallas Maverick forward who has returned home to Chicago for the NBA All-Star Game this afternoon, that he and I had graduated from the same grammar school, William Cullen Bryant on the West Side, though a number of years apart.

"Is that so?" he said, politely but with understandable lack of interest.

"Yes," I said, "and you broke all my records—except one." He looked at me closer. "Oh?" he said. "What was that?"

"I spent three years in the second grade."

He blinked and then laughed, gratefully.

It was true that we had gone to the same school, but none of the rest of it was, particularly the records part, and probably not the second-grade stuff, if memory serves. This was simply one reporter's notion of a little witticism to get over a conversational hump.

I was looking into a matter that had been raised by another reporter. That is, since four of the 24 NBA All-Stars chosen for this afternoon's game are native to this metropolis—as well as Tom Hawkins, who played in the Legends game in Chicago Stadium yesterday—could there then be, like a Chicago-style deep-dish pizza, or a Chicago-style gangland rubout, a Chicago style in basketball?

Isiah Thomas, the Detroit Piston point guard, and another of the Chicago natives in the game—along with Glenn "Doc" Rivers of the Atlanta Hawks and Maurice Cheeks of the Philadelphia 76ers—wasn't sure there was an actual Chicago style of basketball. "But one thing I'm certain of," said Thomas. "We did go at it!"

"Aggressiveness," said Rivers. "Maybe it came from the days of Dillinger, or Capone." He laughed. "I don't know."

Thomas talked about going from neighborhood to neighborhood looking for games. He remembered that he went into Doc Rivers' area, on 10th Street in Maywood, a Chicago suburb, when he, Thomas, was a sophomore in high school and Rivers a freshman.

"You didn't go into a neighborhood and beat people there," said Thomas. "We lost four out of five games to Doc's guys, and then we won the last. They didn't care for that. And they started attacking us. We had gone there with our bikes and couldn't get away. Someone called the cops, and we ran into the rec center. Those guys hemmed us in and threw rocks. That's the way it was." Cheeks recalled how players in Chicago learned to "go to the hoop" in the playgrounds and schoolyards. "You learned to drive and make the shot and get hacked and not call a foul," he said. "If you called a foul, there was sure to be fights, brawls, things like that."

Hawkins remembers his high school coach at Parker giving his players added impediments on drive shots in order to improve concentration. "He'd whip us with the whistle cord," said Hawkins, who played as a pro with the Royals and the Lakers. "And on Sundays everyone went to the court at 71st and South Park, and there were so many fights that guys brought in referees. I don't think the referees lasted too long, either."

Rivers had mentioned that a handicap for young Chicago players was the notorious wind. "That's why you don't see a lot of guys from Chicago with great outside shots," he said. "You can't shoot in that wind, so you drive."

Aguirre disagrees. "I'd just put up my finger," he said, "and test the wind. 'Hmm, gale from the southwest, I'll just adjust the shot a little to the right...'"

Aguirre also believed that the wind was a factor in developing a one-on-one style, which he also felt is a trademark of Chicago basketball.

"It's not that easy to pass," he said, smiling. "You know, the wind factor."

One remembers the wind, and the fights, and the always alive possibility of basketball altercation.

After grammar school, as most readers must be dying to know, this reporter went on to Sullivan High School on the North Side, and played on the basketball team considerably before the high school days of Cheeks,

Rivers, and Thomas, and just after Hawkins, and with considerably less success, though, once, after making a shot in the wind, a defensive player paid me the ultimate compliment. "You meteorologist!" he shouted. I remember one never knew what to expect when traveling to another school for a game. Our coach instructed us never to wander off separately when we left the opponents' premises. The coach at a neighboring school, as part of practice, had his players work on their circle, in the manner of wagon trains, to fend off would-be attackers on the street.

Tuley High School was so tough that no girls would dare go to the game and sit in the stands. Hearsay had it that there was another school so tough no boys would sit in the stands, but I can't attest to that because I never played there, but I did play at Tuley.

At Marshall High School, one of players on our bench was asked by one of the spectators behind him which team he was rooting for.

"Are you kidding?" he said. "Sullivan."

Suddenly he felt something very sharp at his side. It was exactly what he thought it was. A knife.

The player wisely changed his opinion, as well as his seat.

In a park district game, a player once got angry at a call by a referee and left the game. He went home, but it wasn't to pout. That's not Chicago style.

The player went home to get a pistol. He returned to the game. When he did, it was the referee who then left. He fled from the gym, and barricaded himself in the administration office, and wouldn't come out until the coast was clear.

Such was the environment in which some of today's NBA All-Stars and legends grew up, flourished, and lived to tell the tale.

ONE ON ONE WITH
MAGIC AND MICHAEL

February 3, 1990

A ONE-ON-ONE BASKETBALL GAME between Magic Johnson and Michael Jordan, probably the two best and most electric players of the day, would be terrific to see. Mano a mano always is, even if the competitors are refugees from a team sport. But it is Borg versus McEnroe, Ali meeting Frazier, Errol Flynn clanging swords against a sea of pirates.

About an hour before the first Ali-Frazier title fight, in 1971 at Madison Square Garden, the battle between two undefeated heavyweight champions, Bill Cosby sat in the press room with several reporters and talked about the anticipation. "This is so exciting," he said, "that I wish it could go on forever."

To basketball fans, Johnson-Jordan would be in that kind of emotional ballpark.

It was first suggested by the Johnson camp, either by Magic's agent or friends, and came to light several weeks ago. The ears of the Jordan aides-de-camp, and Air himself, apparently, perked up.

Almost immediately there was clatter from both corners. "Well," said a Jordan intimate, "Michael has a lot of confidence. He doesn't think anyone could beat him one on one."

"Magic told someone," came a report, "'Don't bet against me.'" Oh, some rumble! No details had been fixed, but there was speculation about the match's taking place in the off-season and possibly for pay-for-view television and with a charity involved. League officials said that for any such thing to occur, the players must seek approval from them, according to the collective bargaining agreement, as well as each NBA player's contract. "And we'd have a lot of questions about it," said Gary Bettman, general counsel for the NBA. "Would it be properly arranged?

"Where would the money go? What would the rules be?

"Would such a game be in the best interests of the league?"

He said it was unlikely to happen soon.

Nonetheless, the basketball fan dreams. One sees Jordan swirling, soaring, slam-dunking; Magic pounding, posting, popping. Jordan is younger, swifter, but smaller. He is almost 27 years old, 6'6". Johnson is 30, and stands 6'9". Johnson has led his team to a handful of NBA titles. Jordan, on inferior teams, has yet to win one.

Jordan would conceivably be the heavy favorite because of his uncommon moves and bounding ability. Yet Johnson, historically, has done nothing more than regularly triumph. He's as fast as he has to be, as strong as he has to be, and as talented and full in his heart and head of what it takes to win as any athlete has ever been.

Too bad there are so many obstacles, but a schoolyard one-on-one game would be perfect. Eighteen years ago, the NBA had a one-on-one tournament in conjunction with CBS. It didn't quite work. There were commercials that broke up the play, which was taped, and there were even free throws thrown in.

Most games, though, were intense, as one on one ought to be. After all, reputations are at stake, even lifestyles. My favorite game involved Connie Hawkins and Jerry Lucas. Hawkins narrowly won, but Lucas bitterly complained that the officials had fouled up the score, awarding Hawkins an extra basket. A replay proved him wrong. But anyone who ever played one on one can appreciate Lucas' vituperation.

I remember guys doing anything to win, whether playing for a Coke (a soft drink, in those days) or a buck. Big players kept backing you to the basket. Smaller ones stepped on your toes and pulled your shirttail. And of course you called your own fouls. This led to a lot of fouls called, and a lot of discussions, ending occasionally with a fist brandished.

I played with an assortment of people, from Big Red, who would strip to his baggy polka-dot undershorts for a quick game, to Shmutz Schwartz, to someone I once met at a YMCA in Chicago. I arrived just as a game was breaking up. One guy, about 6'1", remained. I asked if he'd like to go one on one for the sweat. He said sure. I began, shot, and missed.

He took the ball and hit a jump shot at the top of the circle. I moved him back and he hit a longer jump shot. I moved him back more and he hit again. It was incredible. We were nearly at mid-court. Now he drove around me for another basket. And this is how the game went. Afterward we introduced ourselves. He said his name was Flynn Robinson.

"Flingin' Flynn Robinson!" I said. Of course! He had only recently retired and had been a feared shooter with several NBA teams, including the Bulls and the Lakers.

Well, it was a lesson to me in the great skills of pro players. I doubt, though, that Flingin' Flynn could have dispatched Michael Jordan, and, as an experienced and wounded hand, I doubt that Michael, as great as he is, could whip Magic. I might even bet a pair of Big Red's shorts on it.

WHEN RUBY MISSED
THE FINAL FOUR

April 1, 1989

THIS IS THE 30ᵀᴴ anniversary of the year that neither Ron Rubenstein nor I played in the Final Four. I recalled this recently when I saw the booklet *Final Four Records*, a history of the Division I men's basketball tournament, published by the NCAA and put out to coincide with today's semifinal games.

In the section, "All-Time Final Four Player Roster," I checked the listing under "Louisville," and there, listed alphabetically several notches below "Pervis Ellison '86" and "Darrell Griffith '80," I found the entry "Ron Rubenstein '59."

Rubenstein was a dark-haired, 6'1" sophomore guard for the University of Louisville. He had seen a lot of action for much of the season, then suffered a leg injury that put him on the sideline. When Louisville played West Virginia and Jerry West in the 1959 NCAA semifinals, Rubenstein was a spectator.

I followed this rather closely. In such circumstances, many of us keep an eye on someone we know. I had played with Rubenstein in parks and schoolyards, and just two years earlier we competed in a Public League high school game in Chicago. I was a member of the Sullivan Tigers and he was a star for our nearby rival, the Senn Bulldogs.

He was one of the best players in the state, a swift, strong driver and deft outside shooter. I guarded him for part of the game, and, with my teeth clenched and my eyes blazing with competitive fire, I helped keep him to about 30 points as Senn beat us rather handily. The fact that

Rubenstein—Ruby, as we called him—didn't play most of the last quarter may have contributed to my holding down his scoring.

He went to Louisville. I went somewhere else, never, it turned out, getting even close to being on a roster in the Final Four. Nor, for that matter, did anyone else I ever played with or against in school, other than Howie Carl, a standout at DePaul, who was in two NCAA tournaments, but with teams that were eliminated early.

No one else, though, not Pickles Bailen or Smelly Hartsman or my red-haired, pigeon-toed friend, Dickie Brandwein, who taught me in playing one on one for money the difference between "Owesies" and "Paysies": if he won, it was Paysies, if I won, he decided after I won, it was Owesies.

So, Rubenstein was unique among my contemporaries in the neighborhood, the only one on a team roster in the Final Four. These are the connections, the sometimes slim threads that often bind us to special events.

Rubenstein, for me, was a kind of distant basketball cousin. In the 1959 semifinal games, West Virginia beat Louisville, and California defeated Cincinnati. The Cincinnati star, of course, was Oscar Robertson. And Rubenstein earlier in the year played against Oscar Robertson, a step in the levels of the game that I found extraordinary, even uplifting.

I once met a former teammate of Rubenstein's at Louisville, Bud Olsen, who told me this story: just before a game against Cincinnati, the Louisville coach, Peck Hickman, gave the team a pep talk that ended with, "And remember, Robertson puts his jockey strap on the same way you guys do." Robertson scored virtually at will as Cincinnati won. In the locker room later, Rubenstein turned to Olsen and said, "I don't care what Coach says, Robertson has to put his jockey strap on differently."

I called Rubenstein in Chicago recently to commiserate about his having missed the Final Four 30 years ago. He laughed and told me about the other time he had a chance to make it there. This was in the Mideast Regional semifinals, against Ohio State, in 1961.

Hickman had instructed how to guard Lucas and Havlicek and Siegfried. When he got to a reserve named Knight, he said, "Remember, play him like he has the measles. Stay away from him. He can't hit the rim." Rubenstein said, "It was a very close game and it got near the end and Paul Franks—remember him, a friend of mine from Senn?—he was listening to it on radio, and told me the announcer said, 'And here comes

Rubenstein up the court with his fancy dribble and—oops, Siegfried steals the ball!'"

Rubenstein laughed softly. "I had to foul Siegfried to prevent a basket," he said. "He made the free throws, and we lost 56–55, and I guess you could say I was responsible, but one of our players did have a couple free throws at the end and missed them." Ohio State went on to the NCAA final, losing to Cincinnati in overtime.

I asked Ruby whom he likes in this year's tournament. "The winner of the Duke–Seton Hall game," he said. "I'm picking the coaches over the players, and I think Duke and Seton Hall are better coached than Illinois or Michigan."

I told him I was picking Duke to beat Michigan in the final. With that, I wished him a happy 30th anniversary, and we said so long.

CAN WE ALL RUN TOGETHER?

January 25, 1993

AT HALFTIME OF TOMORROW night's Knicks-76ers game at Madison Square Garden, there will be another basketball game, one that season-ticket holders had not bargained for.

It will be a brief scrimmage played by black and Hasidic young people from the Crown Heights neighborhood's "Project CURE—Increase the Peace" basketball teams.

Not long ago, the Knicks were approached with the idea for the scrimmage and their enlightened management bought it. The Knicks are calling the evening Racial Harmony Night, with Anthony Mason, the Knicks' home-grown forward from Queens, as the designated spokesman and awards presenter.

The name Crown Heights, however, has a recent history that immediately conjures up anything but racial harmony. In August 1991, after an automobile in a procession that was carrying the Lubavitch Grand Rabbi accidentally struck and killed a black seven-year-old boy, some blacks went on a rampage through the streets of that section of Brooklyn, screaming "Kill the Jews." And somebody indeed murdered one, stabbing to death a Hasidic scholar from Australia.

Tensions that had been simmering for years between the two communities, which live literally side by side, had erupted into the nightmare that many had dreaded. Many citizens in the neighborhood are now deadly serious about wanting to do something to ease the fear and loathing. Playing games together to promote understanding is, they believe, as good a way as any. At least, they feel, understanding must start someplace.

Sometimes it does. Understanding often comes in one-on-one situations. I've thought about this because I've played basketball on various levels, from grade school to high school to college, from the parks and the schoolyards to alleys where, as we grew up in a racially mixed neighborhood, we tossed a rubber ball through a loose drain pipe extending from the roof of a garage.

There was a refrain in the schoolyards that I will always remember. I'm sitting waiting for "next" when a guy walks off the street in his sneakers and asks, "Can I run wichya?"

"Yeah, sure you can," I say.

He's black, he's Hispanic, he's white, he's Hasidic, he might even be a she, for, as time goes on, more and more women are playing basketball in situations like this, and playing well, which was disconcerting to veteran male hoopsters when the new era began.

But change and being thrust into new situations—with different people—can always throw someone off their game. It can crush stereotypes and wipe out clichés.

At Bryant grammar school on the West Side of Chicago, I could jump better than Willie Rockett, who was black, but not as well as Tommy Swope, another black.

In a Christmas tournament for public high schools at the International Amphitheater, my school, Sullivan, an all-white North Side team, played Carver, an all-black South Side team.

The game went on at 9:00 AM. It was freezing outside, and freezing inside in the huge empty auditorium, because the heating system had broken down. We would have played in our parkas if we could have.

None of us ever warmed up, and they beat us 29–27. Afterward, all of us shared the few showers available in the one locker room, laughing together when our jaws unlocked, comrades in cold.

At Roosevelt University, which I attended for two years, the coach of the racially mixed team was Edwin Turner, a gentle and perceptive black man. By strength of character, he maintained respect. He knew what he was doing. He wasn't always right, to be sure, and might take me out of a game when I knew—just knew—that I was about to turn my game around. But it never surprised me, in later years, to find that a black man could coach a pro basketball team, or football team, or could manage a big-league baseball club, as well or as poorly, as a white man.

In the Army, there was a black man, Ron Hamilton, with whom I played basketball on the Fort Gordon, Georgia, base. Hamilton had played at Tennessee State and later the Cleveland Pipers. One afternoon we learned that we could play at an American Legion gym in nearby Augusta. This was in the summer of 1959. Six of us, five whites and Hamilton, joyously drove over.

The doors happened to be locked. We were deeply disappointed. On the way back, as the sun was setting, I noticed a beautiful outdoor court, like a mirage. I shouted, "Stop the car! We're in luck!" But the driver knew better. In that time, if we had played, we would have courted disaster, since blacks in the South then didn't play in games with whites. I had never hated segregation—never hated hatred—any more than I did then. Hamilton remained silent. I felt his anger and frustration.

Years later, I wrote a book with Walt Frazier. Clyde and I used to play one on one together (we will not discuss the scores). I came to appreciate not only his extraordinary physical skills, but also his insights into the game. It was the latter, I am convinced, that made him the champion he was.

"Everyone," Frazier once told me, "has a certain rhythm that he dribbles to."

At one time, there was a prevalent cliché among whites that said this: if a team with mostly blacks was to succeed, it needed a smart white guard. In some of the Knicks' best days, they had white players Bradley, DeBusschere, and Lucas up front, with Frazier or Monroe or Barnett handling the ball—and a brainier backcourt you could never find.

I don't know if "Project CURE—Increase the Peace" will cure the ills. I don't know if Racial Harmony Night will work. But I know it can't hurt.

It is, after all, indefinably sweet when someone asks, "Can I run wichya?" and the answer is, "Yeah, sure you can."

ABOUT THE AUTHOR

IRA BERKOW, A SPORTS columnist and feature writer for *The New York Times* for more than 25 years, shared the Pulitzer Prize for national reporting in 2001 and was a finalist for the Pulitzer for commentary in 1988. He also was a reporter for the *Minneapolis Tribune* and a columnist for Newspaper Enterprise Association. He is the author of 20 books, including the bestsellers *Red: A Biography of Red Smith* and *Maxwell Street: Survival in a Bazaar,* and, most recently, *Summers at Shea: Tom Seaver Loses His Overcoat and Other Mets Stories.* His work has frequently been cited in the prestigious anthology series, Best American Sports Writing, as well as the 1999 anthology Best American Sports Writing of the Century. He holds a bachelor's degree from Miami University (Ohio) and a master's degree from Northwestern University's Medill School of Journalism, and has been honored with distinguished professional achievement awards from both schools. In 2009 he was inducted into the International Jewish Sports Hall of Fame and also received an Honorary Doctorate of Humane Letters from Roosevelt University in Chicago. Mr. Berkow lives in New York City.